DATE DUE FOR RETURN

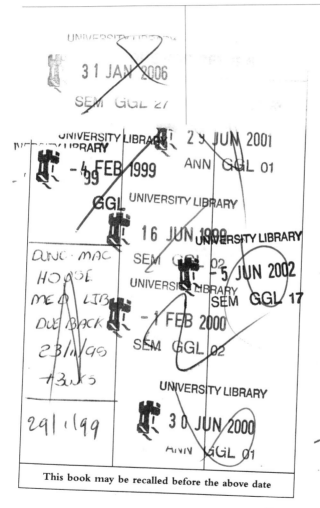

UNIVERSITY LIBRARY

3 1 JAN 2006

SEM GGL 27

UNIVERSITY LIBRARY
UNIVERSITY LIBRARY

- 4 FEB 1999
'99

GGL

2 9 JUN 2001

ANN GGL 01

UNIVERSITY LIBRARY

16 JUN 1999
UNIVERSITY LIBRARY

DUNC· MAC
HOUSE
MED LIB.
DUE BACK
23/11/98
+3UK5

SEM GGL 02

- 5 JUN 2002
SEM GGL 17

UNIVERSITY LIBRARY

- 1 FEB 2000

SEM GGL 02

29 1 (99

UNIVERSITY LIBRARY

3 0 JUN 2000

ANN GGL 01

This book may be recalled before the above date

90014

Clinical psychology observed

UNOTTSCI

Clinical psychology has developed gradually as a separate profession since the Second World War. It has been shaped by its relationship to medicine, British philosophy, and the organisational setting of the National Health Service. Clinical psychologists are trained in a culture which stresses scientific research and its applications. Yet, as David Pilgrim and Andy Treacher insist, the profession's theory and practice lack coherence and consistency.

Clinical Psychology Observed contrasts the confident public persona of the profession with its private insecurity and confusion. The authors attempt to understand this contradiction by examining its historical cultural context and its professional strategies in response to recent radical changes in health care policy. After developing this historical and sociological analysis, the future – if any – for the profession is discussed critically.

David Pilgrim has worked as a clinical psychologist and is now Lecturer in Health and Social Welfare at the Open University. **Andy Treacher** is a clinical psychologist and family therapist at the Royal Devon and Exeter Hospital. He was co-author of *Psychiatry Observed* in 1978.

Clinical psychology observed

David Pilgrim and Andy Treacher

Tavistock/Routledge
London and New York

First published 1992
by Routledge
11 New Fetter Lane, London EC4P 4EE

Simultaneously published in the USA and Canada
by Routledge
a division of Routledge, Chapman and Hall, Inc.
29 West 35th Street, New York, NY 10001

© 1992   David Pilgrim and Andy Treacher

Typeset from the author's wordprocessing disks by
NWL Editorial Services, Langport, Somerset

Printed and bound in Great Britain by
Mackays of Chatham PLC, Chatham, Kent

All rights reserved. No part of this book may be reprinted or
reproduced or utilized in any form or by any electronic,
mechanical, or other means, now known or hereafter invented,
including photocopying and recording, or in any information
storage or retrieval system, without permission in writing from
the publishers.

British Library Cataloguing in Publication Data
Pilgrim, David, 1950–
   Clinical psychology observed.
   I. Title   II. Treacher, Andy
   157.9

Library of Congress Cataloging in Publication Data
Pilgrim, David, 1950–
   Clinical psychology observed / David Pilgrim and
Andy Treacher.
   p.   cm.
   Includes bibliographical references and index.
   1. Clinical psychology – Great Britain – History –
20th century.
   I. Treacher, Andy.   II. title.
   [DNLM: 1. Psychiatry – trends.   2. Psychology, clinical –
trends.
   WM 105 P638c]
   RC466.83.G7P55   1992
   616.89′023 – dc20
   DNLM/DLC   91–25281

ISBN 0–415–07227–1
         0–415–04632–7 (pbk)

UNIVERSITY
LIBRARY
NOTTINGHAM

Contents

Preface

As the title of this book suggests, our self-appointed task is to record our observations of clinical psychology as a profession. One of us (DP) is an ex-clinical psychologist, who is now an academic, the other (AT) is an ex-academic and now a clinical psychologist. This switching between roles has given us a unique opportunity to come to know the profession both inside and out. Given this history of moving in and out of the profession we are reviewing, we do not intend to provide a simple descriptive work – it will not be an apologia for our trade. Equally, whilst we intend to be uncompromisingly critical, we have no intention of being nihilistic about a profession which has inspired certain hopes in our lives, as well as giving us valued colleagues and salaries.

The project was prompted by the recognition that the dominant health care profession, medicine, had had its justified fair share of critical scrutiny. During the 1970s and 1980s, both of us contributed at times to this critique, in relation to psychiatry. It seemed to us that the time had come to turn a similar type of attention upon our own occupational group. This seemed to be appropriate since most of the debates about the coherence and worthiness of our profession, which we had originally wrestled with while we were trainees, remained unresolved. At the same time, we also were aware that we were coming to the end of a dark decade of British politics, which had propelled health and welfare professionals into frenetic activity. Clinical psychology had been shaped by this political context, for good or ill, to defend its existence publicly whilst remaining internally confused.

It seemed to us that this contradiction of public confidence and private uncertainty provided us with three main targets of interest. First, we wanted to find out where our profession came from. Maybe the current profession could be better understood by tracing its historical roots. Second, we wanted to explore how new practitioners were socialised into their profession. Maybe some of the confusion about the role of practitioners might be accounted for in terms of their training. Third, we wanted to examine how the recent social and political context might have influenced the profession and how the latter had responded to the constraints and opportunities it encountered. Maybe some of the trends of self-promotion and professionalisation after 1979 were a product of external cultural and political forces. These three aims structure the book. By the end we hope that you, as a reader, will have been furnished with food for thought about clinical psychology. Even if you do not share our conclusions, we hope you will find the book both challenging and sympathetic towards a profession which could still play an important role in shaping the character of services for a wide range of health and welfare clients.

David Pilgrim
Andy Treacher
London and Exeter, March 1991

Acknowledgements

We are grateful to the following clinical psychologists for their cooperation in providing us with views and oral histories of their trade: Eric Bromley, David Bird, Chris Cullen, Hans Eysenck, Bernard Kat, Ed Miller, Bruce Napier, Glenys Parry, Monte Shapiro and Frazer Watts. Of course, we take full responsibility for the picture we have constructed from their accounts. Some of them are quoted directly, in Chapter 6, from the first author's MSc thesis in sociology at South Bank Polytechnic (Pilgrim, 1990). Thanks are due to his supervisor, Judy Allsop, for her help and encouragement. The extended loan of Barrie Richards' PhD thesis has proved invaluable (apologies for the delay in its return). At various points, some other sociological guidance has been provided by Anne Rogers, Nigel Goldie and Ray Holland.

We would like to thank Sandy Lovie and his colleagues at Liverpool University for facilitating our access to the British Psychological Society archives and Bruce Napier for giving us access, at the BPS headquarters in Leicester, to the minutes of the executive committee of the Division of Clinical Psychology. Finally Don Stein's reflections on the advantages of mental labouring have been appreciated and Liz Mears' word processing help proved invaluable and is much appreciated by Andy Treacher.

Chapter 1

The legacy of psychiatry

Clinical psychology is a relatively recent interloper in the British mental health industry. Its first practitioners only began to appear in the 1950s. In contrast, the medical profession had secured the legal mandate to manage mental disorder a century earlier. This first chapter will emphasise the consequences of the profession of clinical psychology emerging in an organisational context dominated by medicine. In the next chapter other contextual factors, including the cultural traditions of Britain and the impact of changes in the British welfare state, will be examined to try to account for the form and content of the professional development of clinical psychology, once it was formally established by 1960. We hope to demonstrate that medical dominance has had three major consequences: medicine has incorporated psychological theory; it has constrained the autonomous development of non-medical practice; and it has provoked the development of competing bodies of knowledge in clinical psychology.

The pre-conditions of clinical psychology being set up included, and were built upon, those which facilitated the professionalisation of psychiatry in the nineteenth century. Consequently, it is important to put the events during and since the 1950s into a longer historical context. This will be done in terms of three main phases related to the legacy of Victorian psychiatry and the impact of both the First and Second World Wars. At a theoretical level, our discussion below will involve examining the advantages and disadvantages of a Marxian account of the first of these in the work of Andrew Scull, and post-structuralist accounts of later developments in the work of David Armstrong, Peter Miller and Nikolas Rose.

THE ESTABLISHMENT OF THE MENTAL HEALTH INDUSTRY BEFORE 1914

During the nineteenth century two main internal threats to the stability and efficiency of capitalism existed, which provoked centrally directed state action. The first of these was mass physical contagion, which propelled the state into establishing a national network of sewers. The second concern was the threat from 'the dangerous classes'. Criminality, infirmity, sickness and madness were increasingly differentiated and added to the threats of rebellion or revolution. A systematic description of the response to deviance from the state is laid out by Scull (1977, 1979, 1984). Whilst Scull's work has its weaknesses (which we will highlight later), he does provide an important, scholarly overview of the conditions which facilitated the emergence of the asylum system and the profession of psychiatry in Britain.

As noted, mental disorder was only one part of a wider threat to the integrity of the ascendant capitalist system. As well as the mad, there existed the simple and the sick, the lame and the infirm, as well as the frail and the elderly. These had been combined with criminals in an undifferentiated mass in earlier days, when they were lumped together, and responded to a similar way, by medieval feudalism, on a local basis. Through the eighteenth century changes in the economic system facilitated, even demanded that this underclass of unemployed or unemployable people was dealt with differently. Despite this differentiation, it is crucial to note that the various groups shared a vital core characteristic: they were all overwhelmingly drawn from the lowest economic stratum of society. Whilst madness existed in all classes, a clear gradient of incidence was evident, so that it was *pauper* lunatics who populated the growing state asylum system. This gradient was to persevere right through to the middle of the twentieth century (Braginsky *et al.*, 1972).

Scull (1977) describes three main changes in the management of pauper deviance as feudalism gave way to capitalism. First, there was a shift of emphasis from local to *centrally governed* systems of social control of any deviance, be it madness, sickness or criminality. Social relations now built on market principles rather than feudal ownership meant that older bonds of paternalism and *noblesse oblige* were destroyed. Local aristocratic authority was now replaced by the authority of a new capital-owning middle class in central government.

Second, following from this, the containment of deviance in the community in the earlier period gave way to a new emphasis on *segregation* or incarceration. The asylum system built in the nineteenth century was part of the explosive growth of a larger segregative social control apparatus, to be added to the prison system. Note that workhouses and infirmaries were still under local or charitable management. This puts into perspective that criminality and madness were the two largest threats to social stability. Physical illness did not entail central regulation until 1948, with the passing of the National Health Service Act. (For accounts of the emergence of these institutions in the eighteenth century when the response to mental disorder was more *ad hoc* and in private local hands, see Busfield, 1985.)

The third most striking characteristic shift was that, whereas the feudal system failed to differentiate this amalgam threat from the underclass, the nineteenth century witnessed a move towards the *conceptual and physical separation* of different forms of deviance. This entailed, for instance, the prison, criminology, lawyers, police and prison officers emerging as a separate sub-system from the asylum, psychiatric classification of psychopathology, alienists, mad doctors, asylum superintendents and asylum attendants.

Scull dismisses notions that the asylum system and psychiatry emerged as a result of either breakthroughs in scientific knowledge (then as now the medical profession remains mystified about the causes of madness) or humanitarian concern (asylums were and remain degrading environments) or in simple reaction to the growth of urbanisation and its attendant poverty:

> Instead I would contend that many of the transformations underlying the move towards institutionalisation can be more plausibly tied to the growth of the capitalist market system and to its impact on economic and social relationships.
>
> (Scull, 1984, p. 24)

These changes entailed the abolition of the traditional social obligation of the rich to the poor and a shift from the stable parochial exploitation of peasants by aristocrats to the more unpredictable vagaries of capitalist exploitation of the worker in an overarching national, and increasingly international, market system. Scull quotes the assertion of Marx that the latter system 'has pitilessly torn asunder the motley feudal ties that bound man to his "natural superiors".' A direct cause of this rupture was the tradition of local paternalism in response to deviance. Henceforth, the state and its agents (psychiatrists and their ancillaries and their analogues in the prison and infirmary) would now deal directly with those failing to fulfil their role as workers in the productive process. Local charitable responses would be pushed into a secondary role.

Scull's explanation does accept the relevance of contributory ideological considerations, but they are assigned a secondary role. For instance, he notes the anxieties of the ruling class in relation to the inefficiency of the poor law outdoor relief approach. A centrally managed segregative solution may have been considered to be more efficient and less wasteful. Also, asylums might act as factories of correction, which could aim to inculcate 'bourgeois rationality' in the erring poor. Foucault in his competing history of madness and psychiatry places a greater emphasis than Scull on moral rather than economic factors (Ingleby, 1983).

As far as these changes were concerned, the conceptualisation of madness as illness was central to the project of the new profession of psychiatry. Pauper lunatics now became carriers of mental disease, their social status and predicament being re-framed as a medical problem to be managed or even cured. This located the problem of madness *inside* individuals, rather than in a set of social relationships. By the late nineteenth century, medicine had triumphed in defining what madness was (a biological fault) and who should manage it (physicians). Scull (1979) quotes the editorial comment from the *Journal of Mental Science* in 1858, the same year as the passing of the General Medical Act, which summarises this position in an early example of professional boundary making: 'Insanity is purely a disease of the brain. The physician is the guardian of the lunatic and must ever remain so.'

A relevant aspect of the triumph of the medicalisation of madness was that in the first half of the century, before medical dominance was established via the General Medical Act (1858), a failed attempt was made to establish a psychological rather than biological approach to madness. Exemplified by the regime of Tuke at the York Retreat (a charity asylum) at the turn of the century, moral treatment aimed to provide a moral order in the conditions of an 'ordinary household', combining both authoritarianism and kindly paternalism (Castel, 1985; Digby, 1985; Donnelly, 1979). However, this regime failed to transfer to the state asylum system, despite the rhetorical use of it made by reformers promoting the latter. Tuke's main disadvantage was that he was not a physician, yet he used the terminology of medicine. This disability pre-figured a similar weakness of psychological practitioners incorporating medical terminology, first in psychoanalysis and later in clinical psychology. Thus, by the mid-nineteenth century, medicine had driven out successfully competing bids for administrative and therapeutic control of the aslyums by non-physicians. Of greater structural significance was that these vast 'warehouses of madness' were simply not designed to be anything like 'ordinary households'. None the less, this failure did not discourage later similar attempts to humanise the asylum system, when the therapeutic community advocates were to introduce their own twentieth-century variant of moral treatment after the Second World War.

Whilst medicine has been successful in the main in stifling the therapeutic aspirations of non-physicians, it has been in constant battles, some of them being lost, with the legal profession and administrators. In the former case the 1890 Lunacy Act was the first example of the legal contraints on psychiatry (Ewins, 1974; Bean, 1986). However, the 1930 Mental Treatment Act was to restore medical power in this regard despite the introduction of the 'voluntary' status patient.

In summary then, during the nineteenth century, medical hegemony was established over mental disorder. Mad doctors gained a monopoly of legal control over the management of the mentally disordered but also established a dominant model for conceptualising 'residual deviance' (non-criminal rule breaking). This way of conceptualising mental disorder (later to be dubbed variously the 'medical', 'disease' or 'faulty machine' model) was established as legitimate not only within medicine but in the discourse of politicians and the general public. Despite the hegemony of the medical approach to mental disorder, which took on a logic of its own as far as the promotion and maintenance of professional self-interest was concerned, it was the *economic system* which had ultimately determined *where* these activities were to take place (locked away in the asylum).

Before leaving Scull, it is important to underline that his history and others (Foucault, 1965; Sedgwick, 1982; Busfield, 1985) emphasise that madness and its segregation in asylums were at the centre of these early developments. How a new mental health profession, clinical psychology, with no marked enthusiasm for either madness or the asylum, was to cope with and adapt to this historical legacy, when it emerged under welfare capitalism, we will describe and analyse later. In the interim period, the mental health industry became more complicated, so that it could no longer be identified narrowly with the coercive containment of madness in the asylum, as in Scull's account. In the twentieth century the ambit of psychiatry expanded to offer not only involuntary control, which it still does unambiguously today (Rogers and Pilgrim, 1989), but also the promotion of mental health and the amelioration of mental distress in voluntary encounters with patients. Not only is Scull's analysis limited in accounting for this later complexity, but it blinkers him from formulating a positive version of what mental health services should deliver. His pessimistic and even nihilistic conclusions about the failure of modern community care policies (Scull, 1984, part four) are a logical consequence of analysing the mental health industry in narrow economic terms.

THE IMPACT OF THE FIRST WORLD WAR

The nineteenth-century mad doctors, as their name suggests, were preoccupied with admitting, controlling and attempting to cure lunatics in their asylums. (This last activity, though boasted by medical superintendents, was less evident at the end of the century than the increasing seclusion of pauper lunatics in poor conditions (Skultans, 1979).) The systems of description applied to mental disorder at that time were dominated by terms like 'mania' and 'melancholia', which were being gradually superseded by Kraepelin's 'dementia praecox' (1895) and Bleuler's 'schizophrenia' (1911). The German school of classification was not immediately dominant in Britain, though after the First World War Kraepelin's theoretical scheme was to gain and retain favour in the bulk of Anglo-American psychiatry. Kraepelin's clinic, visited in 1907 by Mott, a pupil of Maudsley and founding member of the British Psychological Society, was the spur for the new Maudsley Hospital (opened in 1915 after its namesake gave the London County Council £30,000).

Before the First World War, psychiatrists favoured biochemical or toxic theories of madness. Vulnerability to these pathogens was assumed to be a function of inherited 'weakness of the brain'. Then as now psychiatrists were rich in assertion and poor in empirical evidence for their preferred theories. This hereditarian preoccupation ironically posed the first serious threat to what Doerner (1970) has called the 'self-satisfied approval' with which psychiatry viewed itself at the turn of the century. The threat came in a social context in which there was a de-stabilisation of the fruits of a peacetime economy at home and colonial adventures abroad. (The relevance of the interrelationship between imperialism abroad and social stability at home to psychiatry during this pre-war period is discussed by Baruch and Treacher (1978).)

In 1914, the 'Great War' between imperialist European neighbours brought military violence to their own populations. This violence meant that the main, or at least immediate, priority was no longer the threat to industrial efficiency from the 'dangerous classes'. Now military efficiency was centre stage, and any impediment to this became the main political problem to be solved. At this time, there existed another theoretical framework for explaining mental disorder which had been waiting in the wings to replace bio-determinism. Psychoanalysis had its small collection of practitioners and fellow-travellers by this time, and these were the people (the 'shellshock' as opposed to 'asylum' doctors) who were to challenge the 'self-satisfied' attitude left over from Victorian psychiatry.

Stone (1985) has documented the process by which shellshock became constituted as the central problem of military morale and efficiency, during a war of unprecedented casualties and protracted attrition. Because the mad doctors had taken little or no interest in 'neurasthenia', but instead studied only madness from the citadel of the asylum, they had neither the interest nor the ability to solve the shellshock problem. However, neurologists and psychologists took more of an interest. 'Shellshock' was at first deemed to be a disturbance resulting from the physical trauma to the nervous system of the shell-blast. The term and its implications were first discussed by the psychologist Myers in 1914 (Hearnshaw, 1964).

As a result of the shellshock issue, the limitations of biological psychiatry were publicly exposed. Consequently, a psychological model received its first social opportunity to flourish as a result of warfare for two main reasons. First, as mentioned, the discourse and practices of asylum-based psychiatry, which functioned to resolve the problem of madness in peacetime civil society via segregation, were badly suited to solving the problem of fear in the face of military conditions. These distressed soldiers were not mad, but they were worryingly inefficient and disabled as willing cannon-fodder. Second, a crucial underlying assumption of bio-determinism was that mental disorder (as well as other forms of deviance) resulted from a tainted or degenerate human stock (Skultans, 1979). This genetic obsession, legitimised by the pseudo-sciences of Eugenics and Social Darwinism, was the conventional psychiatric wisdom of the time.

Shellshock posed a serious challenge to this hereditarian consensus. The men who were breaking down under the stress of warfare were not the 'degenerate' riff-raff of the lumpenproletariat, who accumulated in the asylums and workhouses, but were working men who had *volunteered* to serve their King and Country. Of greater significance was that the breakdown rate amongst officers was even higher than in lower ranks. Given this, how could the degenerate stock theory favoured within the bio-determinism of traditional psychiatry be sustained? These men were, after all, 'England's finest blood' (Stone, 1985), rendering such a psychiatric stance tantamount to treason. And so, at least for a while, the unrelenting ascendancy of biological psychiatry was stopped in its tracks. Military conditions had set the scene for a bid for legitimacy for a *psychological* account of mental disorder. Moreover, unlike the earlier failed bid from moral treatment in the early nineteenth century, this new competitor was championed by medical men, not laymen. Many of the shellshock doctors involved in experimenting with psychotherapies (to various degrees based on Freudianism) now made a strong contribution to the discourse about mental disorder. Moreover, they contributed to the expansion of the Psychological Society, which was formed in 1901, and the formation of its first section (the Medical Section), founded the year after the end of the war.

The most important point to note here was that the range of interest of psychiatry was now broadened irreversibly. Armstrong (1980) points out that psychiatric textbooks reflected this shift. In 1906, Bruce's *Studies of Clinical Psychiatry* concerns itself only with insanity. When pre-war textbooks did mention the neuroses, they were given little attention compared to the psychoses (e.g. Cole's *Mental Diseases* published in 1913). Moreover, as that book's name suggests, neurologists commented on and speculated about the physiological roots of 'neurasthenia', to a point where they assumed it resulted from poor nutritional supply to the nerve fibres. So, although the neuroses were considered to be medical disorders, they were deemed to be *neurological* rather than functional in nature. Consequently, medical men were trapped by their own biological reductionism. They had not yet discovered how to reason in psychological rather than biological terms. None the less, as medical specialists, neurologists were taking a greater interest in the neuroses than was the case with their psychiatric colleagues in the asylum.

Thus, immediately prior to the First World War, the asylum-based emphasis of psychiatric practice meant that other branches of medicine were as likely to seek to construct theories about, and seek jurisdiction over, neurosis. In fact, many textbooks post-war still placed the emphasis on the psychoses and it is significant that the main exception was the revision of Stoddard's *Mind and Its Disorders* in its 3rd edition in 1919. Stoddard was no longer an asylum superintendent but a lecturer at St Thomas' Hospital Medical School. In his book, he declared his conversion to psychoanalysis, which was reflected in the high profile now given to Freud's ideas about neurosis.

After the war, this expansion of the psychiatric jurisdiction over neuroses as well as psychoses was formalised by the 1930 Mental Treatment Act emphasising *voluntary* status. This Act 'greatly enlarged the range of aberrant behaviour' being attended to by medical practitioners (Wooton, 1959). At this time, two different tendencies to consolidate the power and status of psychiatry were also evident. One path taken was for the medical psychotherapists and the biologically orientated asylum doctors to coexist but not engage. The former could work in private practice or staff the shellshock out-patient clinics set up after the war. Moreover, they could gain cultural nurturance by segregating themselves, when not in patient contact, in the Medical Section of the BPS, the British Psychoanalytical Society, the Analytical Psychology Club or the Medical Society of Individual Psychology. Indeed, the perception that these doctors had of the BPS by the mid-1930s was that it was essentially, in origins and intentions, a *medical* society. For instance, in 1934, the psychoanalyst and Medical Section Chairman, John Rickman, commented:

A history of the Medical Section of the British Psychological Society must differ from that of other medical societies in one important respect. There is not a doctor in the country who would express surprise at the existence of an anatomical, a physiological, a pharmacological society for he has learnt about these things at his medical school but there used to be very many, and still are not a few, who do not realise what medical psychology deals with, from

what it has sprung and whither it is going... [the BPS] was started indeed by doctors but by doctors who were also doing other things.
(Rickman, 1938, p. 3)

A second strategy for dealing with the potential conflict about biological versus psychological reasoning was to develop integrative models. This middle way could draw upon Pavlov's work, which showed that environmental stimuli and physiological processes could be theorised and empirically explored concurrently. Similarly, Meyer proposed a theory entailing biological 'reaction types' to account for variations in response to similar environmental stimuli. Armstrong (1980), reviewing this eclectic tendency in inter-war psychiatry, notes that even institutions or personnel known for their psychological orientation attempted to incorporate a somatic component in diagnosis and treatment. Commenting here on the *psychodynamically orientated* Tavistock Clinic (which was founded in 1920 with Field Marshal Haig as its first Honorary President), Armstrong says:

The Tavistock Clinic ... together with its associated Institute of Medical Psychology, promoted a unified psycho-somatic approach to diagnosis and treatment. Crichton Miller, the Clinic's founder, published his views on etiology [which included the notion that] the emotions, sepsis, the endocrines and blood circulation all had inter-dependent effects on mental stability.
(Armstrong, 1980)

It should be emphasised that this consolidation of psychiatric power entailed resolving intra-professional tensions about biological versus psychological theorising in psychiatry *and* important moves to pre-empt inter-professional threats. The 'eclectic' and the 'coexistence' strategies can be interpreted now to have had two vital functions. First, they warded off a potential internal conflict which might have damaged the professional well-being of medicine. In training school the shared professional socialisation into loyalty to medicine ensured that public disputes between organised factions of physicians were (and remain) rare spectacles. Second, by retaining a respect for somatic considerations (the traditional territory of medical jurisdiction) whilst incorporating psychological notions, physicians ensured that *non-medical practitioners* were excluded from the treatment business. This issue was prefigured by the earlier dispute within psychoanalysis about 'lay analysis' (in which Freud broke ranks with his medical colleagues and took the side of non-medical analysts). Moreover, it was to ward off, for the time being, an acrimonious conflict between non-medical psychologists and their psychiatric colleagues.

However, these unconvincing amalgamations of psychogenic and bio-determinist theories of mental disorder were not without cost to the profession. Psychiatry failed to resolve important epistemological questions, to which only that most bloody-minded of psychiatric and psychoanalytical mavericks, Thomas Szasz, was to return in later years (Szasz, 1960). Freudian and subsequent psychological models assumed an essential continuity of normality and abnormality. This is inconsistent with the medical assumption that some people are sick and others well. Despite holding this psychological model, medical psychoanalysts have continued to use the language of illness and retained rather than rejected their medical authority over non-medical colleagues.

Another price medical psychotherapists paid was to separate themselves off from dealing with madness. They were guilty (as many clinical psychologists were to become in later years) of dealing with a 'neurotic' population in the main, whilst leaving the mad to the vagaries of hospital-based biological psychiatry. This historical collusion has left medical psychotherapists accused of being élitist (by treating a high proportion of middle-class patients) and precious (by evading the problems of struggling with more disturbed and disturbing clients).

These contradictions were reflected in the adjustments made in the organisation of psychiatric services in the inter-war period. As well as the post-war introduction of more out-patient treatment and the establishment of the Tavistock Clinic, the ideas of the shellshock doctors were to be more influential than those of traditional psychiatrists on the lawyer-dominated Royal Commission on Lunacy and Mental Disorder, set up under the chairmanship of Macmillan in 1924 and reporting two years later. The asylum doctors were so out of favour in government circles at the time that none was invited to sit on the Commission. None the less, despite the out-patient and voluntary status emphasis of the report, which was to inform the 1930 Mental Treatment Act, in practice it was not long before it was 'business as usual' in the asylums (Stone, 1985; Ramon, 1985).

However, the new and permanent eclecticism altered the contours of modern psychiatry in a way which highlighted the limitations of Scull's centralised social control model. Whilst he was correct to emphasise the political economy underpinning psychiatry, social order and disorder are not only constituted and regulated by the centralised coercive power of the state. The 1930 Mental Treatment Act raised issues of community care, out-patient clinics and the importance of voluntary rather than coerced treatment. The new psychotherapeutic models were based essentially on the assumption of a voluntary contract outside hospital, which held out the hope of not merely controlling disordered conduct but also ameliorating its associated emotional pain. Psychiatric surveillance was to become more elaborate and subtle, to include informally sought relationships. Moreover, the very economic system which determined the existence of psychiatry also determined a *moral order*, entailing social control coming from 'below', not simply from above.

The emotional and material stability of family life was linked to 'bourgeois rationality' directly via wage slavery. The financial unit of the family required that its members followed the rules of employment. Consequently, it was important that the conduct of unemployed family members should not impede the efficiency or capability of those at work. Thus, twentieth-century psychiatry has indeed entailed its practitioners acting as agents of social control for the state but *also* they do so at the behest of lay people. Scull's hostility to a 'phenomenological' approach to the sociology of mental disorder (Scull, 1984, Ch. 1) has blinkered him to the reality of this wider source of surveillance and control (cf. Horwitz, 1983). Generally in psychiatric crises it is non-professionals (relatives, neighbours or strangers on the street) who initiate social control. Thereafter, psychiatrists, social workers and the police rubber-stamp their decisions (Coulter, 1973).

To summarise the state of affairs in the mental health industry in the 1930s then, the asylum emphasis was re-established but the emptiness of the narrow biological approach to treatments had been embarrassingly exposed by the Macmillan Report of 1926. Its three pages devoted to treatment complained that asylums were essentially detention centres with a limited number of approaches available which were of dubious efficacy (baths, laxatives for hypomania and paraldehyde and chloral hydrate for 'schizophrenia') (Bean, 1980). Only the organic condition of syphilitic psychosis (General Paralysis of the Insane) had provided any evidence that madness could be treated physically with success (Baruch and Treacher, 1978). However, despite the Commissioners being unable to find a credible treatment technology in asylum psychiatry, they still accepted and thereby legitimised the notion that mental disorder was illness. Consequently, the 1930 Act actually *increased* the power of medicine compared to the 1890 Lunacy Act. The dispersal of even more legal power to psychiatrists was to occur later in the 1959 Mental Health Act. Legal constraints on medicine equivalent to the 1890 Act were not to be ushered in until the 1983 Mental Health Act (Bean, 1986). Thus between 1890 and 1983 there was a sustained increase in formal legal powers of psychiatrists over their patients.

THE SECOND WORLD WAR AND THE BEGINNINGS OF THE PROFESSION

By 1939, the anticipated problems of shellshock and low morale provided a spur to psychological approaches to both military selection and treatment, in the context of an imminent and predictable war. Clinical psychology in a formal sense still remained absent from the scene, though not for long. There was to be no simple replay of the tensions of the Great War between psychoanalysis and the crass biologism of Victorian psychiatry. Not only had this already given way to an unpredictable eclecticism, but 'scientific' psychology was to enter the field of clinical discourse, with its strong emphasis on measurement and objectivity.

Two institutional settings were to be the centres of excellence for new tensions: the Maudsley Hospital and the Tavistock Clinic. Richards (1983) notes that the new profession of clinical psychology also developed at Crichton Royal Hospital, Dumfries, under Raven, but this was a relatively minor event in relation to the central conflict that was to develop between psychoanalysis and methodological behaviourism at the two London centres. The beginnings of the Maudsley Department were physically at Mill Hill Emergency Hospital. The Maudsley had been emptied to accommodate potential civilian casualties at the outbreak of war. The bulk of the Maudsley staff had been transferred to Mill Hill, or Sutton armed services psychiatric units, though some were dispersed elsewhere (e.g. Mayer-Gross went to Crichton Royal in Scotland).

Aubrey Lewis, the medical director of the Emergency Hospital, on the recommendation of Philip Vernon, appointed Eysenck as its research psychologist in 1942 (Gibson, 1981). At the end of the war, the Mill Hill staff were reconvened at their Camberwell base at the

Maudsley. The Maudsley medical school, which was established in 1924, was renamed the 'Institute of Psychiatry' in 1948 and was under the Directorship of Lewis. He organised it to include separate autonomous departments (of psychiatry, psychology, physiology, biochemistry and biometrics). The conscious inclusion of psychology in this set-up demonstrates that it was a psychiatrist who prompted the first steps of British clinical psychology. As with Trethowan later, Lewis was to be an important patriarchal medical advocate of professional development in applied psychology.

In 1950 Eysenck returned from a six-month observation trip to the USA as Visiting Professor of Psychology at the University of Pennsylvania. There he examined the role of clinical psychology, and began to set in motion plans to formalise the beginnings of his own training course. The longer period of establishment of clinical psychology in the USA gave some clues as to how the British profession might develop. The first 'psychological clinic' had been set up in Pennsylvania by Witmer in 1896 and the applications of psychology to psychiatry were well founded by the First World War. Seashore and Sylvester set up another key psychological clinic in Iowa in 1908 and shortly university training courses were running in Clark, Minnesota and Washington. In 1919 the first section to be formed in the American Psychological Association was the *Clinical* section not the Medical section which was formed in the same year in the BPS (Reisman, 1976). However, the conflict over therapeutic autonomy remained unresolved until the mid-1960s even in the USA. In 1954 the American Medical Association declared psychotherapy to be a medical procedure (supported four years later by the American Psychiatric Association). The logic of this position was that psychologists practising psychotherapy were doing so illegally. All of these twists and turns were to prefigure, or mirror, to some degree British events.

At the Institute in the early 1950s, the psychometric role, which posed no threat to psychiatry, predominated. Indeed, the early fifties saw Eysenck continuing to be supported by Lewis in his first steps towards professionalisation. Eysenck was appointed as a Reader in Psychology at the Institute in 1952 and Professor in 1955, with Lewis' support (Gibson, 1981). This suggests that, when clinical psychology began, its psychometric emphasis invited a welcome rather than distrust or disapprobation from the mature profession of medicine. This honeymoon period was not to last long however.

The accounts given by Gibson and Eysenck himself of this period give the clear impression that he was the prime innovator at the Institute of professional expansion, particularly in relation to behaviour therapy. By contrast, Yates (1970) records that Monte Shapiro, the clinical course organiser, was the person who influenced this change. For his part, Shapiro eschews the role, claiming that it was Gwynne Jones (now deceased) who was the most important innovatory force in behaviour therapy (Shapiro, personal communication, 1991). Eysenck does acknowledge that Gwynne Jones was his assistant when presenting a vital paper on behaviour therapy to the Royal Medico-Psychological Association discussed below (Eysenck, 1990). Given that Eysenck was a researcher and did not see patients, the practical development of behaviour therapy could only have been made initially by Gwynne Jones, who reported his interest to a regular seminar group organised by Shapiro. Eysenck's role was to take up this gauntlet and throw it at the feet of psychiatry. His leadership role was characteristically one of popularising and politicking. It was not based upon being immersed in the practical work of the profession, as either a clinician or a trainer. These roles were taken up in a sustained way by others like Shapiro.

During the 1950s the early culture of psychologists at the Institute was associated with three main campaigns to establish a brand new clinical profession. The first of these was the denigration of the dominant pre-existing psychological corpus of knowledge (psychoanalysis) (Eysenck, 1952). This attack on the lack of efficacy of verbal psychotherapy is now well known as a seminal paper for post-graduate students (and many undergraduates) studying psychotherapy outcome research. Usually its qualities are assessed in terms of its innovatory status and its methodological strengths and weaknesses. However, for our purposes here, the emphasis needs to be placed on a wider bid for legitimacy on behalf of a new profession. If psychoanalysis could be refuted successfully, and cast aside as pre-scientific, then a new style of psychologising could be ushered in.

The second, closely linked campaign occurred inside, or rather about, the Medical Section of the BPS. Between 1954 and 1956, the small but expanding culture of psychologists at the Maudsley set about challenging the Section's traditions. This period of turmoil had two interweaving political themes: medical dominance in the section and the psychoanalytical emphasis of its business and journal (the closely linked *British Journal of Medical Psychology*). As agendum 3 submitted by the Medical Section's executive for the BPS Council meeting of 3 December 1956 notes, 'Criticisms of the Journal and implicitly of the Section were first aired by Maudsley spokesmen in 1954 at Society and Council level'. The agendum describes how this 'small minority group ... of clinical psychologists well known for their intolerance of dynamic viewpoints in psychology ... began to take political form.' At a lengthy and acrimonious meeting of the Medical Section earlier that year (22 February) the Maudsley lobby failed to persuade the core group in the Section (who were mainly psychoanalysts) to alter the focus of its business. In the interim period informal talks to resolve the differences between the analytical 'old guard' (represented by Plaut, the Section Secretary) and the Maudsley critics (represented by Gwynne Jones and Shapiro) failed.

Eventually, the old guard resolved explicitly to block the applications of critical clinical psychologists to the Section leading to the extraordinary scenario of a Section which had vetoed only nine nominations in ten years rejecting ten out of fifteen applications in a single meeting (24 October 1956). Amidst accusations of unfairness and ballot rigging, and legal advice being sought by the BPS Council, Summerfield, the BPS secretary, had to write to Plaut (5 November) to inform him of the decision of the Council two days earlier to suspend any further elections in the Section. A full report was demanded of its executive. Eventually normal business was resumed in the Section and the *putsch* from the Maudsley had failed (within a few years clinical psychology, with its own theoretical preferences, had its own division and journal).

The medical psychoanalysts proved to be ferocious defenders of their power base in the BPS. Eventually, the Medical Section (now called the Psychotherapy Section) was largely depleted of its medical membership, which moved to the Psychotherapy Division of the newly formed Royal College of Psychiatrists in the 1970s. It is now, in the 1990s, run by clinical psychologists. None the less, the editorship of the *British Journal of Medical Psychology* has remained in unbroken medical control. What the Maudsley group did in the 1950s was emphasise their role as the main contenders for academic and clinical legitimacy in the professional realm of abnormal psychology.

The third campaign, which was to seal the bid for legitimacy from the Maudsley School of clinical psychology, was that surrounding behaviour therapy. In 1958 Eysenck, assisted by Gwynne Jones, presented a paper to the Royal Medico-Psychological Association (Eysenck, 1958) which affirmed the appropriateness on scientific grounds of psychologists treating neurotic complaints using variants of behaviour therapy. Predictably, this threatened encroachment onto the medical terrain of treatment was received badly by psychiatric colleagues. This push by psychologists to colonise behaviour therapy was to have two decisive implications for the 1960s. First, the new profession at the Maudsley was to assert its scientific professionalism increasingly on the basis of its therapeutic rather than its psychometric credentials. Second, it was to sting the Maudsley psychiatrists into attempting to recover their therapeutic authority. Lewis encouraged two junior colleagues, Marks and Gelder, to secure the behaviour therapy terrain. Amongst other things this facilitated the development of a medically led training course for nurse therapists, still in existence at the Maudsley. This is a good example of how behaviour therapy is compatible with the medical model as it allows for a traditional division of labour, with the psychiatrist diagnosing a problem and nurses being delegated to carry through a prescribed course of treatment. (The medical control and definition of psychiatric nurse training dates back to 1890, when the Medico-Psychological Association outlined its first nurse training curriculum.)

These machinations at the Maudsley in the 1950s were not the whole picture as far as the early days of the new profession were concerned. Eysenck and his colleagues may have trumpeted the end of psychoanalysis as a dominant form of psychological knowledge but this did not mean that it would crumble automatically like the walls of Jericho. Just as the rebuttals of psychiatrists at the Maudsley and in the Medical Section of the BPS were to be met, their Tavistock colleagues retained their own aspirations, which were not to be deflated by the challenge of the contemptuous 1952 paper. The Tavistock Clinic had its own period of post-war optimism, with its returning analytical medical leadership forming 'Operation Phoenix'. The Clinic was to be a model facility for similar organisations to be spawned inside the National Health Service after 1948, delivering out-patient psychodynamic psychotherapy (Dicks, 1970). This was a re-affirmation of earlier hopes following the First World War, when the Clinic was established in 1920. The pre-eminence gained in London in those early days was in relation in the main to problems of childhood (Hadfield, 1935; Miller, 1937).

It is worth contrasting the view of asylum-based psychiatry as being a function of centralised social control, criticised earlier in the work of Scull, with the strong claims made by Miller and Rose (1988) for the profession's diffuse new moral influence in the mental hygiene movement, via the Tavistock Clinic in the 1920s. The movement focused its attention on the alteration of the mental health of populations by emphasising the role of personal habits (particularly child-rearing habits), in much the same way that social hygiene advocates in the nineteenth century argued for public health measures. According to Miller and Rose, this new movement established a psychological frame of reference in large sections of society (from parents to policy makers), meaning that, whatever the Clinic's success in its reactive role (psychotherapy), it had established a vital role in insinuating a state of psychological-mindedness in the post-Victorian generations. Family life in general, and mothering in particular, became the focus of social policy debates both then, incorporating the writings and advice of the Tavistock staff, and later in the 1950s in the works of Bowlby and Winnicott.

Against this background of expertise in the civil realm of family life and parenting, and in the light of the legitimacy of the earlier shellshock doctors, psychotherapists in general, and the Tavistock staff in particular, became prime recruits for the war effort. Following a memorandum from the Royal Medico-Psychological Association (this became the Royal College of Psychiatrists in 1971) in 1938, warning the Ministry of Defence that the imminent war would swamp the administration with shellshock casualties, J.R. Rees, the Director of the Tavistock Clinic since 1934, was appointed as consulting psychiatrist to the army, along with two Clinic colleagues as deputies (Hargreaves and Wilson). In 1939 Rees was elevated, in the rank of brigadier, to Head of the Armed Psychiatric Services. These appointments in themselves demonstrate the pre-existing credibility in the inter-war period of psychoanalysis in general and the Clinic in particular. They also underline once more the functional value that psychological models had for warfare compared with the biological emphasis typical of peacetime civilian psychiatry. This value was reflected in the positive response from the War Office to the innovations of Rees and his colleagues in their war-time work (Rees, 1945).

This Tavistock-led psychological operation for the war effort was directed towards problems of selection, training, morale, treatment and rehabilitation throughout the war years and after (Privy Council Office, 1947; Vernon and Parry, 1949; Morris, 1949). All of these were important for post-war applications of psychology to both psychiatric treatment and industrial relations. In particular, the hybriding of social psychology, systems theory and object-relations theory in psychoanalysis to produce new brands of group therapy (Foulkes and Anthony, 1957), moral treatment (therapeutic communities: Jones, 1952) and organisational and industrial relations analysis (Jaques, 1951) generated a vast range of expressions of psychoanalytically based post-war influences. This array of approaches, when set in the context of medical dominance in psychiatry, indicates that Eysenck's competing bid for legitimacy faced powerful professional and theoretical forces. The persuasiveness of his scientific logic was heavily constrained and resisted by this psychoanalytical-psychiatric legacy.

The Tavistock staff returning from the war were vibrant with the successes and status of their privileged military existence. During their war years they had formed an 'invisible college' (Main, 1957) amongst themselves. With like-minded colleagues (including psychologists and sociologists) they explored the above actual or potential forms of applied (psychoanalytically orientated) psychology. The time was ripe to *expand* and professionalise their Clinic (Main, 1983, personal communication), not shut up shop and retire in the face of Eysenckian attacks. The treatment of adult patients was now to be as important as the pre-war child emphasis. The group therapy experiments of Main, Foulkes, Rickman and Bion at the Northfield Military Hospitals, along with similar work in the Effort Syndrome Unit at Mill Hill by Maxwell Jones from the Maudsley, gave new staff trained in the Clinic a technology and theoretical rationale to treat NHS neurotic patients. The opening of the Cassel Hospital as an NHS in-patient facility to deploy these approaches, under the direction of a Clinic member (Main), gave added impetus to the notion that psychodynamic therapy was here to stay in the state sector of the British mental health industry. Indeed the British therapeutic community movement became the focus for wide, respectful international interest in democratising and humanising the old asylums.

Before leaving these historical explorations, it is worth returning to and summarising the advantages and disadvantages of the post-structuralist accounts of twentieth-century psychiatry. These versions from Armstrong, Miller and Rose above provide us in one sense with a more convincing version of the social reality of the complexity of modern-day service delivery, of which clinical psychology forms a part. They have the advantage of demonstrating that these mental health professions ('the psy complex') provide a mixture of theories and practices which certainly coercively control subjects but increasingly have rendered modern society psychologically minded by *promoting subjectivity*: 'We argue that it is more fruitful to consider the ways that regulatory systems have sought to promote subjectivity than to document the ways in which they have crushed it' (Miller and Rose, 1988, p. 174).

This emphasis has allowed us to go beyond the narrow social control and medicalisation of madness thesis of Scull and understand the ways in which mental health and illness are socially constructed. However, this has two disadvantages as well. First, the *coercive* role of psychiatry, which post-structuralists down-play, is still at the centre of its most blatant oppression of its client group. The growth of the users' movement internationally since the 1960s testifies to this ongoing concern (Rogers and Pilgrim, 1989). Second, emphasising that all the occupational groups within the 'psy complex' are basically in the same business, avoids a sociological account of the incontestable differentials of power, and their consequences, between medical and non-medical staff. Accounts outside post-structuralism, but within the sociology of medicine, can give a more convincing version of the relationships between these occupational groups. These alternatives will be considered in the final chapter.

We hope that, by tracing the elements involved in the establishment and expansion of psychiatry in this chapter, the issue of medical dominance and its importance in determining the shape of the emerging profession of clinical psychology will have been clarified. So, finally, some summary comments will be made on the main professional dynamics in play in the formative period of the 1950s for clinical psychology. What Scull's account implies about more recent developments, and the accounts of the post-structuralists evade or dispute, is the overarching power of medicine. What is clear about the battles waged in the 1950s by the Maudsley group, and by their colleagues nationwide in subsequent decades, is that medical dominance is evident recurrently. The behaviour therapy of the Maudsley School was not offensive in itself to the professional interests of psychiatry in Britain (any more than psychodynamic psychotherapy was at the Tavistock). What determined the flurry of psychiatric reaction to the new profession was that it threatened to encroach upon the therapeutic monopoly of medicine. It should be remembered that, whatever offence psycho-analysis caused to biologically minded asylum doctors, ultimately this could be suppressed in favour of an expanded eclectic profession (which is reflected in the pluralistic sectional organisation of the Royal College of Psychiatrists today).

Whatever justifiable complaints were to be made about Eysenck's reactionary brand of psychology in later years (Anderson, 1969; Billig, 1979), it is fair to say that in the 1950s he, supported by a culture of like-minded Maudsley colleagues, was the progressive champion of an embryonic, scientifically educated, occupational grouping, which was entering a prolonged conflict with a mature dominant profession. The latter had no intention of losing its power, status or privilege to newcomers. Next we will examine factors over and above medical constraints which shaped the formation and development of clinical psychology in Britain.

Chapter 2

Academic traditions, warfare and welfare

The last chapter, necessarily, had to dwell on the power of psychiatry and its impact on the formation of clinical psychology. However, whilst the issue of medical dominance, and how the new profession responded to it, will recur as a key issue in this book, this should not lead to the impression that this is the only historical feature worthy of scrutiny. Three others will be added in this chapter. First, clinical applications were only one part of the development of British psychology. These wider academic features, and the cultural context which channelled them, shaped the content of clinical psychology. Second, the profession emerged in a particular organisational setting after the Second World War. Features of the British welfare state in general, and the National Health Service in particular, have provided opportunities and constraints which have influenced the profession. Moreover, whilst the welfare state expanded in the 1950s, earlier institutional developments such as the regulation of the 'mentally defective' had already determined important building blocks within applied psychology. Third, warfare, as was noted in the last chapter, was to have a significant influence on the shape of modern psychology. The interaction of these three contextual features will be examined in this chapter.

British psychology was formalised as a separate discipline, at least on paper if not as yet fully in practice, on 24 October 1901 at University College, London (Hearnshaw, 1964). There, a meeting was called by Sully, Grote Professor of Mind and Logic at University College. Ten people attended this inaugural gathering of the Psychological Society, including, significantly, four key medical practitioners (Armstrong-Jones, Rivers, McDougall and Mott). The Society did not acquire the prefix 'British' until 1906 when its members discovered another grouping using the same name (Edgell, 1961). In its first year, the Society had thirteen members and it remained a relatively exclusive club until the 1920s. By the outbreak of the First World War its membership stood at only seventy-nine (Edgell, 1961) and by the war's end it still had fewer than one hundred members (Hearnshaw, 1986). The *British Journal of Psychology* was started independently in 1904 by Ward and Rivers and was not taken over as the Society's official journal until 1914, when the membership fee since the beginning of half a guinea was doubled to underwrite the organ's survival. In 1902 Stout had suggested that the Society's proceedings be published in *Mind* but the Committee asked to consider this abandoned their negotiations with the philosophical journal in the light of the imminent initiative of Ward and Rivers. In the very first paragraph of their first editorial in the *Journal* key elements in a bid for legitimacy for a new academic discipline were articulated. They set out the stall for this discipline in the following way:

Psychology, which till recently was known among us chiefly as mental philosophy and was widely concerned with problems of a more or less speculative and transcendental character, has now at length achieved the position of a *positive science*; one of special interest to the philosopher no doubt but still *independent of his control*, possessing its own methods, its own specific problems and a distinct standpoint altogether its own. 'Ideas' in the philosophical sense do not fall within its scope; its inquiries are restricted entirely to *facts*.

(*British Journal of Psychology*, 1904, vol. 1, part 1, p. 1, emphasis added)

This quotation reveals so much about how the new small culture of psychologists viewed their own trade. Note that philosophy, not medicine, was the parent identified as limiting its offspring's growth and how a positive science was now to be concerned with facts. Philosophy continued to retard the differentiation of the discipline in the university system, so that by 1939 there were still only six chairs of psychology in Britain (Hearnshaw, 1964). As psychology increasingly struggled free after the Second World War, this antagonism was to have a severely disabling effect for many years on the capacity of psychologists to address philosophical issues about their work. Positivism and empiricism were to continue to be the ideological motifs of all subsequent branches of psychology (including the clinical branch). The crucial exception to this trend was to be the protection of an alien hermeneutical system (psycho-analysis) within the Medical Section of the Society.

The strong philosophical tradition inherited by the Victorian psychologists, was that of British empiricism. This tradition through Hobbes, Locke, Hume and the Mills legitimised a particular way of practising psychological investigation from the outset. Having said this, the content areas scrutinised by empiricist psychologists after the turn of the century did not necessarily comply with a Victorian orthodoxy. For example, Stout and Sully at the end of the nineteenth century rejected the study of individual characteristics, such as intelligence, which was to be the stock in trade of later psychologists. The twin influences of the upsurge of evolutionary biology and the practical problems thrown up by compulsory education were to act as a pincer movement to guarantee that Galtonian psychology was to contradict, and go into the ascendancy over, the Stout/Sully stance. The dominant tradition associated with British psychology in its first official fifty years was to be that of studying individual differences. In particular in applied form this was to serve the social policy function of classifying and regulating certain parts of the population: criminals, children, races and the mad (Burt, 1927).

Galton (1857–1911) was to initiate this dominant tradition. It was not the inherent superiority of this tradition which legitimised its expansion and maintenance in the first half of this century. Rather, it provided a way of conceptualising and responding to the practical needs emerging from changing socio-economic relationships and it reflected wider ideological forms in late Victorian England. Differential psychology was consistent with the *zeitgeist* of élitism, individualism and ethnocentrism in a social context where imperialism was at its peak. These found an academic expression within both Galton's Eugenics and Spencer's Social Darwinism.

Galton actually inverted the heavily environmentally orientated emphasis of his cousin's theory to argue that it was hereditary factors which accounted for natural selection in the main. Accordingly, he produced *Hereditary Genius* in 1869. In the year of his death, Galton bestowed on University College a new Chair of Eugenics, which was filled by the existing Professor of Applied Mathematics, Karl Pearson. Pearson (1857–1936) devoted his time before and after Galton's death to the systematic study of the relationship between nature and nurture with the specific secondary aim of improving the genetic stock of the English race.

Between them Galton and Pearson developed a credible statistical and psychometric technology to be used by applied psychology in its early days. The former introduced the technique of correlation to assess the relationship between two measured variables (and from this he introduced the correlation coefficient). For his part, Pearson elaborated this initiative by introducing the statistical notions of the normal curve, the standard deviation, multiple correlation, the Chi-square test for goodness of fit and the contingency co-efficient. This aggregate list not only provided a technology to legitimise the new applied profession (both here and in the USA) but also constituted the ideology of that profession: 'a positive science' studying 'facts'. The power of this ideology became apparent in later years when clinical psychologists were to claim their new professional identity. It was this Galton-Pearson legacy which was to clothe this identity (for good or bad).

At the turn of the century, alongside this consolidation of the differential psychology tradition at University College, changes in modes of managing or regulating the population were emerging which were to provide new social opportunities for psychological applications. In addition to the segregative solution for the mentally disabled, now schooling solutions were emerging. In the latter half of the nineteenth century all mentally disabled people were grouped together, under the control of medical practitioners in the asylum system, as 'aments' or 'dements'. The 1890 Lunacy Act entailed 'aments' being framed as a medical problem warranting incarceration.

In 1876, compulsory schooling was introduced. This quickly presented a problem of slower pupils undermining the progress of their brighter peers. In the previous year, the Charity Organisation Society had started a campaign for the separate care of 'improvable idiots'. This continuing campaign contributed to the setting up in 1904 of the Royal Commission on the Care and Control of the Feeble Minded, which published its conclusions and recommendations two years later. The Report claimed that there were around 150,000 'defectives' in England and Wales at that time, many of whom were not classified and managed. It was recommended that, thereafter, each local authority should monitor, diagnose and detain their own 'defectives'. A medical classification was recommended, distinguishing 'idiots', 'imbeciles', 'the feeble minded' and 'moral imbeciles'. The first three were derived from a classification of the asylum superintendent Duncan in 1860. A further recommendation was that a central board of control should be set up to supervise the local administration of the above. These recommendations were incorporated into the 1913 Mental Deficiency Act, which was to govern the administration of the problematically slow until the 1959 Mental Health Act.

At that time, the Eugenics Society (founded in 1907 by Galton) was proselytising about the dangers of the over-fertile feeble-minded weakening the English stock. And, as Hearnshaw (1964) notes, the main textbook of the period (Tredgold's *Mental Deficiency*) emphasised that 'in the great majority of these slum cases there is a pronounced morbid inheritance and their environment is not the cause but the result of their heredity'. Thus, at this point in time, a dominant 'social problem', feeble-minded pauperism and its containment within a newly formed educational system, provided the territory on which applied psychology could build its new profession. Not surprisingly, the psychologists of the day were rejecting the Sully/Stout doubts about individual differences and favouring the Galtonian tradition. The mantle for this tradition in applied form was to be taken on by Cyril Burt.

Burt (1883–1971) was to take over the Chair of Psychology at University College in later years. However, his significance in the first two decades of this century was that he was to carry the differential psychology model out of the employment boundaries of higher education for the first time. In 1913, the same year as the passing of the Mental Deficiency Act, Burt returned to London, after working for five years at Liverpool University with the neuro-physiologist Sherrington. To comply with the new Act, the London County Council had decided to appoint a psychologist (in positive preference to another medical officer). He or she was to be accountable to the local authority inspectorate, not the medical department. (Local medical inspections were initiated in London in 1890 before formal responsibility for all schooling matters was taken over by local education authorities, which were set up under the Education Act of 1902.) The significance of this was that, even if the medical model of diagnosis and classification was legitimised by psychometrics (Ryan, 1972), the employment of applied psychologists working with children for local authorities (the beginnings of educational psychology) was to be established outside medical jurisdiction. This highlighted a contradiction, which was to recur later in the early days of clinical psychology at the Maudsley: psychometrics offered itself conservatively as a diagnostic aid to the medical profession, but the testers themselves also claimed autonomy from this profession.

Burt was employed on a half-time basis and by 1915 he set about conducting a survey of 30,000 children in a London borough in an attempt to find out the distribution of 'backward children' and how to standardise scholastic and non-scholastic tests. Another aim was to determine average and extreme attainments in his sample (Hearnshaw, 1979). Burt's fidelity to the Galtonian tradition was eventually rewarded by two chairs, the first at the London Day Training College (now the Institute of Education) and the second at University College. The latter he inherited from Spearman in 1932 and he continued in that role until 1951. With the inauguration of the medical and educational sections of the BPS in 1919, its membership quadrupled to over 400 within a year (Edgell, 1961) indicating a clear trend: psychology was to expand in the main because of its practical applications not because of its inherent academic credibility. Burt's work was to epitomise this applied expansionism in the profession.

In 1907, Spearman (1863–1945) had been appointed as Reader in Sully's psychological laboratory (set up ten years earlier). The continuing dominance of philosophy mentioned earlier was evident: he was eventually appointed in 1911 to the Chair in Mind and Logic (Hearnshaw, 1964). (The name was changed to 'Psychology' only in 1928.) Spearman emphasised three main aims in psychology: to study abilities and personality; to use psychometric rather than experimental methods; and to study practical 'everday' problems rather than test hypotheses in the laboratory. He also emphasised methodological rigour (another continuing ideological motif in later professionalising branches of psychology) and added factor analysis to the Galton-Pearson statistical paraphernalia. (Burt was to claim in later years that he, not Spearman, invented factor analysis (Hearnshaw, 1979).) These minor disputes were insignificant compared to the cultural and ideological cohesion evident across generations of University College psychologists. This loyalty to the Galtonian cause was produced by each generation conservatively ensuring the trustworthiness of the next before selecting them for appointment.

The consistency of the Galtonian tradition at University College was to be maintained right up to the 1950s, when Eysenck, Burt's pupil, was to incorporate intelligence and personality testing into the first professional practices of British clinical psychology. By this point the profession was to be built upon sedimented layers of eugenic, objectivist and statistical assumptions: the nature/nurture preoccupation; the scorning of subjectivism; the centrality of individual differences; psychometrics; methodological rigour; standard deviations; correlations; chi-squares, etc. etc. These were to constitute not only the bedrock syllabus for neophyte clinical psychologists but also a scientific rhetoric of justification for their status and role in a context dominated by another profession.

Hopefully, a picture is emerging of the dominant professional practices becoming associated with British psychology outside medicine early in this century. This Galtonian tradition was not, of course, to exist in isolation but was to jostle for position with psychoanalysis as far as applications to mental disorder, child development, factory behaviour and industrial relations were concerned over the next forty years. In the latter regard, the school of differential psychology at University College was to predominate earlier than the medically controlled psychoanalysis of the Institute of Human Relations associated with the Tavistock Clinic after the Second World War. This twin tradition development has been by and large characterised by animosity. Certain quaint contradictions were apparent however. Flugel, a psychoanalytical psychologist, worked amicably at University College and Spearman was a founder member of the Medico-Psychoanalytic Clinic opened in London in 1913. Spearman also collaborated with Bernard Hart, a populariser of psychodynamic ideas, on mental tests for dementia in 1914.

Whilst developments in industrial psychology during and after the First World War may seem, at first glance, marginal to clinical interests this was not the case. A central concern of these early studies was the relationship between efficiency and stress. Warfare had demanded psychological expertise on the industrial as well as battle front. In Britain, civilians had to produce the munitions as fast as the soldiers could fire them. The military-industrial complex of 1914–1918 determined the behaviour of non-combatants as well as combatants. Hours worked in the factories by men before the war ranged from 48 to 55 per week. During the war, with a predominantly female labour force, this rate leapt to 70 to

90 hours per week, with some exceeding 100 hours (Hearnshaw, 1964).

In 1915, in response to the consequences of this new set of stressful conditions, Lloyd George, set up the Health of Munitions Workers Committee. Also, a group of psychologists (including Burt) from within the British Association for the Advancement of Science offered reports on the subject in 1915 and 1916. Whilst many of the principles of industrial psychology had been set out by Munsterberg (a German psychologist who succeeded William James at Harvard) in 1913, it was the context of warfare which stimulated an expansion in the sub-discipline. By the end of the war an important new agenda of topics and problems in factory production, related to the health and efficiency of workers, was established. This agenda also provided a new opportunity for the expansion of applied psychology. At that time Myers was promoting the notion that each large British city should contain an institute of psychology to respond to problems in education, industry and mental health.

By 1921, factory owners were seeing the potential benefits for profitability and industrial relations of this type of advice and industrial sponsorship was available to Myers to set up the National Institute of Industrial Psychology. (He resigned from his Cambridge post to chair the NIIP in the following year.) The sponsors in those early years included Cadbury, Rowntree, Tootal Broadhurst Lee, Harrisons and Crosfield, Cammell Laird and the Rockefeller Trust. The NIIP pioneered research and consultancy in time and motion study, staff selection and development, personnel management and marketing. In many ways, the factory (like the hospital) provided an optimal closed system in which behaviour could be studied and manipulated. The terrain of such closed systems meshes well with systematic recording and permits the 'methodological rigour' favoured by Spearman (Spearman was a founder member of the NIIP) in ways in which more open systems do not (as anthropological and sociological field-workers know). Between the wars the NIIP offered its services to a variety of government deparments as well as industry.

An important parallel organisation to the NIIP evolved from the Health of Munitions Workers Committee. The latter was renamed first the Industrial Fatigue Board and then the Industrial Health Research Board, which was subsumed under the Medical Research Council in 1929. The staff of the NIIP and MRC overlapped and its work included research into vocational guidance (Burt and Rodger), personality assessment (Vernon) and incentive systems (Mace). In particular, the consequences of stress and monotony in factory tasks were studied along with their psychoneurotic and psychosomatic consequences.

The development of the NIIP and the MRC had both progressive and conservative implications. The ameliorative reforms of factory conditions they recommended, to reduce the frequency of physical and mental disorder in workers, were welcomed and supported by the trade union movement. However, these 'twin pillars of industrial psychology in Great Britain between the wars' (Hearnshaw, 1964) also legitimised the individualisation of social and economic relationships by working within a psychological framework. Political dynamics (like the inherent conflict of interests between owners and workers) became re-framed as problems between individuals to be managed using psychological technologies. Accordingly, applied psychology was offering a 'technical fix' for political tensions and the experience of alienated labour was rendered a problem of stress, neurosis or adjustment.

These deeply conservative conseqences of applied psychology were to be replayed in relation to mental disorder when this scientistic ideology, along with its associated methods, was transferred to the clinical context. Moreover, psychologists (like their medical colleagues) could play out a highly political role in terms of the management of the population, whilst at the same time disowning such a role by pointing to their 'disinterested' scientific training and credentials. Bearing in mind these military and industrial roots of scientistic applied psychology, let us now turn to the period, introduced in the last chapter, when the clinical branch of psychology was eventually established.

In 1948 the National Health Service was set up by the post-war Labour government. Claims that this type of reform were radically socialist are overstated. The management of sickness in capitalist society had been inefficient and disorganised. Consequently, a variety of non-socialist initiatives had suggested sporadically for many years some version of a centrally regulated health system financed from taxation (the Liberal National Insurance Act of 1911, reports from the British Medical Association in 1932 and 1938, the Beveridge Report 1942). A version of the NHS was set out in blueprint form by the wartime coalition government before Attlee and Bevan were to be elected and take the glory.

None the less, the ideology of the new service (health care financed from general taxation delivered free at the time of need) was to have important consequences for the post-war health professions. This was to be particularly the case for those like clinical psychology which were new to the scene. Scientific rationality and egalitarianism were important strands in the *zeitgeist* of the 1950s. The first of these was so strong that it is noteworthy that the new profession did not immediately formally appeal to legal means ('Chartering') to establish its legitimacy. A limited form of this in relation to registering who could carry out mental testing had in fact been established already following the report of the BPS Professional Standards Committee in 1934 warning of the problem of unqualified people abusing tests. However, by and large, the early clinical psychology practitioners placed their faith in science as the main indicator of their professional credibility. Scientism as a justificatory ideology is still a dominant strand in the profession today, as we will see later in Chapters 6 and 7.

In the case of egalitarianism, the hierarchical and authoritarian relationships associated with medical dominance were to prove personally offensive to a generation of young psychology graduates being socialised in the post-war period. Whilst the older subordinate groups, like nursing, had found occupational strategies to accommodate to medicine, and even these were uneven and tenuous, clinical psychology had no equivalent legacy of norms. Its very lack of history and its graduate status, in a cultural context where egalitarianism was an important aspect of the *Zeitgeist*, was to provide a formula for certain conflict with the medical profession.

What must have been perplexing to psychiatrists was the change of aspirations of the new profession. Following the limited chartering of the 1930s, the psychologists of the early 1950s seemed to embrace the diagnostic assistant role before lurching towards behaviour therapy. Consequently, the psychometric emphasis of the Galtonian tradition had put its practitioners in a position in which they could be (and often were in specific local disputes) hoist with their own petard. This paradox is discussed by Holland (1978) in relation to the doleful reflections in the 1973 Presidential address to the BPS by Tizard. Tizard here rues the days of Myers and Burt and the legacy of problems their brand of psychometric psychology left for the post-war generation:

We can look back then at a whole era in which those who were using psychology in industry, education and the clinical field drew from the prevailing psychological theory of the time the lesson that to apply psychology was to assign individuals to points in a multi-dimensional matrix. This, it was thought, would enable them to be sorted into appropriate categories, for which there were appropriate educational or occupational niches, or appropriate forms of remedial treatment.

(Tizard quoted in Holland, 1978, p. 176)

Tizard, a more socially orientated psychologist, was quite correct to highlight the narrow sterility that the Galtonian tradition was to produce. Equally it cannot be denied that the sorting and labelling of individuals, to regulate their position in society, would have been carried out by some occupational group or other willing to do this work on behalf of the state. However, the University College tradition of course pursued this reduction of humanity to 'points in a multi-dimensional matrix' with a particular scientific gusto. This was a function of the dominant British tradition of empiricism, which tended to limit the horizons of what could be defined as 'proper' psychology. In line with this overarching constraint of empiricism, it is also true that these limited horizons did not affect psychology in isolation from other disciplines.

Anderson (1969) notes that across a variety of academic departments, after the Second World War, British empiricism was being championed by immigrants (the so-called 'white' émigrés – radical or 'red' émigrés tended to settle in Scandinavia or the USA). Essentially the conservative and anti-theoretical character of British empiricism led to the theoretical stock for academia being depleted. For example, in British psychology there was an aversion to theoretical 'systems building' (Hearnshaw, 1964) in favour of the methodological rigour noted earlier. Consequently, theoretical systems like behaviourism or psychoanalysis had to be imported and shaped for home consumption.

Despite the stalwart work of Eysenck in defending the faith of British empiricism within the University College tradition, a struggle for its intellectual pre-eminence in the new profession of clinical psychology was inevitable. The very aversion to theoretical systems building noted by Hearnshaw, and re-affirmed in a more general sense here by Anderson, was to undermine the chances of the

Maudsley school attaining a permanent dominance in the field. Anderson highlights an inherent contradiction of empiricism: it encourages a piecemeal attitude towards science and prioritises methodology over theory. The problem eventually emerges of providing coherent and confident theoretical justifications for empirical projects. Hence the necessary importation of foreign intellectual labour. In the case of early post-war clinical psychology this was exemplified by the Maudsley group of *émigrés* (Eysenck, Shapiro and Rachman).

In the midst of this cultural reconstruction after the war, intellectual counter-currents were set up by the already imported mid-European tradition of psychoanalysis. (Klein had been in England from 1926 and the Freuds arrived in flight from Nazism in 1938.) By the 1950s, England had become the new home for a crucial regrouping of psychoanalytical factions. The vital, internationally noted debates between Anna Freud and Melanie Klein started on the Continent were now being hosted by Britain. The tensions generated led in turn to creative revisions by the middle group of object-relations theorists (e.g. Winnicott and Khan in London, Fairbairn in Edinburgh and later Guntrip in Leeds) who selectively took from both antagonists without fully supporting either. Also, as was noted in the last chapter, physicians had incorporated psychoanalysis and so it was well sheltered by a self-confident medical élite. At the very time that the Maudsley group were seeking to refute the legitimacy of psychodynamic psychotherapy, it was proving to be of continuing relevance to clinicians and the intellectual avant-garde all over the world, with the crucible for these psychoanalytical debates and developments being in Britain. Together this protection by the medical profession and its international intellectual reputation were to buffer psychoanalysis permanently from Maudsley-style attacks.

Although the Maudsley position was not to reign supreme in the long term in the profession, for a good while (up until the mid-1970s) it was to dominate the training of new practitioners. For instance, most of the newly developing clinical courses in the 1960s and 1970s were headed by Maudsley-course graduates. Also, the bulk of the training on these courses until the late 1970s was constituted by a combination of psychometrics and behaviour therapy. Richards (1983), studying the development of the profession up until 1979, sketched three main phases associated with the 1950s, 1960s and 1970s respectively: psychometrics; behaviour therapy; and eclecticism. (In Chapter 6 we will argue that this third phase has been eclipsed now by managerialism.) Only in the third phase, of eclecticism, was psychotherapy to be brought in from the cold, and even then the Tavistock training course in clinical psychology did not survive.

Thus, whilst the Maudsley ideology did not permanently exclude psychotherapy from the ambit of clinical psychology, it came very near to doing so. Whilst this led to the view from within the profession that psychotherapy was a thing of the pre-scientific past, except of course at the Tavistock Clinic, its integrity remained intact within the medical profession. Not surprisingly, therefore, psychiatrists were well prepared to make a bid in the mid-1970s to control and manage the development of NHS psychotherapy services (Royal College of Psychiatrists, 1975), leaving psychotherapeutically-orientated psychologists on the sidelines. By the late 1980s clinical psychologists could do little more than bemoan the consequences of this legacy (Nitsun et al., 1989).

At this point it is worth reviewing why the narrow Maudsley agenda of psychometrics plus behaviour therapy failed to be sustained and why it was overtaken by eclecticism during the 1970s. One factor has just been noted: medical psychotherapy was to ensure that psychodynamic psychology was to be preserved in the NHS. Mental health professionals do not operate for all of their time in occupational space sealed off from other disciplines, so some interdisciplinary support existed for psychotherapists. Also, whilst the Tavistock staff retreated more and more into a ghetto position during the 1970s, there were small pockets of resistance to the Maudsley hegemony in provincial psychology departments. But probably of greater significance was the wider cultural upheaval of the late 1960s and early 1970s. This was the period when mental health became a very popular focus for 'counter-cultural' interest. This time was associated with a dizzy mixture of sexual and student politics, libertarianism, Marxism, feminism, gay liberation, existentialism, eastern mysticism and hallucinogenic drugs.

One widely supported movement within this cultural context was the 'anti-psychiatry' associated with the psychiatric libertarianism of the right (Szasz, 1960) and the left (Cooper, 1967; Laing, 1968). At this point, the scientism of the dominant Maudsley tradition began to look grey and conservative. Suddenly, new opportunities began to open up to disturb the dominance of psychometrics-cum-methodological behaviourism. Young practitioners coming into the expanding profession were faced with the challenge of reconciling these wider cultural influences with the legacy of empiricism. In the early 1970s popular expressions of internal opposition to traditional approaches within the mental health professions began to appear. A popular journal of the time was *Red Rat* which highlighted the reactionary character of psychometric labelling and the social adjustment offered by behaviour therapy. Outside psychology the gay movement was beginning to retaliate against the use of aversion therapy to suppress homosexuality (Beckman, 1974).

In 1973, a group of broadly humanistic psychologists asserted the proper link between academic psychology and psychotherapy. This group, including Shotter, Mair, Bannister and Davis, formed the Psychology and Psychotherapy Association in the hope, amongst other things, of rescuing clinical psychology from the 'aggressive scientism' of the Maudsley tradition. At the very time when the latter appeared to have reached a sufficiently strong position to banish permanently the spectre of psychologists taking verbal psycho-therapy seriously, neophyte practitioners were being offered cultural succour for their interest in that very taboo practice. In addition to the PPA initiative, the works of Laing, Cooper and Bateson (spanning psychoanalysis, existentialism and communication theory) stimulated an interest in family therapy. Revisions of British object-relations theory such as Laing's re-working of Winnicott (Laing, 1960) were to soon find resonances in the confluence of social movements, like feminism, with psychotherapy (e.g. Eichenbaum and Orbach, 1982). Radical experiments in social action incorporating object-relations theory began to emerge outside the state sector of mental health provision for working-class clients (Holland, 1979; Hogget and Lousada, 1985; Holland and Holland, 1988).

These interweaving elements emerging during the 1970s are sketched to highlight the social context shaping the profession by providing it with opportunities and constraints. In the former case, the time was ripe for the remit of clinical psychology to be expanded to incorporate practices previously criticised or evaded. However, the profession still had to retain its scientific credibility, as it had consistently argued that it had a circumscribed technical scientific competence to justify its occupational niche (and the posts, salaries and status going with this). Thus a full-blown embracing of psychotherapy to the exclusion of psychometrics and behaviour therapy was an unlikely scenario. The outcome instead was the hybrid compromise of 'scientific humanism' (Richards, 1983). Eclecticism consequently prevailed, mirroring the revision of the medical model in psychiatry during this period. Baruch and Treacher (1978) discuss the portmanteau model of Anthony Clare which incorporated and defused the criticism of biological reductionism within the Kraepelinian tradition from anti-psychiatric critics (Clare, 1977).

The scientific humanism of the 1970s was expressed in three main ways. First, individual practitioners could be found becoming more and more eclectic. Second, taken as a whole, the profession became pluralistic; that is, clinical psychology contained sub-groups of practitioners, practising with different models, which increasingly coexisted with mutual tolerance rather than the acrimony previously linked to the Maudsley/Tavistock tension. Third, therapeutic practice became associated with more and more attempts to integrate disparate theoretical models. Probably the most unlikely of these bedfellows was 'cognitive-behaviour therapy' or 'cognitive-behaviour modification', which was understandably viewed by theoretical purists as a contradiction in terms (Ledwidge, 1978).

By the end of the 1970s, cognitivism was effectively replacing behaviourism as the dominant model within academic psychology and so it was pretty inevitable that the scientific humanism of the time should be associated with a rapprochement of this type (no matter what contradictions it apparently generated). By the arrival of the 1980s, undergraduates socialised into the ways of these new integrations in psychology applied for clinical courses with an uncommitted, confused or agnostic attitude towards psychological theory. Since they had come through a higher education system with the deep-rooted cultural weakness of British empiricism described earlier, this is hardly that surprising. However, this could be contrasted with the healthy opposition provoked by the Maudsley and University College tradition in the late 1950s and early 1960s. Graduates from this either conformed and perpetuated its aims and values (especially when in the position of heading training courses) or they reacted strongly and re-worked or extended alternative forms of theory. This was most marked in relation to the group which popularised and developed the work of Kelly's Personal Construct Theory (Kelly, 1955; Bannister and Mair, 1970; Neimeyer, 1985). By contrast, the students of the eclectic period had nothing to fight for or against as far as theory was concerned. They added to and reinforced the eclecticism already dominating the culture of their post-graduate trainers, prompting Smail (1982) to describe his profession cynically, but with plenty of good reason, as being 'homogenised and sterilised'.

The style of mental health professionalism during the 1970s was studied by Goldie (1974, 1975). His research just prior to the impact of the deliberations of the Trethowan Committee's investigation of *The Role of Psychologists in the Health Service* (DHSS, 1977) reveals some of the features outlined above. As a sociologist looking at the profession quizzically, Goldie found some confusion about how its identity was being described within the discourse of its leadership. For instance, in the late sixties some were still emphasising the role of psychometrics (modernised via automation) (Miller, 1968; Peck and Gathercole, 1968). These authors were carrying on the tradition in which psychologists had unambiguous monopolistic rights, dating back to the limited registration arrangement of the mid-1930s. The Royal Charter of the Society established in 1965 gave the BPS only a vague legitimacy to regulate psychological practice. Goldie noted that for the first time in the early 1970s the Division of Clinical Psychology was making moves to establish a code of professional conduct and register of practitioners, following a discussion of this by Denburg (1969). However, these rumblings of professionalisation proper did not culminate in full 'Chartering' of psychologists until 1989. In the meantime the identity of the profession still seemed to be bound up more with factions of the profession's leadership arguing about what brand of theory or practice might, or should, be associated with clinical psychology.

In addition to the rearguard action by psychometricians, Goldie also found Dabbs (1972) noting the increasing interest of practitioners in verbal psychotherapy. However, the applied scientist model predominated at the time, in line with the Maudsley formula of legitimacy in clinical psychology being synonymous with some proportion of only two permitted ingredients: psychometrics and behaviour therapy (Ingham, 1961; Gwynne-Jones, 1969; Shapiro, 1969; Eysenck, 1975). Thus even fifteen years before chartering of psychologists, Goldie noted that:

> Many clinical psychologists are increasingly claiming to be 'applied scientists'. Confident in the efficacy of this approach many clinical psychologists are now claiming that they should replace doctors as *the* profession to be in charge of the treatment and rehabilitation of certain groups of patients.
>
> (Goldie, 1975, p. 8)

This conclusion was drawn from a BPS memorandum to the DHSS on the report of the Committee of Inquiry into neglect at Whittingham Hospital. This indicated that the main difficulties encountered by psychiatric patients were not medical but social learning problems and that psychologists were the appropriately trained experts in the latter. However, as was indicated above in relation to the emergence of the Psychology and Psychotherapy Asssociation, the 1970s was by no means narrowly associated with this self-confident scientism. Claridge and Brooks (1973) studied attitudes of applicants to the Glasgow MSc course in clinical psychology. They found that only a minority of applicants emphasised the 'scientific' aspects of their interests. The bulk of them saw problem solving and helping as the main features of their imminent role. Therapy not research was given priority. However, in the case of behaviour therapy the two are deemed to be inextricably linked (Eysenck, 1971) a view challenged as rhetorical by Portes (1971).

With the exception of the minority of psychologists content to practise solely as diagnostic aides for psychiatrists, the majority for one reason or another were growing restless with the limitations of being subordinate to the medical profession. The type of hostile psychiatric reaction encountered by Eysenck and Gwynne Jones in 1958 was to prefigure many local skirmishes throughout the health services in subsequent decades. The disaffection was dealt with by the Trethowan Report (DHSS, 1977). Prior to this, tensions about the NHS role were becoming widely visible as practitioners became more numerous. In the early 1960s there were fewer than two hundred clinical psychologists in England and Wales; a decade later this went up to six hundred, and this figure was doubled by 1982. Although the profession is small compared to the thousands of nurses and medical practitioners in the NHS (at the time of writing there are still only around two thousand practitioners), the expansion of the profession combined with its members' assurance (or arrogance) of being graduate scientists did not ensure a quiet life for psychiatry. The latter has been in a permanent crisis of legitimacy since the storms of anti-psychiatry. Its poorly argued case for its own type of applied science (Birley, 1990) along with conceptual critiques of 'mental illness' (Ingleby, 1980) and its loss of a territorial base, with the demise of the large mental hospital, have made it a ready target for any group, professional or lay, wanting to find fault with psychiatric theory and practice. However, psychologists did not respond uniformly when faced with such a large target to hit. The vulnerability of psychiatry as a contradictory and pre-scientific paradigm was well buffered by the *legal* mandate it claimed for itself. The 1959 Mental Health Act gave psychiatrists the confidence to claim that they were condemned to a leadership role in the field of mental health as a function of their legal responsibilities. The strategies that professions subordinate to psychiatry (psychology, social work and nursing) then developed were determined essentially by this primary medical mandate to have authority over patients and non-medical colleagues alike.

In a wider study of these strategies, Goldie (1977) points out that non-medical professionals took up three main positions – of compliance, eclecticism or radical opposition. Individual psychologists could thus be found negotiating the first role by continuing to be psychometricians. The second role would entail negotiating a local division of labour so that they would find a niche seeing neurotic patients leaving the mad to their medical colleagues (the formula favoured by Eysenck (1975)). The third stance would be in terms of challenging medical theory and practice by entering into conflict with their psychiatric colleagues, or by leaving the hospital to practise independently of consultant authority. By the late 1970s, the latter faction were very visible and noisy (Pilgrim, 1983). Many psychologists sought to work in primary care or non-psychiatric settings. In these environments, acrimony was less likely in relation to the medical profession because there was a clearer distance, in terms of role expectations, between the two groups. For instance, psychologists were not seriously trying to usurp the role of the general practitioner as they might usurp that of the psychiatrist, in line with the Whittingham memorandum noted above. Against this background, the Trethowan Report was published. This will be discussed in Chapter 6, but before that we will deal with the socialisation of trainee clinicians. Through exploring the origins and development of the scientist-practitioner (or scientist-professional) model within the profession, we will attempt to demonstrate the underlying contradictions that clinical psychologists inherit when they are inducted into the profession.

Chapter 3

The origins of the scientist-practitioner model

It is not an easy task to explore the evolution of clinical psychology training in this country. For a profession which is preoccupied with being scientific, and hence claims to base its work on published research, there is a dearth of literature on training. Indeed, it is difficult to gauge the profession's level of interest in training issues. Judging from the published record there seems to have been remarkably little real debate. For example, an analysis of the articles appearing in the *Bulletin of the British Psychological Society* in the period from 1949 to its replacement by the *Psychologist* in 1988 provides no evidence that any sustained debate took place. Occasional articles were published but these did not address any of the major dilemmas that are integral to the training of clinical psychologists.

Admittedly the *Newsletter of the Division of Clinical Psychology* and its successor, *Clinical Psychology Forum*, have published articles on training but almost without exception these articles have been concerned with the pragmatics of training. Various working party reports from the BPS Committee on Training in Clinical Psychology have also been published from time to time but these are characterised by meticulous attention to detail coupled with a strange inability to acknowledge that the training of clinical psychologists is problematic.

In this chapter we will attempt to explore training from a historical point of view. This task is fraught with difficulty because we have had to rely mostly on published papers and documents in order to construct a history of the developments that have taken place during the last forty years. A more adequate history will unfortunately have to wait upon a much more intensive research project which would also utilise oral history techniques. Reviewing the published record is important but it is obvious to us that publications do not necessarily reflect the developments that take place. Psychologists are renowned for their inability to agree with each other and yet at the same time it is usually only psychologists from the more prestigious centres who tend to publish. It is therefore inevitable that the 'true' history of developments within the profession is extremely difficult to write if the history is constructed from published material. This chapter is therefore very vulnerable to criticism on these grounds but we nevertheless feel it is important because nobody else has, as yet, attempted to understand training from a historical point of view.

Predictably, we will start our historical reconstruction by examining the work of H.J. Eysenck. Eysenck was undoubtedly the most important spokesman for the profession of clinical psychology in the immediate post-war period – it was his views that strongly influenced the early development of training in this country. Interestingly, his first paper on this topic was published in 1949 (in the American equivalent of the *British Psychological Society Bulletin*). This paper, entitled 'Training in clinical psychology: an English point of view', is a trenchant attack on the American way of training clinical psychologists. Eysenck challenged both the findings of the important Committee on Training in Clinical Psychology of the American Psychological Association (1947) and the influential Josiah Macey Jr. Foundation conference on Training in Clinical Psychology (1947). We will pay particular attention to this paper because it is almost unique in addressing many of the central dilemmas of training.

The essence of Eysenck's disagreement with his American colleagues is contained in the second paragraph of his article.

> The main conclusion of the APA report lies in the stress 'of the need for preparing the clinical psychologists with a combination of applied and theoretical knowledge in three major areas: *diagnosis*, *therapy* and *research*'
>
> (Eysenck, 1949, p. 123)

To which Eysenck ripostes:

> Equally briefly it is our belief that training in therapy is not, and should not be, an essential part of the clinical psychologist's training; that clinical psychology demands competence in the fields of diagnosis and/or research, but that therapy is something essentially alien to clinical psychology, and that, if it be considered

desirable on practical grounds that psychologists perform therapy, a separate discipline of Psycho-therapist should be built up to take its place beside that of Clinical Psychology.

(Eysenck, 1949, p. 173)

It is important to stress that Eysenck's position was shared by many leading psychologists. For example, John Raven, a psychologist working at the Crichton Royal in Scotland, was also vehemently opposed to psychologists being involved in therapy. Writing in the *Bulletin of the British Psychological Society* in 1950 he argued that:

It is not the clinical psychologist's function to put other people right either by treating them therapeutically or by fitting them into appropriate social situations.

(Raven, 1960 cited by Hetherington, 1981)

Raven tenaciously held on to his position so that when he published a book in 1966 (following his retirement) he still maintained that the psychologist's main task was to understand clients – therapeutic involvement could only contaminate this process (Raven, 1960).

The subsequent evolution of clinical psychology was (as we know with the benefit of hindsight) predominantly linked to clinical psychologists establishing themselves as therapists who could claim to be responsive to clients' needs. Eysenck's position therefore appears decidedly quixotic. Nevertheless the arguments he uses to dismiss the American position are very intriguing – they raise a number of issues that are still central to the dilemmas facing clinical psychology. First of all, Eysenck was at pains to refute the arguments in favour of therapy that the APA mobilised. In the wake of the Second World War, with its enormous numbers of 'neuropsychiatric' casualties (to use the then current term), the APA insisted that there was an enormous social need for more therapists to be trained – clinical psychologists could obviously help make up the deficit. Eysenck refutes this position with characteristic disdain:

We must be careful not to let social need interfere with scientific requirements; ultimately psychology cannot simply go where social need requires, unless it wishes to be led into a cul-de-sac. A science must follow its course according to more germane arguments than the possibly erroneous conceptions of social need.

(Eysenck, 1949, p. 173)

Eysenck's self-appointed role as defender of clinical psychology as a science appears to be an historical anachronism, especially viewed through American eyes. It is ironic to think that Eysenck's paper was published in 1949, the very year that a key conference on training was convened by the American Psychological Association (with financial backing from the National Institute of Mental Health and the US Public Health Service). This conference held at Boulder, Colorado, was crucial in determining the subsequent evolution of training in the US but conference members were clear that the whole future of clinical psychology was necessarily bound up with its ability to meet social needs.

> Clinical psychology in recent years is an excellent example of the interaction of a professional group and social needs . . . the recent professional developments in clinical psychology were largely non-instigated (by the profession), and following World War II were compounded by recognition of the need for more and better-trained persons to minister to the mentally and emotionally disturbed. . . . As a fairly young profession, clinical psychology is in both an enviable and a precarious position. There is no doubt about the immense, unmet social need for more and better mental hygiene services, including research. The tasks before clinical psychologists lies in adopting such policies in their training institutions that are best calculated to provide services that can demonstrate social usefulness.
>
> (Raimy, 1950, p. 19)

Eysenck's policy was essentially a manifesto for the development of a very different profession. Developments in clinical psychology were destined to overturn his position but the underlying tensions concerning the scientific role of clinical psychologists remain largely unresolved forty years later.

It is for this reason that Eysenck's early writings are important. Our concern is not to slip into the error of producing an *ad hominem* critique of Eysenck but to use his work to highlight important epistemological issues that have bedevilled the training of clinical psychologists.

Having despatched the APA's first argument to his satisfaction Eysenck then turns to the second one – which is summarised by the following quotation from the APA report:

> Our strong conviction about the need for therapeutic experience grows out of the recognition that therapeutic contact with patients provides an experience which cannot be duplicated by any other type of relationship for the intensity and the detail with which it

reveals motivational complexities. A person who is called upon to do diagnostic or general research work in the field of clinical psychology is seriously handicapped without such a background; a person who is called upon to do research in therapy ... cannot work at all without such a background.

(APA, 1947, cited by Eysenck, 1949, pp. 173–4)

Eysenck's dismissive reply to this position is worth quoting in full since it reveals the crudeness of a positivist position which was characteristic of the profession at that time.

To a scientist, a statement of this kind must be anathema. It is traditionally conceded that the value of scientific research is judged in terms of its methodology, the importance, within the general framework of scientific knowledge, of the results achieved, and the possibilities that other scientists can duplicate the experiment with similar results. We wish to protest against the introduction of a new kind of evaluating device, namely, the background training of the scientist. To say that research ... into the process and effects of therapy ... cannot be carried out at all by persons who are not themselves therapists appears to us to take the concept of research in this field out of the realm of science into the mystical regions of intuition, idiographic 'understanding', and unrepeatable personal experience.

(Eysenck, 1949, p. 174)

It is tempting to be drawn into this debate – Eysenck clearly has every right to be concerned about the impact of psychoanalytic training on the ability of clinical psychologists to undertake research but we would argue that his uncritical acceptance of the 'scientific' framework of psychology did not allow him to examine the underlying issue addressed by the APA. It is therefore not surprising that he fails to explore the APA's position in any depth and abruptly turns to exploring the grounds for supporting what is effectively the 'scientist- diagnostician' model rather than the 'scientist-professional' or 'scientist- practitioner' model of the APA. He lists no less than six major arguments for excluding therapy from the clinical psychologist's role.

His first argument addresses the crucial question of the division of labour within the field of mental illness:

[S]pecialisation of function is an inevitable condition for advance. The team of psychiatrist-psychologist-social worker constitutes such a combined attack on a problem ... the psychiatrist is responsible for carrying out therapy. The psychologist for diagnostic help and research design, and the social worker for investigation of social conditions in so far as they affect the case.... There are far too few persons competent in their own sphere – be that psychiatry, psychology or social work – to allow any but the most exceptional to combine several functions. But training courses are run for the average practitioner, not for the rare and isolated genius. It follows that training in clinical psychology should concentrate on those areas in which the psychologist can make his most significant contribution to the psychiatric team.

(Eysenck, 1949, p. 174)

Writing in 1991 we find it anachronistic that a clinical psychologist should so readily accept a division of labour which tacitly accepts the professional dominance of psychiatry. But clearly Eysenck was unaware of the trap contained in his formulation. His position as a key contributor to the newly founded Institute of Psychiatry blinded him to the uncomfortable realities of the historically determined division of power that actually existed in multidisciplinary teams. The rational 'scientific' arguments of Eysenck about how such a team could be constituted were markedly naive and accurately reflected the crucial weaknesses of Eysenck's own brand of theorising. The scientism and ahistoricism of his own theorising could not equip him to understand how an emerging profession would have great difficulty in establishing its modus operandi in the face of opposition from other well-entrenched professions with axes of their own to grind.

But we need to remind ourselves that Eysenck's essentially reductionist view of mental illness underlined his acceptance of the primacy of the psychiatrist's role in providing therapy. In order to establish his second argument against clinical psychologists undertaking therapy he therefore merely quoted a leading psychiatrist's view of the matter:

In this question we may quote Dr. D.G. Wright of the U.S. Naval Hospital, Great Lakes, Illinois, who points out that 'the psychiatrist's part in defining the kind of pathological processes at work must be decisive. A great many pathological processes have significance only to the physician, and are in the first place illnesses which, although manifested by emotional and mental symptoms, are caused directly by injuries, diseases, and other organic processes in the brain'.

(Eysenck, 1949, p. 174)

By adopting such a conformist (but of course 'scientific') attitude to psychiatry Eysenck helped create a milieu which enabled clinical psychology to develop. Ironically the rapid development of behaviour therapy during the next ten years resulted in a dramatic switch in Eysenck's position. Behaviour therapy was ideologically and conceptually a perfect vehicle for expanding the role of the clinical psychologist into the therapeutic arena since its claims to be based on 'scientific' principles enabled clinical psychologists of Eysenck's positivistic stance to adopt its methods uncritically. Therapy based upon the 'scientific' principles of learning theory could be legitimately bolted on to the structure of clinical psychology and any thought of personal training for therapy could be neatly sidestepped because a behaviour therapist is essentially an applied scientist who dispassionately advises treatment programmes based on scientific principles. The therapist (like the scientist) is trained in methods that are allegedly 'objective' and hence the subjectivity of the person who is the therapist can be neatly ignored. Within this model the therapist, of course, has no gender, no politics and no beliefs other than the scientific ones inculcated by the training programme to which s/he has been exposed.

The most significant body of therapeutic knowledge which was available to clinical psychologists in the immediate post-war period was, of course, psychoanalysis, not behaviour therapy, but Eysenck was implacably hostile to psychoanalysis. Eysenck's reasons for objecting to psychoanalysis are well known – his attack on its efficacy beginning in 1951 is too well celebrated to detain us here, but it is not surprising to discover in his 1949 paper that he is vehemently opposed to the APA's suggestion that clinical psychologists should undergo personal therapy. Eysenck is absolutely emphatic that clinical psychologists should have none of it because any form of personal therapy would involve undermining the clinical psychologist's ability to be scientifically detached. The force of Eysenck's argument is well illustrated in the following quotation from his paper.

According to the APA, 'psychologists must come around to the acceptance of some kind of intensive self-evaluation as an essential part of the training of the clinical psychologist. We are not prepared to recommend any special form of such procedures, although some of us believe that wherever possible this should take the form of psychoanalysis. . . .' The reader may more easily see the danger in this recommendation (which itself is an almost inevitable consequent of the premise that clinical psychologists should do therapy) if he glances at the following statement made by one of the best-known psychoanalysts in this country whose experience in the field is probably unrivalled: 'The transferences and counter-transferences developing during training analysis tends to give rise in the candidate to emotional conviction of the soundness of the training analyst's theories' (Glover, 1945). In other words, it is proposed that the young and relatively defenceless student be imbued with the 'premature' cystallizations of spurious 'orthodoxy' which constitute Freudianism through the transferences and counter-transferences developing during his training. Here indeed we have a fine soil on which to plant the seeds of objective, methodologically sound, impartial and scientifically acceptable search!

(Eysenck, 1949, p. 175)

Clearly Eysenck's point is a challenging one. The role of personal therapy in training in clinical psychology remains largely unresolved to this day. The majority of courses do not require trainees to undertake personal work of any sort but we would argue that this reflects both the uncritical acceptance of the Eysenckian tradition and the influence of behaviour therapy which does not place such a demand on the neophyte.

His fourth objection to clinical psychologists becoming therapists is really a pragmatic one – he argues that a thorough training in research and diagnostic testing is in itself 'a full-time occupation' *(sic)* and that the addition of a third type of training would merely result in a lower level of skill and knowledge in all three levels. Curiously Eysenck is not prepared to debate whether courses could be lengthened to cope with this third strand in training. For him the case is apparently so self-evident that such issues do not warrant any discussion.

His fifth objection is more telling – and more interesting since it raises a crucial issue about the selection of trainees which remains unsolved (and unresearched) to this day. With characteristic bluntness he argues that:

students who are interested in the therapeutic side are nearly always repelled by the scientific flavour of research training, while conversely the students who are best suited and more successful on the research side betray little interest in active therapy.

(Eysenck, 1949, p. 175)

He admits that this position is based on personal experience rather than research but implies that research findings would support his position. He therefore suggests that 'here is a powerful reason for restricting training in clinical psychology to diagnosis and research.'

His sixth objection overlaps with his fifth. He insists that the APA's inventory of the necessary characteristics of the right kind of person who can become a clinical psychologist is remarkably comprehensive. According to Eysenck the APA's list of attributes includes 'superior intellectual ability and judgement, originality, resourcefulness and versatility, curiosity, insight, sense of humour, tolerance, "unarrogance", industry, acceptance of responsibility, trust, cooperativeness, integrity, self-control, stability', and a variety of qualities whose operational definition would be even more difficult such as 'ability to adopt a therapeutic attitude'. Ironically this list of the virtues needed by a clinical psychologist is extraordinarily like Clare's grandiose list of the attributes required by psychiatrists (see Baruch and Treacher, 1978).

Having made the predictable positivist point that the 'qualities' or 'faculties' listed by the APA will prove difficult to validate or measure reliably he is obviously concerned that such characteristics would not serve to distinguish clinical psychologists from 'the lawyer, the doctor, the teacher, or any other professional person'. He then adds the final *coup de grâce* by insisting that 'as a job analysis this list is perhaps typical "of the retreat from science" implicit in the adoption of the therapeutic attitude'.

We can only speculate about the personality characteristics that Eysenck's scientist-diagnostician *should* have since he doesn't bother to explore them but it is genuinely difficult to see which of the APA's characteristics Eysenck's ideal scientist-diagnostician should avoid adopting.

Reading between the lines, at that time (1949) it was the *therapeutic attitude* that seems to have been an anathema to Eysenck. But what would a clinical psychologist be like without the characteristics that are crucial to establishing effective rapport with clients?

Fortunately, Alice Heim, another clinical psychologist of much the same generation as Eysenck, has ironically documented the personality characteristics of the Eysenckian scientist-diagnostician. In her paper 'The proper study of psychology' she tells the following true story which puts Eysenck's position neatly in perspective:

> Some years ago I was invited out to dinner by a long-standing friend who wanted me to meet the parents of a 16-year-old boy who had recently received career guidance at his grammar school. The parents told me that their son, John, had taken a battery of tests preceded by and followed by interviews with the careers master, Mr. Brown. In addition, John and his parents had filled in the customary biographical inventories.
>
> In the second interview, Mr. Brown told John that he had done exceedingly well on most of the psychometric tests and the other measures. In fact, he was in the top decile on mathematical ability, verbal reasoning, spatial perception and mechanical aptitude – on grammar school norms. The only area in which he showed poorly was in dealing with people. Mr. Brown believed that John had difficulty in effecting communication: John's parents confirmed all of this: they were impressed by the accuracy and vividness of the picture Mr. Brown had outlined. What perplexed them was the vocational advice which, in the circumstances, he had given their son. His first choice for John was that he should become an experimental psychologist!
>
> I had the unenviable task of explaining to John's parents that Mr. Brown must have met a number of experimental psychologists and been struck by the resemblance of their psychological profile to that of John. Academic or experimental psychologists do tend to combine marked scientific and intellectual gifts with a singular lack of empathy and understanding for other people.
>
> (Heim, 1979)

Admittedly the anecdote does not involve Mr Brown positively recommending John to become a clinical psychologist but Eysenck's stress on the clinical psychologist's need to be an experimental scientist of course implies that John would (at a post-graduate level) be a good recruit to Eysenck's 'scientific' profession.

Eysenck himself would not be at all embarrassed by Heim's anecdote because he has argued that the best psychologists are usually out of touch with everyday life. In his book *Uses and Abuses of Psychology*, Eysenck (1953) explains this conundrum by insisting that there are two types of psychology.

> German philosophers ... [contrast] *verstehende* psychology and *erklärende* psychology, i.e. a common-sense psychology which tries to *understand* human beings, and a psychology which tries to *explain* their conduct on a scientific basis.
>
> (Eysenck, 1953, p. 222)

Having established this distinction he then adds the following rider which is far more problematic than Eysenck would allow:

> It is often said that psychology has a long past, but a short history; it is the common-sense type of psychology which has been the stand-by of writers, philosophers, and all others who had to deal with human beings, and which accounts for the long past, but it is the explanatory, scientific type of psychology which arose towards the end of the last century which is referred to as having had the short history.
>
> (Eysenck, 1953, p. 222–3)

Eysenck, of course, is notably a contributor to this short history so he is prepared to dismiss the alternative tradition:

> The 'understanding' psychologist is trying to gain an intuitive insight into the working of another person's mind on the basis of his common-sense knowledge of human nature. He may have derived his knowledge from self-observation and introspection, or from the observation of other people in a great variety of situations, or even from reading Shakespearian plays and modern novels; there is no denying that he is often amazingly astute and accurate in his intuitions. This type of insight based on wide experience and probably natural aptitude and interest in human beings, is a very valuable quality in many walks of life, and almost indispensable in the psychiatrist, the personnel manager, the social leader, and the politician. *However, valuable and useful as it may be, psychological insight and understanding by themselves have nothing whatsoever to do with psychology as a science*, just as little as facility in dealing with physical 'things' is an essential asset for the physical scientist. From observation I venture to assert that many of the greatest psychologists are if anything below average in this quality of 'insight' into human motives and purposes, and

similarly physicists of the highest standing are frequently incapable of adjusting the carburettor in their cars, or even of fixing a burned-out fuse. The expectation frequently voiced, namely, that psychologists should have learned a lot about 'human nature' ... is quite unjustified. The psychologist knows no more about 'human nature' than the next man, and if he is wise he will not let his claims outrun his discretion.

(Eysenck, 1953, p. 224–5, emphasis added)

It is, perhaps, of little importance whether academic experimental psychologists are competent at understanding and/or relating to people or not – they can survive well enough within academic institutions which are reasonably well insulated from the vicissitudes of everyday life, but we are naturally profoundly sceptical about whether such paragons of scientific virtue should be involved in clinical work with clients.

It is, of course, no accident that Eysenck's scientistic position should lead him in the direction of decrying such things as a 'therapeutic' attitude. Eysenck's approach is in fact anomalous because it prevents the person of the scientist-practitioner from being a possible object of scientific scrutiny. Indeed his bias against therapy at this time, compared with his stance a decade later, is so strong that he actually accepts the position that the majority of clinical psychologists should be trained solely as psycho-technologists. He therefore quotes approvingly an article in the *American Psychologist* by a 'doctor of medicine' (Gregg 1948) who insists that the PhD degree is unnecessary for most clinical psychologists who need to satisfy the demand for 'persons with general experience and reasonable competence'.

Eysenck translates this view into a proposal for a two-tiered training. Stage one would give an adequate theoretical and practical knowledge of psychometric techniques and 'psycho-technology' and would equip trainees so that they could fulfil the 'routine everyday needs of the community'. The diploma or certificate level of training would take one or two years and would follow a bachelor's degree in psychology. The clinical psychologist emerging from this training would be called a 'clinical psychologist, junior grade'.

Stage two training would consist in research training resulting in a PhD. Only a small minority of stage one psychologists would complete this level of training (hence earning the title 'clinical psychologist, senior grade'). The research undertaken by such a psychologist should in Eysenck's view be relevant to clinical psychology but should 'preferably be of a fundamental rather than of an applied nature'.

It is, for us, difficult to come to terms with the élitism of Eysenck's position. As a largley self-appointed spokesman for an emerging profession it is surprising that he should espouse such an undisguised élitist position in relation to members of his own profession. The élitist nature of Eysenck's position is even more clearly demonstrated in another article published by him in the *Journal of Mental Science* (forerunner of the *British Journal of Psychiatry*) in 1950. This article is particularly fascinating since it is clearly a tactical one designed to appeal to psychiatrists as allies in developing training for clinical psychologists.

Since the article is mostly a rehash of the earlier *American Psychologist* article we will concentrate only on its final section which contains some remarkable arguments about the relationship between psychiatry and clinical psychology.

Eysenck begins his argument in this section by insisting that psychiatrists and clinical psychologists are essentially soul mates.

> The writer believes that the emergence of a large, well-qualified group of clinical psychologists will be of considerable usefulness to the psychiatrist.... The old and always untenable view which regarded psychiatrists and psychologists in some sense as rivals is surely ready to be thrown on the scrap heap. The general public fails to distinguish between the two disciplines and it may truly be said that they sink or swim together ... the more effectively psychiatrists and psychologists learn to work together the greater that prestige and the higher that status are likely to be.
>
> (Eysenck, 1950, p. 723)

We would argue that the historical record does not support Eysenck's position – clinical psychology and psychiatry as professions have continued to clash, reflecting the basic historical truth that psychiatry (like its parent discipline medicine) has always sought to control professions that are ancillary to it.

Interestingly, David Smail (writing in 1973) reflects upon the state of the discipline at the time Eysenck was writing and comes to a very different conclusion, as the following quotation reveals.

> Clinical psychologists were dwarfed by a medical guild whose powers, self-determination and freedom of action must be almost

unique – the state of psychological knowledge . . . did not permit psychologists to adopt anything but a secondary role. The physical methods of treatment appropriate to so-called mental illness obviously necessitated possession of a medical degree, and non-physical methods stemming . . . largely from the psycho-analytic school could only be practised by people (mostly doctors) who had undergone a lengthy and expensive initiation. In other words, the licence to practise treatment was based on a system where authority accorded to would-be healers on the basis of their belonging to the appropriate (medical) club.

(Smail, 1973)

Eysenck's position, which failed to address the central issue of medical dominance, may well have simply reflected his own uniquely privileged position at the Institute of Psychiatry. But it is important to stress that this position was not just a rationalisation based on the weakness of clinical psychology. He genuinely believed that clinical psychologists should function as clinician/researchers like himself.

The ending of Eysenck's paper is in many ways even more problematic than earlier sections because he chooses to quote a particularly élitist argument from R.B. Cattell, an influential expatriate English psychologist who made his career in America.

Cattell has pointed out in commenting on the disparity between what is and what should be, that clinical psychology is 'a field of unequalled intellectual challenge; yet it has actually recruited, in addition to its truly competent, a multitude of camp followers of an amateurish status, unaware of the main issue, and large enough in numbers to drown out the voices of those who are. It may be asked, at least in these days of shortage of plumbers, if clinical psychometry has not robbed the community of some who might have learned competently to assemble a faucet or understand a domestic water system. Certainly one may doubt whether in the history of applied science there has ever been an era in which so many have known so little about so much.'

(Cattell, 1948, cited by Eysenck, 1950, p. 723)

The content of Cattell's statement is remarkable enough but it is the way that Eysenck uses it that is even more remarkable. In fact he does not comment on Cattell's statement at all. Instead he appeals to psychiatrists to insist that the psychologists they work with should be highly trained:

Psychiatrists can help us in separating the sheep from the goats by insisting on the highest possible qualifications and the best possible training in clinical psychologists employed with or under them.

(Eysenck, 1950, p. 724–5)

Forty years on this appeal to psychiatrists by Eysenck seems anachronistic, but clinical psychology as a profession was clearly in such a weak position that it had to seek allies particularly within medicine and psychiatry. But Eysenck's position, in fact, had a sting in its tail because he was quite prepared to attack the scientific credentials of medicine. In order to do this he turned to Cyril Burt who had recently criticised the medical profession for poaching work from psychologists:

There has been a widespread tendency to assume that the doctor must himself be not only officially exempt from any taint of charlatanism but also a scientific expert on every kind of human ill. Magistrates and government departments often seem to share this feeling about the scientific prestige attaching to the medical practitioner as such. . . .

Quite a number of 'medical psychologists' have claimed, not merely that they are the proper experts in the field of educational and industrial psychology but also that they are the right people to investigate the fitness of applicants for the universities, of entrants to the Civil Service, and of candidates for commissioned rank in the Army and other services.

(Burt, 1949, cited by Eysenck, 1950, p. 724)

Again Eysenck makes no comment about Burt's argument (so the reader must assume that he sees it as unproblematic). Instead he approvingly agrees with Burt's solution to the problem.

[I]nstead of trying to sweep all human and social problems into its net, the profession of medicine should, now as in the past, seek more and more to hand over its outlying fields to specialists appropriately. But, of course, increasing specialisation will call for increasing co-ordination, increased differentiation for increased integration. The paramount need is for specialist teams.

(Burt, 1949, cited by Eysenck, 1950, p. 724)

It is no surprise that Burt, the leading educational psychologist of the time, should be cited by Eysenck (who had, in fact, been trained by

Burt in the first place). Clearly they were united in trying to win a demarcation dispute with medicine and psychiatry. As psychologists there were attempting to establish that it was the scientific training of psychologists that was paramount in deciding who should control the 'outlying fields' which were not central to the tasks of medicine and psychiatry. In fact Eysenck's solution to this problem is clearly aimed at establishing the superiority of psychology.

> Because of their complementary functions and because of the inability of the general public to differentiate between them, psychiatrists and psychologists have everything to gain, and nothing to lose, by the closest possible integration of knowledge, experience and working methods; the closer this integration, the more likely is the ultimate emergence of that unified body of knowledge which alone will be worthy of being called a science of psychology, and of that agreed body of principles of pathology, prognosis and treatment which alone will be worthy of being called the applied science of psychiatry.
>
> (Eysenck, 1950, p. 725)

Eysenck's attempt neatly to solve the division of labour issue between psychology and psychiatry was doomed to failure for a number of reasons. Perhaps the most fundamental concerns the organisational base of clinical psychology. As many commentators have pointed out, clinical psychology is the prime example of a profession whose history and destiny is entirely intertwined with that of the NHS itself. (See Summerfield (1958) who recognises this point in his summary of the state of clinical psychology in the late fifties.) Eysenck's Delphic prognostications about the future role of clinical psychologists reflect the fact that he was an academic safely closeted in a research institute within a university. The realities of the NHS are quite different from academia. Above all else the NHS is not a rationally organised vehicle for delivering optimum health care. It is a rambling, Byzantine structure subject to a whole range of contradictory forces including the whims of its managerial and political masters and mistresses.

Eysenck's notion of the two-tiered profession of clinical psychology – the psycho-technologist (concerned solely with diagnosis) and the researcher (concerned with the development of theory and evaluating effective therapy) was never tested in practice, but it is easy to see why the proposal remained a utopian dream. The clinical psychologist as psycho-technologist posed little problem to psychiatry but the clinical psychologist as researcher had profoundly different implications. For the NHS to have paid clinical psychologists to be researchers would have required a quantum leap in the functioning of the NHS. As Magaro, Gripp and McDowell (1978) have argued in their very challenging book *The Mental Health Industry: A Cultural Phenomenon*, health care systems are not rationally or scientifically organised – they are cultural phenomena owing their allegiance to dominant cultural ideas. 'Therapy systems live, not by proving their usefulness, but by conforming to changing intellectual ideas' (Magaro *et al.*, 1978, p.ix). We have no space to explore this issue any further but it is important to draw attention to Barbara Tizard's recent exploration of the link between research and policy making (Tizard, 1990). Her highly sophisticated approach to the issue serves to throw into relief the naivety of Eysenck and a host of other researchers who remain trapped in a scientistic framework that assumes that science has a magical power to influence social policy. The relationship between science and social policy is extraordinarily complex but if we were to look specifically at the influence of research on, for example, a much more specific area like psychotherapeutic practice then we would find that there is little evidence supporting the idea that clinicians are actively influenced by research (Treacher, 1983).

Turning once again to Magaro *et al.*'s important point, we would argue that the 'changing intellectual ideas' current in the period when the NHS (and clinical psychology) came into being were not consonant with Eysenck's rationalist-scientific stance which placed a premium on interconnected programmes of mostly laboratory-based research. The appalling state of the health care system, and the mental hospitals in particular, is not reflected in Eysenck's thinking, which seems so far removed from the needs of patients. The urgency of the task facing the NHS predictably swept aside any notions that fundamental research in health care and/or abnormal psychology could have a place in a state health care system which was perpetually underfunded and continually struggling to achieve minimum standards of health care.

We have examined Eysenck's position in some detail because of the influential role he played in shaping the evolution of clinical psychology in this country. His intransigent stand against clinical psychologists undertaking therapy is remarkable considering his major role in popularising behaviour therapy from about 1958 onwards. But, as we have already pointed out, behaviour therapy skills could (at a conceptual level at least) be bolted on to Eysenck's scientist-diagnostician without too much difficulty. Eysenck's opposition to clinical psychologists having a therapeutic role can therefore be shown to hinge around his opposition to psychoanalysis. Psychoanalysis was an anathema because, first, it was held to be ineffective and, second, it involved sustained personal reflection on the part of practitioners.

Eysenck, in the context of attacking psychoanalysis, is quite prepared to insist that a research role is incompatible with the role of a therapist, but he dropped this objection opportunistically in 1958 when behaviour therapy began to compete with psychoanalysis as a major method of therapy. Of course it could be argued that behaviour therapy is a very different form of therapy which requires much less personal commitment from the therapist, but nevertheless the basic question remains unanswered – can an effective therapist also be an effective researcher and vice versa? The scientist-practitioner model insists that the roles should be combined but, as we shall see in our next chapter, there is absolutely no reason to assume that the majority of clinical psychologists ever successfully combine both roles.

We have dwelt on Eysenck's views about training because his ideas permeated the Maudsley course which had a disproportionate influence on the development of clinical psychology. For about fifteen years the course was the main conveyor belt for training clinical psychologists; its graduates also played a very significant role in contributing to the development of further courses in clinical psychology. However, it is important to stress that the Maudsley model was not the only one that existed. Two in-service training programmes were in place when Eysenck wrote his article. Summerfield (1958), in his summary of the state of clinical psychology in the late fifties, documented the fact that both the Tavistock Clinic in London and the Department of Psychological Research at the Crichton Royal Institution in Dumfries had well-established courses that trained clinical psychologists. The Tavistock course was, like the Maudsley course, predominantly concerned with psychological assessment but the tests used were mostly projective ones and the theoretical orientation of the course was predominantly psychoanalytic, although the work of Gestalt psychologists (especially Lewin) was also influential (Sutherland, 1951). The Crichton course was more eclectic but again emphasised assessment, not treatment, as the main role to be undertaken by clinical psychologists.

The Crichton course became an integral part of the University of Glasgow Diploma in Clinical Psychology course which began in 1960. Gathercole, Kear-Colwell and Ben-Harari (1962) were amongst the first students to graduate from this course. They provide an interesting inventory of the topics taught on the course. The first year was based in the Department of Psychological Medicine of the University of Glasgow at the Southern General Hospital. It is therefore perhaps not surprising that the course outline reads more like a course in psychiatry than in clinical psychology. The longest course was psychiatry (88 hours), including 28 hours of case demonstrations, but neuroanatomy (58 hours) and neuroanatomy dissection (24 hours) featured strongly and neurophysiology teaching was allocated 61 hours (30 hours of lectures, 31 of practicals).

The lecturing load (387 hours) in the first year was heavy and the students commented on this because it tended to limit their clinical training. This was confined to training in test administration and interpretation which was expanded and developed in the second year of the course which took place at the Crichton. The clinical psychology training in the first year was undertaken by R.M. Mowbray who relied on a tutorial system to teach a series of topics including learning theory and its application to psychotherapy, thinking and its pathology, and problems of research in clinical psychology. In fact, supervision of both behaviour therapy and psychotherapy was also offered so that the course was clearly breaking new ground and equipping trainees for a much more active, therapeutic role.

The flavour of the Maudsley course in the 1950s can be gleaned from a short article submitted to the *Bulletin of the BPS* by Monte Shapiro who was the senior lecturer in charge of the course (Shapiro, 1955). The credo of the course is effectively summarised by the following quotation:

> The theoretical aim of the training is the understanding of the application of scientific method to the solution of clinical psychological problems. This approach ... has a number of consequences:

(i) ... It means that no test or psychological treatment can be accepted for routine use unless there is a minimum amount of information concerning its validity and standardisation.

(ii) It is not possible at the moment to rely exclusively on any particular theory of neuropsychiatric disorder as none has been validated. Students are introduced to various theories and presented with relevant factual data. However there is an increasing emphasis on the use of the relatively well validated generalisations of academic psychology as guides to the investigation and treatment of psychological abnormalities. ...

(iii) Considerable attention is devoted to the teaching and application of experimental method to the solution of clinical psychological problems, with special emphasis on the investigation and treatment of the single case.

(Shapiro, 1955, pp. 15–16)

Clearly the course's emphasis was in step with Eysenck's concept of the clinical psychologist as diagnostician-researcher. Shapiro's inventory of lecture topics contained in his paper revealed that therapeutic methods had no place in the syllabus. (Admittedly, Remedial Teaching Techniques were listed but only three hours of teaching were devoted to this topic compared with 60 hours of statistics and 95 hours of topics concerned with testing.) Shapiro also emphasised that the thirteen-month course was not sufficient to train a fully fledged clinical psychologist. A minimum of two further years of research training (leading to a higher degree) was essential.

It is clear from Shapiro's presentation that Eysenck's goal of producing a 'senior' grade clinical psychologist was not achieved by the Maudsley course. In effect the course was training a 'junior' grade psychologist because the research component was minimal and did not include the writing of a thesis. Subsequent developments in the Maudsley course, particularly its expansion from thirteen months to two years (Shapiro, 1962), went some way to filling this gap. Provision was made for writing a clinical research thesis but the allocation of time was clearly too limited to allow an effective researcher to be trained.

Shapiro's brief summary of the Maudsley course is valuable in giving the flavour of clinical courses in the fifties and sixties but it is also important to examine his own work because it made as significant a contribution to the training of clinical psychologists as

Eysenck's. Fortunately Yates (1970) has provided an interesting first-hand account of Shapiro's contribution to shaping clinical psychology. Yates was a graduate of the Maudsley course who then became a staff member staying for six years (1951–1957). His account appears in his book on behaviour therapy but it is important to point out that, according to his preface, Eysenck did not agree with his account probably because it stresses the important role that Shapiro, not he, played in developing ideas about the potential role of clinical psychologists.

Yates points out that the Psychology Department at the Maudsley was split into a Research Station (headed by Eysenck) and a Clinical-Teaching Section (headed by Shapiro but with a staff of ten). According to Yates, Eysenck exercised a great influence on the course through his conceptions of the basic role of the clinical psychologist as a fundamental research worker and his rejection of the role of pseudo-psychiatrist (diagnostically and therapeutically) which some clinical psychologists adopted. However, Eysenck's grandiose project of attempting to explain abnormal behaviour in general by special reference to the dimensions of neuroticism, psychoticism and introversion-extraversion was of little practical significance to the everyday clinical activities of clinical psychologists. Curiously, Yates does not himself explore this point but it is clear that he felt that Shapiro's work filled the vacuum created by Eysenck's work. Eysenck's essentially nomothetic approach could be of little value to a clinician faced by the complexities of an individual client so Shapiro's single-case approach seemed more capable of making a valid contribution.

According to Yates, it was Shapiro's influence that led initially to major changes in clinical psychological testing. Shapiro, in the course of a long series of staff seminars, worked out in great detail an alternative to the 'battery' testing approach prevalent at the time. The essence of the new approach is summarised by the following key quotation taken from an early paper, which itself was the first in a long series published by Shapiro.

> First of all, the features presented by the patient, his life history and medical history and test results are integrated. In this the discussion between the psychiatrist, social worker and psychologist play an important part. As a result certain formulated problems emerge.
>   The next move is to advance hypotheses which will explain them. . . .

The third step the clinician takes is to ask himself what effect the truth of each of his hypotheses will have on the treatment and disposal [*sic*] of the patient. If any of these hypotheses are not likely to have an effect on treatment and disposal, he will be disinclined to test them.

Finally, the clinician has to decide how he is going to test the various hypotheses.

(Shapiro, 1951, p. 755, cited by Yates, 1970)

Yates is not at all perplexed by the glaring scientism of Shapiro's position. He accepts that the clinical psychologist should be a researcher; he is therefore quite content to expand Shapiro's comment by adding his own supportive commentary:

The most important points to note so far are that the clinical psychologist is responsible for formulating his own meaningful hypotheses about a particular patient ... that he must assess the relevance of what he is proposing to do in relation to treatment and disposal [*sic*] of the patient, and that his hypotheses and procedures may be quite different from those of direct interest to the psychiatrist. Furthermore, he will not necessarily be at all interested in arriving at or considering a formal diagnosis of the patient.

(Yates, 1970, p. 17)

We would argue that the emphasis in the two quotations is slightly different. Shapiro implies that the clinical psychologist's hypothesis testing can be in accord with a team decision about the underlying causes of the patient's problem, while Yates correctly acknowledges that the situation may be more complex, i.e. the psychiatrist's formulation may not agree with the psychologist's. Of course, in the a real everyday situation such a disagreement would most probably lead to the psychologist backing off because the psychiatrist's view of what should happen was likely to prevail because he or she was in charge of treatment.

Yates is surprisingly oblivious to this difficulty – he is intent on pursuing his (and Shapiro's) argument to its logical conclusion by insisting that:

the clinical psychologist must be an experimental psychologist, though not of a conventional kind. In testing hypotheses ... he must, in effect, *treat the patient as the object of an experimental investigation*.

(Yates, 1970, p. 17 – emphasis added)

As an example of this approach Yates cites some work by himself, Bartlet and Shapiro concerned with a child's failure to acquire learning skills (Bartlet and Shapiro, 1956). The study revolved around analyses relating to the various modalities involved in learning to read. Special standardisation data had to be collected using specially constructed tests. The time-consuming, even obsessional, nature of this type of study is well documented in Shapiro's review of single-patient studies (Shapiro, 1963) but Yates insists that despite their evident weaknesses they did make a contribution to subsequent developments in the field:

> The significance of this approach lay in subsequent developments. If the experimental method, involving as strict objectivity as possible, and the formulation of meaningful questions derived from knowledge of general psychology could be applied to the elucidation of the basic causal factors underlying abnormalities of function manifested by a single case then it very soon became obvious that the same techniques could be applied to the *treatment* of the disorder. In other words by drawing an empirical and theoretical general psychology it should be possible to carry out controlled, laboratory-type experiments in an effort to manipulate systematically *and change* the abnormal behaviour.
>
> (Yates, 1970, p. 17)

So according to Yates, the development of behaviour therapy was naturally congruent with Shapiro's project of creating clinical psychology as an applied science based on scientific principles.

Behaviour therapy necessarily enters our argument at this stage because it was behaviour therapy that provided an effective rhetoric which enabled clinical psychology in this country to establish its claims to be an independent profession, legitimately contributing to the umbrella of professions that were active within the mental health services. The Eysenck/Shapiro bid to establish the clinical psychologist as psycho-diagnostician/researcher was inevitably abortive. The *real politik* of the mental health (illness) services of the time provided no space for the emergence of a profession which would challenge the professional dominance of psychiatry.

In fact, Yates comes quite close to formulating the problem in the same way as we do here, but he is too inducted into the Maudsley position really to understand the conflict between different parts of his argument. For example, in a section of his chapter entitled

'Dissatisfaction with the role of the clinical psychologist', he argues
that diagnostic testing is mostly a waste of time because the tests used
are either invalid or yield answers which could have been reached
more quickly by other means.

But why should clinical psychologists spend most of their time
engaged in these supposedly diagnostic activities which have so little
validity? Yates' answer to this conundrum is immensely revealing:

> The adoption of the role of diagnostrician ... seems to have
> resulted partly from feelings of professional insecurity on the part
> of the clinical psychologist, partly from the desire to communicate
> meaningfully with psychiatrists by means of a supposedly common
> language, and partly from the demands of psychiatrists for such
> diagnostic services in line with the tenets of the medical model.
> The psychiatrist, in fact, has himself perceived the appropriate
> role of the clinical psychologist as that of a medical ancillary,
> whose primary purpose in life is to assist in arriving at a diagnostic
> category into which the patient can be fitted, particularly in the
> cases of doubtful instances.
>
> (Yates, 1970, p. 11)

Yates, unlike Eysenck, is much clearer about the role of psychiatry in
shaping the early development of clinical psychology. But, unsur-
prisingly, his solution to the identity crisis experienced by clinical
psychologists is identical to Eysenck's. However, in attempting to
establish his argument he makes a remarkable admission which, in
our opinion, effectively exposes the Achilles heel of psychology both
at the time he was writing (1970) and in the 1950s when Eysenck was
attempting to establish a legitimate clinical psychology.

> If we reject this diagnostic i.e. pseudopsychiatric role as
> unsatisfactory and unnecessary what then should be the role (or
> roles) of the clinical psychologist? The answer must surely follow
> directly from a consideration of the nature of his training and
> qualifications. It is a remarkable state of affairs that several years
> are commonly spent in teaching the embryonic clinical
> psychologist the fundamental empirical knowledge (of which in
> spite of the sceptics, there is now a vast amount) in sensation,
> perception, learning, motivation and so forth, together with the
> principal theoretical systems (which, in spite of their diversity of
> language, do have a great deal in common) only to find that this

basic body of knowledge and theory is virtually ignored as soon as the psychologist moves into the clinical field. It is not, of course, suggested that the application of this knowledge is not extremely difficult, and it is recognised that obstacles are, or would be, placed in the way of psychologists who attempted to do this by unsympathetic or ignorant physicians or psychiatrists. But it is plainly the responsibility of the clinical psychologist to demonstrate that he has something to offer other than a pale copy of psychiatric procedures – and, by and large, clinical psychologists have not met this responsibility.

(Yates, 1970, p. 12)

We would strongly reject Yates' claim that psychology had a secure knowledge base in the sixties when he was writing. (His book is dated 1970 but it was effectively written in the mid-1960s.) One of us (AT) completed his first psychology degree in 1963. The degree course was a ragbag of conflicting theories and paradigms which studiously taught me (AT) virtually nothing of significance about everyday life. The course that taught me least was unfortunately the clinical psychology course. This course, taught by a convinced disciple of Eysenck, presented clinical psychology as a highly abstruse experimental science – patients were just experimental subjects whose IQs or sedation thresholds were of much more significance than their personal histories.

Unfortunately we haven't space to refute Yates' position in a detailed way, but we would nevertheless argue that Yates' claims (like Eysenck's and even Shapiro's) are merely scientistic rhetoric. The bitter truth is that most experimental psychological knowledge is either trivial or contradictory or both. Paul Kline's recent uncomfortable book *Psychology Exposed or the Emperor's New Clothes* is salutary reading for anybody who believes that psychology has anything valuable or consistent to say about everyday life (Kline, 1988). Interestingly, Kline has been a close collaborator of R.B. Cattell, but that does not prevent him from arguing that Cattell's lifetime project in attempting to understand human personality was based on a misconception. (For Cattell we could, of course, read Eysenck since their nomothetic approaches are essentially similar from a methodological point of view.)

Kline's book is, of course, by no means unique. Other critics of psychology have lambasted it for its failures to increase understanding of human behaviour. For example, Beloff (1973) has insisted that psychology has yet to establish a single fact about human behaviour. We haven't space to pursue this type of criticism any further in this book but it is crucial for us to confront another aspect of Eysenck's scientism. Eysenck, along with many other theorists, assumes that 'scientific' knowledge (based on experimental investigation) is clearly distinguishable from other forms of knowledge. But how secure is the 'scientific' base of this type of knowledge?

Broad and Wade (1985) in their book *Betrayers of the Truth – Fraud and Deceit in Science* have effectively shattered the myth of scientists as impartial pursuers of 'truth'. Broad and Wade do not, in fact, pay much attention to psychology in their book, although, not unexpectedly, they do explore Burt's fabrication of data in his papers reporting the degree of heritability of intelligence. However, there is one section of the book which does cause immense difficulty for advocates of the scientist-practitioner model. This section is concerned with a crucial feature of the scientific endeavour – that data should be readily available for scrutiny by anybody who has a mind to examine them. Wolins (1962) reports a study that involved an investigator writing to thirty-seven authors of papers (published in psychology journals) asking them for the raw data on which the papers were based. Of the thirty-two authors who replied, twenty-one reported that their data had been 'misplaced, lost or inadvertently destroyed'. In the end only nine authors sent data that could be used in the study. Only seven of these arrived in time for them to be analysed but three of these contained gross errors in their statistics.

Craig and Reese (1973) undertook a replication of the Wolins study – they wrote to fifty-three psychologists who had published articles in journals in a given month. Nine refused point-blank to provide raw data, saying that they were either lost, destroyed or unavailable. Eight did not reply and only half the sample even offered to cooperate in some way – twenty either sent data or a summary analysis, but the remaining seven offered the data only if certain conditions would be met.

Clearly these findings are very unsettling. Most clinicians quite rightly find much clinical research either methodologically unsound and/or irrelevant to their work as clinicians. Much research is ephemeral and out of date before it is even published, but if researchers are so reluctant to share their data with other bona fide researchers then it is only natural that clinicians should be highly suspicious of the reliability and validity of research findings. Broad and Wade clearly document the current imperative to publish at all costs. Academics are now forced to produce papers much like food factories produce sausages.

We would insist that psychology is still a pre-paradigmic science with no agreed methodology; hence its ability to provide a secure basis for a practitioner remains suspect. In the 1940s and 1950s when Eysenck and Shapiro were attempting to establish a 'scientific' legitimation for the role of clinical psychology their task was a very difficult one because there was virtually no link between theory and everyday practice. Eysenck's nomothetic approach had almost nothing to offer the clinician, while Shapiro's obsessionally detailed single-case approach was too time-consuming to be practicable and assumed that an unrealistic level of rational negotiation could be achieved within multidisciplinary teams. Interestingly, Shapiro himself has recently agreed that the approach he espoused was impracticable (Shapiro, 1985).

The gap between theory and practice certainly preoccupied contemporary commentators in the 1950s and 1960s. Unfortunately, there are very few written accounts to substantiate this point, but by happenstance Shapiro's top-down view of training (which we have already summarised) was put into perspective by a consumer account published three years later. Fortunately for us, Dabbs (1965) provided a brief account of what it was like to be a member of the Maudsley course in the mid-1950s. He stresses the excellence of the academic teaching but adds the following rider about meeting clients for the first time:

> When the time came for us to interview our first patients, I am sure I was not alone in realising with shattering clarity that although I considered myself to be well informed about psychological tests, I was a complete novice at dealing with people. No-one had attempted to provide any understanding of the dynamics of the testing situation or even the basic techniques of establishing rapport.
>
> (Dabbs, 1965, p. 17)

According to Dabbs the course enabled every student to leave with 'an excellent grounding in academic psychiatry and objective [sic] clinical psychology'. This meant that 'it was possible to apply scientific method to specific clinical problems and provide reliable information upon which psychiatrists could formulate their opinions'

(Dabbs, 1965, p. 18). But Dabbs felt that this type of approach created a situation in which 'the patient as an individual had been "forgotten" during the investigations and was relegated to the status of being the source of test findings' (Dabbs, 1965, p. 18).

Curiously Dabbs was also a trainee on the Tavistock course so he was in a unique position to compare the two types of training.

> The change in intellectual environment was quite as remarkable as one might have expected. The training programme was far less formalized, so informal in fact that for some time I doubted its existence. A more limited range of psychological techniques was employed and the approach was essentially clinical rather than academic. . . . [O]nly the barest systematized training was employed, and the bulk of teaching was carried out through the medium of case discussion. The orientation was decidedly psychoanalytic and one wondered what the newly graduated trainees made of it all. . . .
>
> It was difficult for me to accept the apparent lack of concern about small statistical inconsistencies in the test results (a passion with Maudsley psychologists). The focus of interest was the patient's problems and the clinical psychologist's task was seen as elucidating these difficulties. Psychological testing was employed largely to broaden the scope of the clinical picture and to provide implications about the general therapeutic approach.
>
> (Dabbs, 1965, p. 18)

At a theoretical level Dabbs clearly found the transition from the Maudsley to the Tavistock very jarring, as the following comment demonstrates:

> The psychological and philosophical orientation of the basic tenets held by the majority of senior staff . . . [at the Tavistock] . . . appeared to be grossly absurd to one so recently emerged from a scientific background. Yet there was no doubting the general high quality of clinical work being carried out. It was interesting to observe how the most vocal and doctrinaire Kleinians seemed the least sophisticated in the philosophy of science. It was almost the reverse of my experiences at the Maudsley where psychoanalytic theory was most vehemently attacked by those who only had the barest academic knowledge of the subject.
>
> (Dabbs, 1965, p. 18)

Unfortunately Dabbs does not explore the contrast between the two courses any further. Nor does he evaluate how he managed (if at all) to synthesise his learning experiences from two such different courses. He is more concerned in his article to warn against the dangers of courses becoming too academic. He was writing at a time when the BPS was involved in the detailed work involved in establishing an examination for a diploma in clinical psychology. He felt that there was a danger of in-service courses being dominated by university-based academics who would not give sufficient emphasis to the need for trainees to gain experience and competence in clinical settings.

He also felt that both the two-year MA course at the Maudsley and the two-year course at the Tavistock would be inclined to produce a rather specialised type of clinical psychologist who would not be able to cope with the vicissitudes of working in a wide range of settings (e.g. industrial rehabilitation units or mental subnormality units).

Interestingly, Dabbs' concerns were echoed by a number of other clinical psychologists, including Mahesh Desai who was a key figure in forming the Co-ordinating Committee of Senior Psychologists in the NHS and the Division of Clinical Psychology. In the course of giving his Chairman's address to the first scientific meeting of the DCP in May 1966 he also addressed the academic/practitioner split which preoccupied Dabbs. Having reviewed the evolution of clinical psychology in the USA, he has the following to say about the ways that training departments operate:

> In the training departments the academic and clinical teachers differ in their values, the former regarding themselves as pure, vigorous scientists; the latter regard the academician's view-point as inappropriate to clinical problems and situations, and his research activities as oversimplications with little relevance to clinical needs. Even the assumptions of what psychological science is, are challenged. ... According to my view, to the extent that academic departments continue to be wedded obsessionally to rigid concepts of 'Scientific method' and accordingly confine themselves to studying only those aspects of human behaviour which are amenable to the method, to that extent they continue to exclude some of the most important areas of the subject matter of psychology which should be the whole range of human experience and behaviour. Methods have to be adapted to subject matter, not vice versa, and unless this is done students leaving academic

departments are bound to find considerable difficulty in relating their academic studies and equipment to many of the most important needs of everyday life situations and not least to clinical problems and situations.

Some students suffer conflict of loyalties as well as conflict of self-identity, in terms of scientist versus professional rather than scientist *and* professional roles. ... Many students have complained, after completion of their training, that they have found themselves ill-equipped to deal with the demands of service situations and they have suggested the introduction of much more practical service experience in the training programme.

(Desai, 1967, pp. 32–3)

Desai's concern about the role conflict experienced by trainees is echoed in another paper published in roughly the same period. Claridge and Brooks (1973) undertook a survey of applicants for the Glasgow MSc course in clinical psychology. Their primary motivation seems to have been a concern to establish why so many graduates from the course were not staying in NHS posts but they were also concerned about the role conflict experienced by their trainees. The loss from the NHS of clinical psychology graduates had been clearly documented the previous year by Kear-Colwell (1972) who, according to Claridge and Brooks, had provided evidence that the key element in the job dissatisfaction expressed by psychologists hinged around the vexed issue of whether the contribution of the psychologist should be mainly academic or mainly practical. Claridge and Brooks' survey is very revealing because it demonstrates that the vast majority of applicants for the Glasgow course wanted to become clinical psychologists because of an interest in therapy. When asked their reasons for entering clinical psychology 12 per cent did so because of research possibilities while 87 per cent did so because of possibilities for therapy.

In interpreting their overall findings Claridge and Brooks concluded that:

[Our] results seem to provide some early evidence of the later role confusion and job dissatisfaction likely to be experienced by those ... entering clinical psychology. On the one hand many appear to see themselves as sophisticated behavioural scientists having the appropriate critical and research skills. On the other hand their predominant ambition seems to be to work as practitioners.

Inevitably this will be mainly in settings where professional colleagues will have received a training which is vocationally more relevant, even though the psychologist may perceive it as academically less substantial and pertinent than his own. He [sic] may therefore tend to find himself as a highly trained academic caught, without a *unique* therapeutic contribution to offer, between the two existing major caring professions of medicine and social work, each of which is already carrying out some of the functions he aspires to perform.

(Claridge and Brooks, 1973, p. 125)

One obvious solution to this paradoxical situation is to make clinical psychology courses much more vocational in their emphasis. Claridge and Brooks rehearse this solution but immediately back off from advocating it because of the obligations that they assume university courses must discharge:

It must be borne in mind that any marked shift in the emphasis of training would prove a dilemma for the university based courses. . . . On the one hand they are required to prepare students to perform – mainly within the NHS – those vocational functions which clinical psychology as a profession decides are appropriate. At the same time they must maintain the academic standards of abnormal psychology as a scientific discipline and be in a position to offer appropriate postgraduate opportunities to less vocationally oriented students. Already . . . there are signs that the demands of the former are leading to a neglect of the latter. Given the very limited number of places available . . . any further shift in that direction would seriously endanger the important role that the psychologist has demonstrated he can play as a basic scientist in the abnormal field.

(Claridge and Brooks, 1973, p. 126)

It is, of course, an extremely debatable point that Claridge and Brooks raise here: are university courses in clinical psychology obliged to maintain the academic standards of abnormal psychology? The sudden introduction of the term 'abnormal psychology' into the article is very intriguing – in our opinion Claridge and Brooks are caught in the same trap that ensnared Eysenck in the late 1940s. In Britain it has proved impossible to create a viable profession devoted to the study of abnormal psychology. Eysenck's original attempt to prevent clinical psychology from developing as a therapy-providing profession was overtaken by the formation of the NHS – a service that desperately required skilled therapists not researchers. Claridge and Brooks' attempt yet again to argue in favour of the need for fundamental research is curiously naive – for example, they fail to examine past attempts to achieve this goal and the solutions they propose are very unconvincing.

The first suggestion they make is that post-graduate courses should be separated into ones that deal with the research aspects of abnormal psychology and ones that deal with service aspects. But they then undermine their own argument by suggesting that:

> [T]his [separation] carries certain difficulties, not the least of which is the lack of career outlet for individuals taking the former kind of course since presumably they would not meet the professional requirements at present imposed on existing courses in clinical psychology.
>
> (Claridge and Brooks, 1973, p. 126)

Having made (and effectively withdrawn) this suggestion, they then make two more:

> Another possibility is to state more explicitly, and perhaps encourage, differences in the content and emphases of present courses allowing the interests of different kinds of psychologist to be catered for. A similar degree of flexibility in the content of training might also be encouraged within the individual courses themselves, again making it possible for students to follow, within certain limits, their own indications towards the more academic or more practical aspects of abnormal psychology.
>
> (Claridge and Brooks, 1973, p. 126)

Both these suggestions are clearly fraught with difficulty and at no point do Claridge and Brooks really tackle the crucial question that training research workers is a lengthy and exacting task which cannot be effectively achieved unless very real resources are mobilised.

We have explored Claridge and Brooks' paper in some detail because we see it as a pivotal paper which reflects the period in which it was written. The late 1960s/early 1970s was a transitional time for clinical psychology – the scientistic tradition of Eysenck and his disciples like Claridge was still strong but clinical psychologists had yet to gain a sure identity as therapists. This sense of transition is well reflected in the conclusion of Claridge and Brooks' paper:

In conclusion we think it is fair to say that in the future psychologists will make an increasingly varied contribution in the field of abnormal behaviour. Their contribution as basic scientists is, we believe, already well-established. Their exact role as practitioners has yet to be worked out. In view of this greater flexibility, rather than greater standardization, in training policies would seem to be required. In practice, and as far as the university courses are concerned, this means a greater recognition of their dual obligation to train not only service clinical psychologists but also academic abnormal psychologists, to meet the needs of the kind of individual predominating in ... [our] sample ... but at the same to attract a proportion of more research-orientated graduates who can be encouraged to apply their skills to problems in the abnormal field. The latter, we suspect, were grossly under-represented among our applicants, a sign perhaps that clinical psychology has already too narrowly defined its scope vis-a-vis so-called mainstream psychology.

(Claridge and Brooks, 1973, p. 126)

As we will see in our next chapter, clinical psychology courses have indeed shown some aspects of the flexibility that Claridge and Brooks called for but it is also true that the profession has not evolved along the research path that they valued so highly. Our reading of the history of clinical psychology leads us to the conclusion that it was precisely the fleshing out of the clinical psychologist's role as an active practitioner, able and willing to engage in therapy, that in fact contributed to the rapid development of the profession. Initially, it was behaviour therapy that provided the vehicle for filling the vacuum created by the Eysenck and Shapiro approaches. As we have already argued in an earlier section of this chapter, neither of these approaches created a viable model for relating theory to (therapeutic) practice so the introduction of behaviour therapy techniques was of crucial importance to a profession which sought to expand its role and escape its dependence on psychiatry.

Behaviour therapy was not initially developed by the Maudsley School. Their preoccupation with theory held them back from making a breakthrough that was long overdue. In fact the term behaviour therapy was not coined until 1954 (by O.R. Lindsley). Yates records this early usage by Lindsley but insists that it was Lazarus who was primarily responsible for establishing its consistent use four years later in 1958. In America it was Skinner's work that spawned behaviour modification, but perhaps the most crucial early work in the field was published by a South African psychiatrist, Wolpe, who used a neurophysiological model (reciprocal inhibition) and not a learning theory framework to underpin his approach (Wolpe, 1958).

In fact, as Yates (1970) carefully documents, there were scores of earlier studies applying principles of conditioning to various forms of abnormal behaviour. Pavlov himself published several studies of this type but Bekhterev, Ivanov-Smokensky and Krasmogorski also contributed similar papers, so, according to Yates, 'the possibility of an objective, experimentally-based approach to abnormalities of behaviour, derived from knowledge of the principles of conditioning, was recognised very early' (1970, p. 14).

Yates doesn't explain why a school of therapy did not emerge in Russia to reflect these developments. Some American psychologists (including J.B. Watson) did initially respond to Pavlov's early work but the really important theoretical contribution to the field was made by the learning theorist Hull in the 1940s. So the puzzle remains – why was behaviour therapy as a clinical discipline a Western invention and not a Russian one? Ironically an American psychologist, Salter, did publish a book called *Conditioned Reflex Therapy* in 1949 but this book is overlooked by Yates.

Portes (1971), in his penetrating critique of behaviour therapy, provides a useful framework for understanding how and why behaviourism emerged as a major framework for understanding human behaviour. Portes, as a sociologist of knowledge, approaches behaviour therapy in a completely different spirit from Yates who sees the emergence of behaviour therapy as merely another milestone in the progress of science. In the first part of his paper, Portes effectively demonstrated that the literal application of behaviouristic theory to complex human disorders was a nonsense. It would be tempting to explore these arguments again but they are too well known to detain us here – instead, we will concentrate on the latter part of his article in which he explores the reasons for behaviour therapy's emergence as a powerful force within the mental health arena. Or as Portes puts it:

> Behaviour therapy's claims to objective success alone do not seem to justify its emergence and rapid acceptance. From the standpoint of the sociology of knowledge, the question is what factors in the

surrounding cultural context have determined the preference by those involved, therapists and patients alike, for the image of man conveyed by behaviour therapy over competing ones? Its better 'fit' into existing social structural arrangements seems a function of its rational simplicity (the person is a consequence of a few logically consistent principles) and its greater claim to scientific status (its principles as derived from experimental research).

(Portes, 1971, p. 311)

Buy why should a theory/therapy that denied subjectively obvious thought processes and emotional complexes (albeit in the name of science) achieve such importance? Portes insists that the answer lies in a tangible process documented especially by Weber (1958, 1965) and Sorokin (1937) who argue that there is an inexorable trend towards rationalism within modern society. Portes argues that 'scientificism' (scientism is the word we prefer) is an important facet of this trend. Behaviour therapy's well-trumpeted claims to be effective and to be based upon the 'principles' of learning theory are seen, through Portes' eyes, as an ideological smokescreen which enables practitioners within this tradition to establish the superiority of their approach in the face of competition from other approaches.

Clearly the painstaking work of Shapiro and his collaborators, who published scores of papers demonstrating the application of experimental psychology to clinical case material, made an important contribution to creating a new rhetoric for clinical psychology. As Yates himself points out, Shapiro did not pursue a therapeutic approach as actively as might have been expected but nevertheless his influence was very important. It is no surprise that clinical psychology courses rapidly adopted behaviour therapy training as one of their main topics although it is important to stress that psychologists did not succeed in monopolising the development of behaviour therapy in this country.

A paper published by Liddell (1977) neatly illustrates this point. According to Liddell a DCP working party report (DCP, 1975) attributed the interest that psychologists were taking in psychotherapy to the development of behaviour therapy. And yet the same report recorded that 71 per cent of practising clinical psychologists had received little or no training in behaviour therapy. Liddell also reported the discomforting news that clinical psychologists lagged behind other professionals (such as nurse therapists) not only in lacking recognised behaviour therapy training but also in failing to develop any sort of policy concerning the development of their therapeutic role.

By the mid-1960s, clinical psychology training in this country had begun to encompass behaviour therapy techniques but the length of training was unaffected by the change in role that began to occur as clinical psychologists became more involved in therapy. The rhetoric of the scientist-practitioner model became more noticeable but the success of courses in actually producing effective practi- tioners was questionable, particularly if comparisons were made with developments in America. We have already noted Eysenck's claims about the superiority of British training but the historical record does not convincingly support his case, although it is clear that American training programmes also had their problems. Ironically, it is American clinical psychologists not British ones who are trained in ways that conform to Eysenck's 'senior' grade psychologist – an issue that we explore in our next chapter.

Chapter 4

The scientist-practitioner model – problems and paradoxes

In order to develop our investigation of the significance of the scientist-practitioner model to British clinical psychology it is necessary to review briefly the deliberations of the famous conference held at Boulder, Colorado, in 1949. This conference clearly marked a further stage in the professionalisation of American clinical psychology. Raimy (1950), in his book documenting the conference, points out that it was in the wake of the Boulder conference that the American Psychological Association adopted a much stricter definition of what a clinical psychologist should be:

> To obtain uniformity in terminology and to present the public and allied professions with a definition of persons qualified to do independent professional work in this field the conference recommended (with only one dissenting note) that:
> The title clinical psychologist should be used only by persons who have received the doctoral degree based upon graduate education in clinical psychology received from a recognised university.
> (Raimy, 1950, p. 37)

This position statement is the origin of the scientist-professional model which contemporary British training courses aspire to, but we would stress that this American model is saliently different from Eysenck's original model. He would, of course, agree with the scientist part but the professional part of the model encompasses the idea that psychotherapy should be a core activity of the fully trained clinical psychologist.

The Boulder recommendation was clearly designed to sort out the sheep from the goats. The conference report points out (in a passage reminiscent of Eysenck) that 'many members of such allied professions as medicine and social work ... may mistakenly regard the psychometrist, who is variously trained in the administration of tests, as a representative member of the profession' (Raimy, 1950, p. 37). But the more fundamental reason for the recommendation was the feeling that 'such a step will in the end safeguard the public as well as the profession against the still greater evils that are bound to arise if the profession cannot define what the title 'clinical psychologist' stands for' (Raimy, 1950, p. 38).

The Boulder conference was a watershed in American clinical psychology training because it introduced an academic model of professional training which delegated the responsibility for both didactic preparation and practical (internship) training to departments of psychology (Pottharst, 1973). As Pottharst comments, the Boulder conference is known to most psychologists for its emphasis on the *scientist* aspect of the model. Training in research was stressed because of the generally perceived lack of reliable knowledge about personality and the effectiveness of assessment methods and psychotherapy. But Pottharst insists that other recommendations by the Boulder conference focused very clearly on the *professional* side of the equation. We have already pointed out that psychotherapy training was stressed but so was a graded sequence of field training experiences. Professional ethics were also strongly emphasised and the APA and state associations were recommended to press for licensing and certification. The development of accreditation procedures and the public listing of APA-approved training programmes were also recommended.

So the Boulder conference marked a further step in the professionalisation of American clinical psychology but, as Pottharst points out, the Boulder recommendations were in practice quite flawed. The Achilles heel of the Boulder approach was its failure to focus on how students were to achieve clinical competence. According to Pottharst:

> Boulder required training programmes to implement the scientist-professional concept in courses, in general program emphasis, in a third-year internship, and in the dissertation. But responsibility for acquiring professional competence beyond bare entry-level skills *was placed on the student* [emphasis added] in his or her postdoctoral years, as was the responsibility for even the internship in a number of programs.
>
> (Pottharst, 1973, p. 39)

This deficiency has been highlighted by Rachman in comparing the relative merits of American and British methods of training clinical psychologists:

> The most serious weakness of North American courses is the large gap between the high quality of university instruction which is provided and the poor and often unsupervised clinical training which the students obtain. The courses are badly unbalanced and the scientist has squeezed out the practitioner. In many instances, the students are required to make such arrangements as they can for their own clinical training – the university training courses absolve themselves from the responsibility for developing or even selecting clinical training sites, monitoring them, or evaluating what the student has learned.
>
> (Rachman, 1983, p.xiii)

Given this structural weakness it is not surprising that graduates of such courses find it difficult to combine the roles of scientist and practitioner. However, dissatisfaction with the implementation of the recommendations of the Boulder model resulted in a further series of conferences being held. It is not our purpose to trace all the twists and turns of the evolution of American training but the complexities of American training are well reflected in the proceedings of the Vail (Colorado) conference (1973). The major recommendation of this conference in fact directly contradicted the original Boulder conference recommendation:

> It is the judgement of this task group that the development of psychological science has sufficiently matured to justify creation of explicit professional programs in addition to programs for training scientists and scientist-professionals.
>
> (Korman, 1973, p. 99)

And the appropriate degree to be awarded to this new professional was to be the Doctor of Psychology (PsyD). But the report is careful to make a distinction between the PsyD award and the more traditional Doctor of Philosophy (PhD) award:

> Where primary emphasis in training and function is upon direct delivery of professional services and the evaluation and improvement of those services, the Psy.D. is appropriate. Where primary emphasis is upon the development of new knowledge in psychology, the Ph.D. degree is appropriate.
>
> (Korman, 1973, p. 101)

It is not easy to establish clearly why the Vail conference recommended this shift but Darley, in his interesting opening address to the conference, does provide some clues (Darley, 1973). A few years earlier Darley himself was responsible for publishing a very embarrassing statistic which showed that the sharing of scientific information within psychology was effectively confined to a mere 10 per cent of qualified psychologists. But, as Darley points out, the findings for clinical psychology are even more embarrassing:

> My colleague Paul Meehl, speaking of the 'eternal hope' fallacy in graduate training, has pointed out that even though the modal number of publications of clinical psychology Ph.D.s is zero, faculty members lamely refute this fact by saying that maybe training in research hasn't worked, but 'we have to keep trying anyway' (Meehl, 1971). The fact is that research, however defined, will only and forever be an activity of a very small number of people.
>
> (Darley, 1973, p. 6)

Milne, Britton and Wilkinson (1990), in an article to which we will refer in more detail later in this chapter, have recently brought this discussion up-to-date by neatly summarising the dismal history of research productivity.

> One of the most common survey findings has been that the modal frequency of publications is zero (e.g. Prochaska & Norcross, 1983; Marrow-Bradley & Elliott, 1986; Martin, 1987; Barrom *et al.*, 1988). In addition, some evidence suggests that practitioners hold a negative attitude towards research, as reflected in the general disaffection of clinicians with what they often regard as a largely irrelevant research literature (Allen, 1985; Barlow *et al.*, 1984). Furthermore there is an acknowledgement of considerable difficulties when and if the clinician attempts to consume or produce research. It is ranked below more pressing service commitments (Allen, 1985); has a tendency to be inapplicable and inconspicuous, and hence to attract little support from colleagues or managers (Watts, 1984); has tended to try and draw on an inappropriate research methodology (Barlow *et al.*, 1984); and has tended to run up against organisational constraints, such as unrealistic ethical committees (Salkovskis, 1984).

In short, there have been problems in research production, consumption and utilization. These have been attributed to characteristics of psychologists (e.g. amount of training received) and to environmental determinants (e.g. number of paid hours available for research). A recent report (in *Clinical Psychology Forum*) bore out these points, in relation to Basic Grade Clinical Psychologists in the U.K. (Head & Harmon, 1990).

(Milne, Britton and Wilkinson, 1990)

Given the consistently dismal research record of clinical psychologists in the twenty-five or so years following the Boulder conference, it would appear that the Vail conference's recommendation in favour of a PsyD was a case of realistically choosing to close the door after the horse had bolted. If a research role is not a central role as far as the majority of clinical psychologists are concerned, then it is logical not to insist on a PhD as a ticket of entry to the profession. So perhaps the PsyD proposal was instituted for pragmatic reasons rather than the 'scientific' reasons the Vail report would have us believe?

Our digression to explore briefly the history of American clinical psychology training has revealed that American clinical psychologists have been prepared to rethink radically the research component of the scientist-professional model. But this is not true of their British counterparts. As we will demonstrate in the next section of this chapter, British training programmes have consistently espoused the scientist-professional model and in doing so have glossed over the difficulties that are intrinsic to the model.

The complacency of British clinical psychology can be strikingly illustrated by referring once again to Rachman (1983). We have already referred to his writing in this chapter but it is significant to note that the writing we have cited was a preface to a contemporary book on British clinical psychology. In this preface he has the following to say about the British model:

Most of our experience has been in the field of teaching clinical knowledge and skills and it is my strong impression that the training provided by the British University courses is excellent and probably is unmatched in any other country, European or American. British universities have succeeded admirably in pursuing the scientist-practitioner model that was originally endorsed at the Boulder Conference many years ago. While still pursuing the general aim, the British universities diverged from the American ones in not accepting the need for clinical training to be based on a lengthy Ph.D. course. The British teachers also diverged by insisting that clinical teachers should continue to carry out their own clinical work and should be seen to do.

No doubt Rachman is correct in stressing the value of British teachers having a foot in both research and practice, but is he really accurate in saying that the training programmes are successful? If we follow the rest of his argument through, we can, in fact, demonstrate that he effectively shoots himself in the foot:

> The competence and confidence with which most graduates leave the British training courses reflect the enormous efforts which most of these students put into their concentrated two-year training course. And when it is argue . . . that these concentrated two-year courses are too tightly packed, that it is unreasonable to expect students to complete research projects while gaining a professional training, one has simply to turn to the record. The overwhelming majority of students . . . complete them successfully and then go on to practise with at least reasonable success, and often with a great deal of success. Judging from Dr. Hemsley's as-yet-unpublished report on the research activities of clinical psychologists, disappointingly few graduates undertake research after they have completed their training. . . . It should not be concluded from these figures that the emphasis placed on research training has failed and, therefore, is misguided. It may be necessary to provide such experience for the many in order to encourage the few. There is the further argument that a period of carrying one's own research is an excellent foundation for evaluating the professional literature. Carrying out a research project increases one's sense of realism, among its other benefits.
>
> (Rachman, 1983, pp.xii–xiii)

There is, of course, a glaring fallacy at the centre of Rachman's argument. The completion rate of research projects cannot be taken as a criterion of success for the model if *most graduates subsequently fail to undertake research*. Indeed the reverse could be argued, i.e. that forcing students to undertake an exacting research project at the same time as they are trying to develop their clinical skills may be an aversive experience for the majority of them so they never attempt to undertake research ever again! The fact that the majority of students complete their courses can be attributed to a number of things including their very high levels of competence prior to coming on the course and the undeniable fact that they are highly motivated to complete the course in order to become practising psychologists.

A further weakness in Rachman's position hinges around his failure to examine concretely whether courses can possibly train students adequately in research skills, given the very small number of hours that can be devoted to research training.

Paradoxically we can use the same evidence to argue the reverse of Rachman's case – the scientist-practitioner model in both America and Britain is largely a failure but leading clinical psychologists persist in claiming it is successful because it is a crucial part of the profession's rhetoric in establishing its superiority *vis-à-vis* other professions such as psychiatry, social work and nursing. Training, of course, contributes crucially to justifying this rhetoric – clinical psychologists can point with pride to their three-year undergraduate training in experimental psychology and their two- or three-year postgraduate training, especially when they are trying to justify their excellence, but this way of arguing is essentially of the sheep-dip type – it studiously overlooks whether the goals of training have been achieved or not.

We insist on taking a different stance on the question of the scientist-practitioner model. Despite its glib espousal by leading clinical psychologists it is a role fraught with difficulties. On a day to day basis it is rare for a clinical psychologist to be able to function according to the model. A recent survey by O'Sullivan and Dryden (1990) provides grist for our argument. They surveyed all the clinical psychologists in the S.E. Thames Regional Health Authority in order to find out how they divided up their time. The most frequent activity was therapy (40 per cent of the working week) with assessment taking up a further 6.9 per cent of their time. Not unexpectedly to us, research was the least frequent activity, taking up 5.8 per cent of their time. The productivity of the clinical psychologists (in terms of published papers) was very similar to that of their American counterparts since 49.4 per cent had never published a paper (although 23.5 per cent had published three or more papers). 4.4 per cent of the sample did not spend any of their time on research activities.

Protagonists of the scientist-practitioner model like Rachman will no doubt see these results as indicative of the model's success, viz. nearly 25 per cent of psychologists are involved in publishing research despite the many contradictory work pressures to which they are exposed. Unfortunately, O'Sullivan and Dryden do not tell us anything about the work settings of the 'publishers' versus the 'non-publishers' but we would expect, admittedly on the basis of American research, that it is likely that 'publishers' will have an academic affiliation because research productivity is normally proportionate to the extent to which psychologists have access to research facilities in academic settings. Findings like this would, of course, enable advocates of the scientist-practitioner model to argue that it is the lack of facilities that is responsible for the model breaking down but we remain unconvinced. As we noted earlier in this chapter, Eysenck originally insisted that psychologists are either researchers or therapists but only exceptionally both. Unfortunately, we can find no research which addresses this issue although our own personal experiences of clinical psychologists lead us to agree with Eysenck – typically, successful and productive researchers are not active therapists. They may well be interested in therapy but engage in little therapeutic activity themselves. Equally, it is rare for active therapists also to research.

The controversy over the failings of the scientist-practitioner model has been given a new lease of life by the publication of a paper, by Milne, Britton and Wilkinson (1990), which we have already cited. Milne acknowledges that there have been 'problems in research production, consumption and utilization' but insists that this is because research has been too narrowly defined.

> When 'research' has received a wider definition so that it includes things like preparing accounts of service evaluation for local consumption and publishing in non-refereed journals, a some-what closer approximation to the ideal of the scientist-practitioner has emerged.
>
> (Milne *et al.*, 1990, p. 27)

The results of the study are undoubtedly interesting. For example, Milne reports (once again) the classic finding that the majority of respondents have never published in any sort of journal (academic or non-academic). However, 55 per cent had presented research findings at meetings and 41 per cent had published in academic journals. Consumption of research was documented by asking respondents how often they read journals. 20 per cent read an academic journal each week, 45 per cent monthly and 25 per cent quarterly. When asked whether research influenced their practice, 16 per cent replied 'a lot', 14 per cent 'moderately', 34 per cent 'to some extent' and 9 per cent 'a little' or 'not at all'.

Milne *et al.* interpret their findings as indicating that psychologists may produce, consume and utilise research to a significantly greater extent than had been indicated by prior surveys. However, a number of cautions need to be made. First, the research is based on self-report measure so that its validity is problematic. Second, Milne makes no attempt to evaluate the research reported by his respondents. It is well known, for example, that even full-time clinical researchers have difficulty in carrying out methodologically adequate clinical research (Maher, 1978).

In an important article the American reviewer Barlow (1981) in many ways anticipated the type of argument put forward by Milne. But we believe he has a far more realistic view of the relationship between research and practice. He points out the continuing divorce between what clinical psychologists espouse and what they actually do. He cites an earlier paper by himself (Barlow, 1980) which reports that full-time behaviourally orientated clinicians are no more inclined to integrate clinical research into their work than their non-behavioural colleagues. This is a very interesting finding given the claim of behaviourists to base their work on scientific research.

Various solutions to this problem of the divorce between practice and research have been advocated, as Barlow points out:

> [S]ome have argued that the more realistic approach to training in clinical psychology is to ensure that professionals understand the workings of science so that they will readily consume advances in clinical research to the benefit of their clients. Wollersheim (1974), arguing for the continuation of research training in clinical programmes, observed that this will at least ensure that clinical psychologists are sophisticated consumers of psychological research rather than 'crystal ball gazing' practitioners.
>
> (Barlow, 1980)

But even this more modest goal has proved elusive, particularly in the area of psychotherapy and behaviour change, as is readily evident in the writings of prominent psychologists. For example, Matarazzo, in an important statement, said: 'Even after 15 years few of my research findings affect my practice. Psychological science per se doesn't guide me one bit. I still read avidly, but this is of little direct practical help. My clinical experience is the only thing that helped me in my practice to date' (Bergin and Strupp, 1972, p. 340). Garfield and Kurtz observed a sharp increase in recent years in the number of clinicians calling themselves 'eclectic' which may imply a disenchantment with *tend to rely on experience.* conceptual underpinnings of psychological knowledge and a reliance on clinical procedures discovered on a trial-and-error fashion, as implied by Matarazzo (Bergin and Strupp, 1972, p. 148).

Now, clearly, Barlow's view clashes with the more optimistic one put forward by Milne and his colleagues. We certainly incline to Barlow's view because our own experiences of discussing the scientist-practitioner model with a wide range of colleagues lead us to believe that there is generally very little direct application of research findings to practice. Barlow's point that clinicians trust their own experience first and foremost seems correct to us, but we would also agree with Cohen's finding that discussions with colleagues are crucial sources of information and influence as far as most clinicians are concerned (Cohen, 1979). We also have good reason to doubt the validity of Milne's findings because we suspect that they are subject to considerable bias because of the pressures within the profession to present the work of clinical psychologists as scientific.

Frosh and Levinson (1990) have recently undertaken a survey that provides interesting support for our position. They sent out a questionnaire on clinical skills training to supervisors in the N.W. Thames region. Respondents were told that the regional inservice course organisers were hoping to develop a more coherent clinical skills training component to the course and that the questionnaire explored the need for clinical skills training, the identification of appropriate skills and the most appropriate form of implementation of such a training component. In commenting on the results of their survey Frosh and Levinson clearly demonstrate just how insignificant was their supervisors' stress on the importance of the scientist-practitioner role:

> The questionnaire results ... [show] ... that clinical supervisors are willing to identify a range of skills which they regard as central to the training of clinical psychologists. Not surprisingly many of these skills are in traditional core areas of clinical psychological practice, techniques of formal assessment and behaviour and cognitive interventions. ...
>
> On the other hand there are some striking gaps in areas thought to be crucial for clinical psychological practice ... only 11 per cent of supervisors regarded 'combining research and practitioner roles' as a central skill and no one nominated research either as a

skill to be learnt on placement or even as one which should have been taught previously. This finding calls into question the extent to which the common characterization of clinical psychology as a research-based profession is borne out in the real world.

(Frosh and Levinson, 1990, pp. 22–3)

We see this finding as a clear example of the rhetorical nature of the scientist-practitioner model. Milne and colleagues asked their supervisors directly to what extent they utilise research findings to inform their work and they obtained a (surely) compliant response which supports their contention that the scientist-practitioner is quite strongly adhered to. Frosh and Levinson ask essentially the same question (albeit very indirectly and in the context of training) and discover that the vast majority of supervisors do not attempt to link practice to research. This, needless to say, is an extremely uncomfortable result but we believe that it is an honest one which actually reflects the day-to-day practice of busy front-line clinical psychologists.

Returning to Milne's findings once again – it is crucial to point out that he found that men were much more likely to undertake research than women ($p < 0.001$) and higher grade psychologists were much more likely to undertake research than lower grade ones ($p < 0.001$). He unfortunately doesn't point out that most higher grade psychologists tend to be men, a reflection of the historical domination of men within the profession, an issue to which we will return in our final chapter. Nevertheless, these findings are extremely interesting and add grist to an argument that insists that research in clinical psychology is largely a careerist pursuit – as we have seen, research cannot be shown to influence practice but research publications on a psychologist's curriculum vitae are highly significant in achieving regrading and better appointments.

Our brief history of the scientist-practitioner model is, we think, sufficiently detailed to establish that it is fraught with difficulties. However, these difficulties are studiously overlooked by the profession of clinical psychology, particularly in situations which require the leading spokespersons of the profession to establish the credentials of the profession when it is under threat. For an exploration of the most recent example of this turn to p. 152 where we explore the way that the profession used the MPAG investigation of the profession to attempt to justify its credentials for carrying out work that made it unique within the NHS.

The extent to which the profession ignores the difficulties of the scientist-practitioner model can also be gauged by exploring how the profession presents itself to its intending recruits. Since 1980 there has been a clearing house responsible for organising a clearing house system (along UCCA lines) which helps applicants to apply for clinical psychology courses. Each year a handbook is published; this inventories all the courses and contains submissions from all courses that are accepting trainees during the current year. We have consulted the 1989 and 1990 handbooks (University of Leeds, 1989, 1990) in order to construct the following table which contains the key phrases which describe the courses.

MSc and in-service courses in clinical psychology
Key phrases abstracted from statements of course philosophy

Birmingham

> Scientist-practitioner model.
> Cognitive behavioural (teaching input) but an attitude of 'critical open-mindedness' to a range of approaches and theories is encouraged.

Edinburgh

> Flexibility is regarded as an essential attribute (for trainees) . . . in a profession which is developing as rapidly as clinical psychology. The course is cognitive-behaviourally orientated.

Exeter

> Strong orientation towards community approaches . . . [and] . . . community psychology.
> Students are encouraged to develop an integrated model for undertaking therapy . . . ideas and techniques derived from several major schools are part and parcel of the model.
> Need for practitioners to modify their approach to suit the needs and problems of the clients they encounter.

Glasgow

> The aim of the course is to produce not only good clinicians but good scientists.

Cognitive behavioural approach is dominant ... but there is also a substantial teaching input based upon other psycho-therapeutic approaches.

Leeds

Strong emphasis on becoming an applied scientist.
The course might [sic] be said to be broadly science based and behavioural in orientation but ... aspects of dynamic psychotherapy ... [are] provided.

Leicester

The practice of clinical psychology ... [is] a craft: a blend of science and art. Competence involves not only the skilled use of particular methods and techniques but also the ability to employ theoretical knowledge in a creative and imaginative fashion.

Liverpool

Course is eclectic ... the overriding theme being the application of theoretical notions and experimental findings to clinical problems within the framework of a problem-solving approach.
Consideration is given to the complete spectrum of theoretical models, the keynote being their applicability to any given problem.
Emphasis ... on the development of communication skills.

London (Institute of Psychiatry)

The aims of the course are to enable trainees to apply the methods and findings of psychology to both case work and clinical research.
Emphasis on an applied scientific approach to clinical problems.
Course is predominantly behavioural ... although several staff members are exploring cognitive approaches to therapy and non-directive methods.

London (University College)

> The course aims to provide a broad training in clinical practice and research.
> [NB This is the complete statement of aim.]

Manchester

> The course is essentially behavioural . . . some attention is also given to cognitive methods but the course does not strive to be eclectic.
> The model of the applied scientist is encouraged.
> The approach to casework emphasises full assessment followed by the generation and experimental testing of clinical hypotheses.

Newcastle

> The course aims to provide an opportunity for growth in basic knowledge of psychology, development of clinical skills and the awareness of health care organisations.

Oxford

> The course does not profess to have a single, distinctive theoretical orientation but seeks to encourage trainees to sample . . . [a] diversity of theories and practices

Plymouth

> The principal orientation of the course is behavioural and cognitive although trainees are exposed to a wide range of models and techniques in order to encourage flexibility and openmindedness.
> An overriding aim is to produce professionals capable of promoting high standards of patient care through clinical practice, teaching, research and effective communication.

Surrey

> The course emphasises the scientific approach to investigation and treatment but is cognitive behavioural in orientation.

Teaching explores other models and . . . placements ensure that trainees . . . [can] develop in areas of their own preference.

North East London Polytechnic

No statement of aims.

East Anglia

The aim of the course is to combine high academic standards with extensive clinical experience.

North West Thames

[The course] provides a well balanced and comprehensive training in all aspects of clinical work. To this end it ensures that trainees are aware of the major theoretical approaches and they may choose to gain experience of any of these in greater depth.

South East Thames

Particular attention is given to developing an integrated approach . . . linking clinical, academic and research components.
Trainees are introduced to a range of theoretical models . . . and their application in NHS settings.

North Wales

The course offers . . . a chance to acquire skills from a wide theoretical spectrum.
It aims to promote an open minded approach tempered with rigorous scientific evaluation of different psychological theories and their applications.
The scientist/practitioner model . . . is endorsed.

South Wales

The course [aims to]

1. Prepare (trainees) to solve a broad range of service-related problems.

2. Acquaint trainees with the aims, concepts and methods of clinical psychology.
3. Introduce trainees to important aspects of . . . [NHS] administration and organisation.
4. Encourage a self-critical approach to professional activity.

Wessex

> The course has an explicit commitment to a model of the learner as an active adult participant whose task is to link psychological theory and practice.

Our inventory of the way that courses present themselves to potential consumers is illuminating. What impresses us most is the differing versions of clinical psychology that are encompassed in these proposals. Perhaps the most striking contrast is between the Manchester statement of aims and the Leicester one. In fact, the contrast between these two courses is so startling that we have decided not just to summarise their aims but to allow the two statements to speak for themselves.

Leicester

> The span of knowledge relevant to clinical psychology is evergrowing and often fragmented, and the trainee clinical psychologists (and the Course contributors) are presented with the difficult task of achieving a 'working synthesis' – a map to chart their thinking and actions. Despite its crucial importance we do not believe that it is possible to rely on a scientific map alone – i.e. the model of clinical psychologist as applied scientist. We think of the practice of clinical psychology, whether it be direct therapeutic work with patients in the clinic or clients at the community level, or indeed policy development – as a craft: a blend of science and art. Competence involves not only the skilled use of particular methods and techniques, but also the ability to employ theoretical knowledge in a creative and imaginative fashion. We wish to see our trainees able to operate within a wide range of developmental, social and behavioural science knowledge and capable of applying such knowledge in a wide variety of practical situations.

Manchester

> The course is essentially behavioural in orientation and aims to provide students with a comprehensive in-depth training in this approach. Some attention is also given to cognitive methods but the course does not strive to be eclectic. There is specific focus upon procedures derived from experimental research and the model of the applied scientist is encouraged. The approach to case work emphasises full assessment followed by the generation and experimental testing of clinical hypotheses.

The Leicester statement seems to us to reflect real concern about the complexity of the clinical psychologist's role while the Manchester one reflects a fossilised regurgitation of a position originally formulated by Shapiro (amongst others) at least thirty years ago (and briefly explored by us in Chapter 3). The Manchester course espouses the most rigorous (and we would argue) unworkable version of the scientist-practitioner model. It is perhaps no accident that the course that is so emphatically in favour of the scientist-practitioner model is also the most behavioural. We would see this correlation as a clear example of the point that we made in the last chapter – that it was behaviour therapy that initially provided the most significant vehicle for expanding the scientist-practitioner role into the once despised domain of therapy. We also feel that it is no accident that the Leicester course, which perhaps draws upon more conceptual traditions than even the very wide-ranging Exeter course, is the most sceptical about the scientist-practitioner model. To insist that clinical psychology is a craft, a blend of science and art, is anathema to many clinical psychologists who insist that the practice of clinical psychology is, and should be, grounded solely in scientific research.

The course aims we have inventoried here could form a scattergram located in two-dimensional space. One dimension could be labelled 'degree of emphasis on the scientist-practitioner model' and the other 'degree of emphasis on the behavioural model versus degree of emphasis on an eclectic approach'. Another way of looking at the courses is in terms of some evolutionary dimension – with some courses apparently remaining static over a considerable period of time while others seem to have developed an ability to reflect the evolving nature of the role of clinical psychologists.

Another aspect of these courses concerns the degree of consensus they represent. Given the complexity of psychology as a parent discipline and the wide-ranging nature of the models available within clinical psychology it is no surprise to us that there is no clear agreement between the courses about the major goals of training but nevertheless we cannot resist commenting on the presentations by UCL, NELP and the East Anglia.

The failure of these three courses to formulate their goals in any meaningful way may reflect badly on the course convenors, and we wonder how potential trainees can possibly be attracted to courses that don't bother to clarify their goals even in the minimalist way asked for by the clearing house. We are also left speculating about why their presentations are so weak. Lack of energy or lack of agreement between course members seem to be the most likely explanations. Or is it more profound that this?

Do the psychologists who run these courses lack identity to such an extent that they can't formulate goals for their own courses? Or is it simply a pragmatic matter – that they do not wish to define their goals so that they do not limit themselves in any way when they actually get down to devising curricula?

But there are much wider issues at stake. It is, of course, damaging that a profession that prides itself on its scientific approach should be incapable of agreeing that its training courses should adopt the same basic viewpoint. Defenders of the current system will point to the fact that most courses are eclectic. Apart from those that adopt the label themselves, there are several erstwhile cognitive behavioural courses that allow trainees to experience other frameworks. However, this position overlooks the essential anarchy of the current position. Each course effectively goes its own way – there is no effective mechanism for agreeing a common philosophy although courses do have to conform to a number of criteria in order to be accredited by the Training Committee of the British Psychological Society. These criteria are effectively structural ones which pay very little attention to the underlying dilemmas involved in training clinical psychologists.

One of us (AT) has recently been a kind of participant observer in the process of accreditation because of involvement in the Exeter course as a clinical tutor. The accrediting panel that visited Exeter in July 1990 was suitably diligent but there was a conspicuous absence of any discussion of central issues that urgently need resolving, e.g. can clinical psychologists be adequately trained without undertaking personal work? Can clinical psychologists who are trained eclectically gain sufficient identity to be able to function effectively or are they likely to be confused by an overload of contradictory information? The panel's concentration on organisational issues was important – any course needs to be well structured and well organised – but it is curious that so little attention was paid to the content and philosophy of the course.

We assume that the panel's behaviour was not accidental – to raise issues that are central to the dilemmas of training is just not cricket. Such issues are painful for a profession that has to contain major disagreements within its ranks. Intriguingly a trainee psychologist has recently coined a useful collective noun that can be used to describe any group of clinical psychologists that meet together. The name coined (by an unnamed trainee) is a 'disagreement' (reported by Taylor (1989) in her MSc thesis). It is a useful term because it draws attention to a very wide range of contradictory opinions that are current in the profession.

The different strands within British clinical psychology have been neatly documented by O'Sullivan and Dryden (1990) in the paper we have already cited. The psychologists in their region-wide study had participated in twenty different training courses and were classifiable under eight possible headings: behaviour (*sic*)/learning, cognitive, psychodynamic (Freudian and NeoFreudian), eclectic, systems, person-centred (Rogerian), existential and other. The following table, gleaned from O'Sullivan and Dryden, gives a thumbnail sketch of a sample of British clinical psychologists.

Table 4.1 First-choice theoretical orientation (figures in percentages)

Behaviour/learning	22.2
Cognitive	13.5
Psychodynamic	21.0
Eclectic	31.6
Systems	6.2
Person-centred	2.4
Existential	0.0
Other	3.7

O'Sullivan and Dryden's figures are useful since they demonstrate how varied psychologists are in terms of their therapeutic orientation. As we have already seen, many training courses actively encourage eclecticism so it is not surprising to find that this category is the most popular one. Some clinical psychologists would argue that it is precisely the profession's variability that is its strength but others have argued that there are important dangers inherent in this eclecticism. Smail (1982) in his often cited paper, 'Clinical psychology – homogenized and sterilized', has attempted to explore these dangers at a number of levels:

> It is my impresssion that clinical psychologists as a group have over recent years become weary of philosophical debate concerning the 'models of man' [sic] which we espouse. In contrast to earlier years, we seem on the whole quite happy to let epistemological and moral issues lie unquestioned while we get on with the practical business of 'delivering' clinical services to an increasingly wide range of client groups that demand them. This, though, seems to me to constitute a dangerous state of affairs, both for ourselves as a profession and for those to whom we offer our services. More precisely, the danger is that, while we can't avoid having a philosophical stance on intellectual and moral issues, it has become merely implicit, but nevertheless continues surreptitiously to guide and shape our activities in ways we may at some future time come to regret.
>
> (Smail, 1982, p. 345)

We would argue that within the area of training epistemological and moral issues have indeed been shelved. The strongly and forcefully articulated position originally put forward by Eysenck forty years ago has been replaced by a typically English pattern of muddle and compromise. The scientist-practitioner model allied with behaviourism at least makes intellectual sense because behaviourism insists that it has a scientific (research) basis but how, for instance, can the hermeneutic framework of psychoanalysis be integrated with the empiricism of the scientist-practitioner model?

As we have documented earlier in this chapter, American psychologists *were* prepared to face the difficulties that beset the scientist-practitioner as the role of clinical psychologist changed from psychometrician/diagnostician/researcher to therapist. British clinical psychologists, perhaps because of their original even stronger grounding in the abject scientism of personality theorising and psychometrics, have espoused the scientist-practitioner model more rigorously than their American counterparts. The vulnerability of the profession because of its closely symbiotic relationship with the NHS must undoubtedly have contributed to the tenacity with which the model has been retained but the strongly empiricist intellectual climate of Britain has also played a part.

We believe that Smail is basically correct in arguing that crucial issues have been avoided. The BPS through its Training Committee for Clinical Psychology has played a significant organisational role in making sure that training courses meet a number of basic organisational criteria but at the same time the Committee has not faced up to the historical issues that have accumulated as the profession has changed. Clinical psychologists have become increasingly involved in psychotherapy and have become increasingly involved with complex clients. Training courses have responded to these challenges by becoming increasingly eclectic but the structure of the courses has not basically changed in order to reflect the new roles that psychologists must face. The Training Committee has been preoccupied with content issues, e.g. do trainees get enough experience of different client groups (children, the learning disabled) or do they undertake enough research? What has not been adequately faced is that the rules of the game have changed. Effective training is not achieved by just bolting additional courses, or additional experiences of different client groups, on to a structure that was originally designed in a period when clinical psychologists were much more peripherally involved in client care.

The original psychometrician-diagnostician role was essentially a peripheral, paramedical role. Psychologists had a penchant for wearing white coats and functioned in a way very comparable to radiographers or any other paramedic whose expertise provided information that was utilised by another profession (medicine and/or psychiatry). It is highly likely that the type of psychologist that was attracted to this peculiar role themselves preferred to be distant from people. Needless to say, such psychologists created training courses that tended to institutionalise this distancing from clients albeit in the name of scientific objectivity.

But clinical psychology has not developed in a vacuum. Developments within psychoanalysis, the development of more client-centred approaches (e.g. the humanistic school of Carl Rogers) and particularly the emergence of behaviour therapy created a new context in which the role of clinical psychologists changed. Psychiatric hegemony was challenged both from within the profession (by notably Laing and Cooper) and from without. But the basic stance of training courses did not change. Above all else the *person* of the clinical psychologist never became a legitimate area of discussion within psychology. This is why the clinical training courses that we have inventoried in this chapter contain no real mention of personal training. Trainees will develop skills and theoretical understanding but at no time will they be expected to understand themselves in any coherent way. Training in interviewing skills, in establishing rapport, in having some experience of psychoanalytic work – all are more or less acceptable but the clinical psychologist remains a scientist not a self-reflecting practitioner. She or he is concerned (within the rhetoric of the model) in learning to apply to clients techniques that are derived from scientific principles.

In order to flesh out our argument on this crucial point and avoid possible accusations of dogmatism we urgently need to explore what trainees (the consumers of training) have to say about the training courses they undertake. Trainees' views will be summarised in chapter five but it is important to end this chapter by briefly commenting on the use of the term trainee. It is a curious and unsatisfactory term for a psychologist who is, after all, technically at least halfway through training. Ironically the recently completed regrading system within clinical psychology has resulted in psychological technicians being renamed 'assistant psychologists' but trainees remaining trainees, and yet the majority of trainees have been assistant psychologists prior to joining training courses. This type of insensitivity to would-be entrants to the profession is sadly endemic to training courses which have a tendency to infantalise course members.

Chapter 5

Clinical psychology training – the consumer's view

Regrettably, it is true to say that trainees' experiences of clinical psychology courses are very rarely documented or paid attention to in any systematic way. If we examine the published record over the past forty years or so it is possible to discover an occasional account of training written by an ex-trainee. For example, in Chapter 3 we have already reviewed Dabbs' account of his training experiences. However, the only organised attempt to collate such experiences that we can discover was published in the *Newsletter of the Division of Clinical Psychology* in March and October 1977. Ten clinical psychologists (drawn at random from lists of trainees graduating in 1975) wrote brief accounts of their experiences.

Two of these ten accounts are anonymous – this appears to be puzzling at first sight but on reflection we can understand why. Trainees quite naturally find it very hard to criticise the courses they are participating in openly because they are, after all, in a power relation with staff members. They are reliant upon staff because staff have a large say in whether they graduate – they also need references from staff members when they begin applying for jobs. Trainees' relationships with their supervisors are even more fraught – trainees are often forced to tolerate bad supervision because they are dependent on a good report from their supervisor in order to achieve a pass on their placement. It takes a great deal of courage for a trainee to criticise the standard of supervision on a current placement. When the placement has been completed the trainee, quite naturally, feels disinclined to risk creating a row by communicating her or his experience to the course staff. To risk making an enemy of a psychologist who is potentially a future colleague (following the graduation of the trainee) is a real danger so trainees tend to keep quiet about their problems. Unfortunately, they often tend to internalise the problems they are experiencing – thinking that it must be something they have done that is the source of the problem they are experiencing on placement. This discussion enables us to understand why two of the ten psychologists remained anonymous. To criticise their training courses so soon after graduation also runs the risk of offending managers and colleagues with whom they are currently working.

The ten accounts provided by the psychologists are very different and it is an almost impossible task to summarise them accurately. However, since trainees' views are so often ignored in the literature on training we have decided to focus on them in as much detail as possible.

Barry Richards' (1977) account is perhaps the most intriguing. He openly admits that he has decided to discontinue working as a clinical psychologist because he is able to research clinical psychology itself. However, he insists that his training was not helpful in enabling him to perform his current role as a clinical psychologist.

> [T]he current practice of clinical psychology is a range of heterogeneous and often conflicting tendencies, reflecting, as it must, conflicts within psychology and ultimately within society as a whole. . . . General statements about 'the skills of the clinical psychologist', 'the psychologist's contribution' etc. are spurious insofar as they suggest a coherent body of knowledge and technique which is shared by, and unique to, clinical psychologists; they suggest that psychologists can be as mystified about their work as anybody else, and confirm that a tendency of the dominant ideology . . . (within the profession) . . . is to minimise dissensus.

Not unexpectedly he concludes that his training experience did not equip him to have a clinical role:

> Any meaningful role that I can identify for psychologists rests on training experiences largely outside the purview of this or that training course and not in fact specific to clinical psychology.

Richards' dissatisfaction with his training is clear and it is not surprising that he did not stay long in the profession. Ironically his account is immediately followed by a totally contrasting account by 'Anon Somewhere in England'. As a trainee, this psychologist undertook a training leading to the award of the British Psychological

Society Diploma. She/he was based in a large subnormality hospital and then took a job in the same hospital. The supervisory experience gained was reported to be 'excellent' but it is clear that as a trainee the psychologist felt very isolated:

> On the negative side there were few opportunities to mix with and gain support from others in the same position . . . my training has fitted me superbly for the job I am doing . . . because I trained in the same situation. However, it has not necessarily fitted me for movement within the job and I now wish I had had the opportunity of a broader-based training.
>
> I end on a plea for more organised area services or departments to be responsible for in-service training. . . . I should also like to see provision for disinterested personal tutors i.e. not attached to the same hospital as the trainees – as well as supervision.

It's important to add that since this account was written (in 1977) courses have become much broader and better organised – and it is very rare for clinical psychologists to be trained via the diploma route unless they are participating in a formal in-service training programme. The account is nevertheless relevant to current training because it raises the problem of personal tutors. Trainees often feel that they have no real support from courses because everything they do is monitored either by course staff or supervisors. A personal tutor system manned/womanned by psychologists who are not involved in the training course has been introduced by some courses (e.g. Wessex).

The third account from Gregg Dring (1977) makes two basic points – the first (in agreement with Anon's account) stresses the need for a broad range of experiences to equip the trainee for her/his future role. The second stresses the need for personal relationships which will enable the trainee to undertake the personal changes that are fundamental to being a successful clinical psychologist:

> I believe that learning to be a clinical psychologist requires personal changes . . . and that these occur only when . . . [the trainee] experiences a certain type of relationship. The position is suggested by some theory (Rogers, 1957) and is consistent with some evidence (Truax and Carkhuff, 1967). The organizer of a training course can try to meet the need to provide facilitative relationships in two ways. The supervision situation may fulfil this function as may the trainee's peer group.

Dring's own experience of supervision was mainly disappointing – a position shared with trainees from other areas that he met during his period of training:

> Looking back I picture in my mind's eye my supervisors (for whom I find I still feel affection) and immediately I visualise numerous barren hours, with, I think, dissatisfaction on both sides, deteriorating at last into an empty ritual. . . . This happens because of the things which have remained unsaid.

> What remained unsaid in supervision? Here I am helped by my memory of my most effective supervisors. The two from whom I learned most were those who exposed their psychological models most shamelessly to view. Those from whom I learned less seemed to take the view that supervision should come naturally and was not exactly an application of psychology. Behind this view, I think lies a belief that it is 'not quite nice' to apply psychology to one's colleagues. If I am right this points to rather deep mutual anxieties about the supervision relationship; anxieties which are not acknowledged.

Dring's proposed solution to this problem is to insist that the supervisor must negotiate a model of supervision with the trainee – a valid enough point in theory but it overlooks the unfortunate fact that many supervisors have very rudimentary ideas about how to supervise, so the notion of negotiating a way of supervising with the trainee could be potentially valueless.

Dring ends his reflections on training by making a plea for utilising the energy that can be released if trainees are helped to function as a peer group:

> The peer group . . . is the second potential source of facilitative relationships . . . I doubt if many courses contain mechanisms to maximise this function although there certainly are things which can be done. These range from the simple, such as arranging for the group to continue meeting when otherwise a long break may occur (as in the summer vacation); to the slightly [sic] more complex, encouraging the group to meet as an encounter group once a week, to the great act of faith, giving the group responsibility for planning and carrying out its own teaching. I am inclined to believe that all investments in this field will produce results whereas the safe policy of 'teaching' infantilizes the students and produces no more learning.

As a footnote to Dring's important comment it is necessary to add that some courses have developed ideas similar to Dring's. Some forms of group experience are provided but we should hasten to add that no course has really followed his radical suggestions of using the trainees as a learning cell. Clinical psychologists, despite their pretensions as scientist-practitioners, are often surprisingly unaware of either adult learning methods or the psychology of learning (Milne 1983).

The next account of training is by Richard Adams (1977). He is an enthusiastic advocate of the scientist-practitioner role and takes a fellow ex-trainee, Crockatt (1976), to task for arguing that the clinician role needs to be separated from the scientist role:

> Crockatt (1976) maintained that the clinical shift away from scientist and towards clinician is necessary. Personally, I see the two roles as complementary, even interdependent, and feel that a greater integration of the two . . . is necessary for the profession to develop a clear identity.

We shall be examining Crockatt's alternative view later in this chapter but it is clear from Adams' account that his own training was problematic. In evaluating his own training experiences he argues that 'practitioner' habits were developed more strongly than 'scientist' ones, although ironically he felt that none of his placements were long enough:

> Having failed to acquire an automatic scientist/researcher response during training, I find myself wanting in this area: early enforced use of the model would have increased the ease of using it now. Perhaps 'enforced' is too strong a word but the science model was not a central theme in my training, and I feel in retrospect that such a fundamental orientation should have been constantly in focus throughout.

It is difficult for us not to see Adams' position as anything other than naive given the enormous difficulties a clinician faces if she tried to base her clinical work on research. However, we will not pursue this point any further here because we have given adequate coverage to this issue in Chapter 4. Instead, it is important for us to record another important facet of Adams' account. Very candidly he reports that:

> I also developed a belief that psychologists were much cleverer and more versatile than anyone else and that it was only a matter of

time before we were running the NHS.... I had become too psychology-department oriented. The characteristics of this problem include distrust of other professions; a belief that psychologists have the answer to most problems; underestimation of the intelligence of non-psychologist colleagues; more interest in hospital politics than patient welfare; and other such destructive attitudes. This led me to be somewhat overconfident in my approach in my first job ... but fortunately I took a post which was more-or-less single-handed, and was forced to accept not only that psychologists are not the cleverest people in the clinical team but also that there are situations where other professionals may actually be able to make a more useful contribution than the psychologist. Having spent between six months and a year sorting this one out, I was more-or-less ready to start work.

It's refreshing to read such an honest account from a psychologist. In general, clinical psychologists are not renowned for their ability to be self-reflective but while we admire Adams' candour we also note that he is unaware that adherence to the scientist-practitioner model is one factor that can contribute to clinical psychologists feeling superior to other professions.

The next account by Adrian Skinner (1977) is amongst the shortest and is perhaps the frankest:

And now ladies and gentlemen, for 64,000 dollars, the star question: How does your training help you in your present role? ... 'Well, the contestants do not seem to be able to answer that one and so they get tonight's consolation prize – a lifetime of moving sand-dunes with a teaspoon'.

Skinner elaborates his challenging opening by arguing that:

The central problem is that we are taught, mostly, by specialists eminent in their own field and any one trainee has access to only one or two of these on his or her course. One then arrives in the field armed with, say, an intimate knowledge of the finer points of behavioural analysis and you can only use it once in a blue moon. If the speciality of your course is not your interest, then you are on your own, brother (and at present this is a common situation). Placements are a different kettle of fish, in that the same restrictions do not apply, and that is where the real learning goes on.

Why a great deal cannot be done about this situation is because no-one can agree on what clinical psychology is.

Ironically Skinner appears to be in favour of the anarchic situation he records because his conclusion is one that preserves the status quo.

It would be fatal to try and regulate training over much, unless we want a generation of identikit psychologists – it is the opportunity for the individuality which gives clinical psychology its (sometimes crazy) uniqueness. We are neither wholly a profession, as in law, or wholly scientists, as in nuclear physics. We are practitioner-scientists and for each person there is a different balance of the two. Perhaps, as Don Bannister has said, to try and 'train' at all is a dangerous occupation as one's whole system is liable to be turned upside down in a few years – and that is why most of us are out here with our teaspoons.

The sixth account, by Peter Holden (1977), echoes many of the points made by Adams because he feel that his lack of research training meant that he floundered when he took up his first post in a primary care setting. He felt that his course was well organised and comprehensive but the research element in the course was problematic because 'there was seldom any ongoing research among the established staff on which first to wean oneself'.

However, paradoxically for an in-service training course, his major criticism of his training was that the course was geared more towards academic learning than clinical experience.

Of course one cannot dispute the notion that they must go hand in hand, though paradoxically from a logistic point of view they were rarely matched. When I was attached to the Subnormality Hospital for example, I was being taught in the lecture room about Kelly's Construct Theory and Ellis' Rational Emotive Therapy . . . since a matching process was acknowledged as being impossible, we were expected to learn our psychology from the lecture course and obtain some experience from our supervised placements.

I cannot help thinking what an inappropriate way this is to carry out practical training of service psychologists. It is disjointed and impersonal, quite apart from being educationally out-of-date. Looking back it is my belief that I learned far more from central supervisors than from the lecture course, not just in terms of clinical experience but of basic academic content as well. There were the supervisors who took their training role seriously enough to take time to discuss both academic and practical issues with me. Much more emphasis should be placed on the training function of supervisors and far less on formal teaching. This is not to relegate formal teaching completely but to reduce it to the minor role, thereby promoting attachment to individual placements and supervisors as the primary focus for training. Lastly the relationship between supervisor and trainee must not be overlooked. My experience varied enormously but where this was good, I was happier, worked harder and learned more. By far the majority of my learning during those three years took place within an open and positive relationship with conscientious supervisors.

The seventh account by Sue Gray (1977) is in many ways a mirror of Holden's account and yet at the same time part of it echoes part of Adams' account. Gray trained at the Institute of Psychiatry (Maudsley) but had taken a research job since graduating. Once again it is difficult to summarise her comments so we rely on quoting directly from her account:

The Maudsley course is strong on measurement techniques and statistical analysis; students are encouraged to be almost obsessionally objective in their assessment of pathology and treatment outcome. This approach turns out to be of great value in my . . . [research] . . . job but I suspect that a clinician in the NHS who is obliged to work with a team of other professionals all operating from different schools of thought might find he needs to be a little more flexible. Unfortunately one failing of the Maudsley course is that, although traditional psychiatry is taught, the students are not encouraged to use the language of psychiatrists. Whether we like it or not psychologists are obliged to work with psychiatrists and it is necessary to communicate with them even though criticism may also be needed at times. In adopting this almost aggressively high-principled scientific approach the psychologist runs the risk of cutting himself off from other professions and sacrificing some of the benefits of a more cooperative relationship.

Gray appreciated her training in clinical method which was 'taught well' but adds a footnote that if she had been working in a more general hospital setting she might have appreciated a little more experience in non-behavioural methods! Surprisingly she found the scientific emphasis of the course quite weak as the following quotation illustrates:

> Experimental design and interpretation of data was dealt with to some extent on the clinical course but I must give most credit to my Nuffield Science training at school and to my first degree course for the foundations of my present knowledge of scientific method.

Overall her positive comments about her course are clouded by some very negative comments which echo Drings' point about traditional lecturing methods infantilising trainees:

> My final comment is a more personal one relating to the transition from the student-role to that of a worker. Having been in a student or trainee role for so many years, I was slow to realise that to make a career of academic research it is necessary to be assertive and speculative and to proffer expertise in a variety of areas despite the fact that one feels painfully aware of the gaps in one's knowledge and suspects that there must be other more experienced workers who could deal with a theoretical issue more knowledgeably and efficiently than oneself. I feel now that whatever assertiveness and intellectual confidence I gained under the flexible individual teaching system at my first University was not developed further at the Maudsley. Rather, it was somewhat undermined by the 'back to school' atmosphere, engendered by the complicated and rigid teaching system and the emphasis on lectures and examinations. I would have preferred the course to have given students more freedom and control over the academic aspects of their training in order to develop a sense of responsibility and confidence as fully in academic work as in the area of clinical practice.

We think that Gray makes a profound point here. Our fairly wide experience of talking to trainees from different courses confirms Gray's point very strongly. It is generally true, we believe, that trainees feel alienated from the academic side of the course but much more involved in (if often frustrated by) the clinical side. The difference in experience can be attributed to the fact that trainees generally feel much less infantilised in clinical settings than in academic settings. In clinical settings they are often welcomed as members of clinical teams and if their supervisors are respectful of them they feel more secure and can function effectively. Gender issues are also usually very relevant to the academic/clinical split since most academic departments are even more dominated by men than clinical psychology departments. Since the majority of trainees are now women this issue is becoming more acute. Many women trainees feel unsupported and find it difficult to find role models within the profession.

The eighth account is simply by 'Anon'. Surprisingly, he or she is positive towards his/her training despite some quite negative criticisms of details of the training received:

> The teaching of clinical skills and therapy techniques was rather arbitrarily taught on the placements, and could have been more systematically dealt with on the course. Supervision of clinical cases was rather sketchy and much of the time I was left to plan and carry out treatment programmes alone. There was very little training in psychotherapy and generally too strong an emphasis on assessment techniques.

Curiously the weakness of supervision had a positive side because Anon reports that:

> Because clinical cases were so poorly supervised I learnt to work independently at an early stage, to take full psychological responsibility for clients' treatment and to make decisions quickly. This is no argument for poor supervision but I do now feel glad that I learnt to take responsibility for my work as a student.

Reading between the lines of Anon's account it is possible to see how he/she survived training – other trainees may well have gone under if they had been exposed to the same regime but clearly the course was successful in helping Anon achieve success at undertaking research in an applied field. Another success of the course was achieved through Anon's ability to cope with the wide range of placements offered by the course:

> Having access to a wide variety of supervisors and other clinical psychologists in the region gave me a chance to decide my own preferences for many aspects of their job – from actual clinical skills and techniques right through to keeping records, writing reports etc.

Clearly Anon had considerable survival skills which enabled him/her to utilise what the course provided. A less secure trainee might well not have survived the ordeal. Some hint of how this was achieved is included in the final comments that contribute to Anon's account:

> Generally I feel positive about the training I received, though I know a real appraisal of its true qualities is impossible. I feel that what is most important and difficult to develop in a new, first job is generally learnt through contact and discussion with a wide variety of people. I refer to such things as 'professional' attitudes and priorities, how to organize one's timetable, how to relate to other professionals, hot to 'take on' administrators and to cope with committees and how to cope with heavy psychotherapeutic demands on oneself. Perhaps dealing with these problems could be systematically built into a training (and I would strongly recommend this) but I basically feel that what counts is the people you meet and who become important to you, rather than a well-taught series of lectures on the latest therapy techniques.

The next account by Adrian Gaggs (1977) is a short and quite sharp criticism of the Leeds course, which is seen by him as aimed at awarding an academic degree in clinical psychology rather than an actual professional qualification. Since the account is so brief we reproduce it almost in full:

> I feel that the following things were lacking:
>
> 1) In depth training in behavioural therapeutic techniques.
> 2) An almost total lack of any real training in psychotherapy.
> 3) A lack of group experience.
> 4) A definite need for more detail of the administrative structure of the NHS, hospitals, etc. and how it affects day-to-day running in actual job experience. So much of one's time in the profession seems to be taken up with meetings, with hospital administration, etc. It seems to me that actual strategies could be discussed about psychological techniques of persuasion and communication. Surely it is a paradox that the profession which purports to have access to psychological insights into processes of communication should be so poor, on the whole, in the realm of communicating its own point of view to administrators.
> 5) A need for more feedback on actual therapeutic experience

undertaken during the course e.g. feedback on therapy tapes or treatment programmes.

6) Room for more training and experience in subnormality... Most problems, in fact, in subnormality seem to involve communication problems between psychologists, nurses, administrators and so on, particularly where setting up behavioural programmes or rehabilitation schemes are concerned. The course dealt quite well with the background and theory of subnormality but very little with how to put programmes into operation in the real life setting.

Gaggs' points numbers five and six are almost exactly echoed by Linda Smith (1977) in the tenth account. As we have already commented, the area of subnormality, or learning disability (to use the more current term), is now a central part of clinical psychology training, but it is still an open question as to how well training courses deal with the organisational aspects of the NHS, which several of the other ex-trainees also comment on.

Smith's account is generally positive but there is a curious sting to its tail:

On the positive side, I did receive a broad grounding in clinical psychology, and a fairly wide range of experience in well-supervised placements. In this sense, courses do ensure some sort of minimum standards of training. Clearly it would be impossible to organise courses which could prepare psychologists to meet the vast number of different problems that are encountered in different hospitals. Thus there is of necessity a lot to be learned in the Basic Grade years. . . .

On the whole I can say in all honesty that I did enjoy my clinical psychology training course. This was probably due to the fact that as I already knew something of the reality of practice of clinical psychology, I had perhaps a more realistic idea of what the training and practice would involve, and so was not as disillusioned as some of my colleagues on the course. Furthermore, having experienced one year at a college of education, I was aware that there were worse post-graduate training courses than those to be found in clinical psychology.

It is, of course, notoriously difficult to convert descriptive accounts of the type we have recorded here into data which can be quantified and we have not attempted a content analysis of these accounts in order to provide a coherent summary of the themes and issues they contain. Our method has involved quoting what we consider to be key sections of the accounts – this method, of course, opens us up to an accusation of bias but we are quite willing to defend our position. Our historical analysis of the evolution of clinical psychology has, we feel, demonstrated that there are a number of unresolved issues that the profession has failed to face. It is therefore not surprising for us to find that trainees – people who are undergoing professional socialisation – should be able to reflect these tensions more honestly than qualified practitioners whose occupational loyalty is secured.

Before reflecting on the ten accounts in an overall way it is important to point out that they probably represent a 10% sample of the population of trainees graduating in 1975. (We would estimate that approximately a hundred trainees would have graduated in any year during the mid-1970s.)

The trainees' accounts of their training experiences are clearly very variegated but it is important for us to point out that many of the issues raised about the breadth of experience (of different client groups) have been addressed by the BPS Committee on Training in Clinical Psychology (CTCP) so that it is undoubtedly true that trainees will now get a broader experience than their counterparts did in the mid-1970s. Child-focused, adult-focused and learning disability-focused placements are now compulsory. It is also true that training is generally much more coherently organised. Until the early 1980s there were four main routes to becoming a clinical psychologist: 1) by means of a university or polytechnic-based course (awarding an MSc or its equivalent), 2) by means of an in-service training course (awarding the BPS Diploma in Psychology), 3) by means of an individually negotiated training programme (involving supervision by at least senior grade psychologist) – this method also involved sitting the BPS Diploma examination, 4) by means of a specialist training in child-focused problems (leading to the award of an MA or its equivalent).

This latter route involved becoming trained either as a child clinical psychologist (at the University of Nottingham) or as an educational psychologist (three London-based educational psychology training courses had a sufficiently large clinical training component to also be recognised by the Whitley Council). In fact the BPS withdrew recognition from these four courses in 1982, arguing that clinical psychologists needed to be generically trained (BPS, 1982).

The bureaucratic nature of this decision is aptly documented by Newsom, Newsom and Gilham (1983) who quite naturally fought to retain recognition for their Nottingham course. Newsom *et al.* quite rightly raised the issue of whether generic training could possibly equip a clinical psychologist for the complexities of working with children and their families. They pointed out that a psychologist on a generic course who had worked for as little as six weeks with children could qualify to work with children as a clinical psychologist while their own year-long trained graduates could not. What also infuriated the Newsoms was the failure of the BPS to undertake any consultation with the specialist courses before taking what they considered to be a precipitate and hurried decision.

We will return to this issue later on in this chapter when we discuss the pitfalls of generic training but an immediate concern is to turn back to the ten ex-trainees' accounts. The issue of depth of experience (i.e. did training actually prepare trainees sufficiently for their future role?) is the next issue to be considered.

It is clear from the accounts that trainees had very different experiences. Some felt reasonably prepared but others felt totally unprepared. Others again felt that the course did not prepare them and yet paradoxically they felt competent because they were able to find a way of exploiting the course in order to find their own path to competence.

In terms of being prepared as scientist-practitioners the findings are again contradictory. Some felt prepared, others did not, but some failed to make any real comments on this issue.

The quality of supervision emerges as very variable. The Committee on Training in Clinical Psychology has focused a lot of attention on this issue and since 1982 has published a set of rigorous guidelines (CTCP, 1982). Fortunately a detailed study by Sharrock and Hunt (1986) enables us to comment upon the continuity of this issue within clinical psychology.

Sharrock and Hunt circulated all the courses in Britain – they received eighty-eight replies (fifty-eight from women, thirty from men) from eighteen courses. Trainees were asked to rate their experience of current supervision on three scales – satisfaction, usefulness and relaxed atmosphere. The respective mean scores were 5.4, 5.6 and 5.5 (on a seven-point scale). Satisfaction and usefulness correlated very highly (0.80) but satisfaction and relaxed atmosphere produced a lower but still highly significant correlation of 0.49. These results are not surprising to us – again from our experience of talking to colleagues there is a general consensus that supervisory standards are improving so that older clinical psychologists tend to report worse experiences than younger ones with the most newly qualified reporting the best experiences. However, Sharrock and Hunt are not complacent about their results, because, for example, twenty-one of the eighty-eight respondents reported that they did not receive regular supervision (despite the CTCP regulation that supervision should be weekly for a minimum of 1 hour). Similarly, while the majority of the trainees observed at least some of their supervisors' work, twenty-eight did not and twenty were not observed working by their own supervisors. Perhaps the most crucial finding of the whole study was the consistently high correlations between the items designed to gauge the 'atmosphere of supervision' and satisfaction. For example, supervisors' empathy to trainees' emotional needs correlated 0.59 with satisfaction and no less than seventy-four of the eighty-eight trainees rated this aspect of supervision as being important to them.

Sharrock and Hunt conclude, on the basis of a stepwise multiple regression analysis, that four aspects of supervision are of significant importance in contributing to satisfaction with supervision. These four aspects are empathy to trainees' emotional needs, sufficiency of supervision, tactful use of criticism and focus on specific details of cases.

Unfortunately we cannot detect any recent published survey that has examined the overall attitudes of trainees to their training experience. However, it is important to reflect a little on the likely significance of more specific surveys like Sharrock and Hunt's. Empirically orientated psychologists will no doubt say that clearly the results are favourable and demonstrate that clinical psychology training – at least as far as supervision is concerned – is heading in the right direction. But we would caution against drawing easy conclusions from this type of data. After all a significant minority of Sharrock and Hunt's respondents (18 per cent) were dissatisfied with their supervision and, interestingly, there was a tendency for older trainees to be more dissatisfied than their younger colleagues. For us the crucial question is – how is satisfaction constructed? To take a personal example, during training one of us (AT) worked with three supervisors – two supervised in a traditional way (cases were discussed in some detail on a week by week basis) while the third (a family therapist) provided *in vivo* supervision of cases and in group sessions also used trainees' videotapes as a key element in training (so there was direct feedback about what trainees had actually achieved in sessions with clients).

If I (AT) had been asked during each of these supervisory experiences whether I was satisfied or not with supervision then my answer would have been very different because the unusual, hands-on style of supervision was the second of my three experiences. I enjoyed and was satisfied with my first experience (traditional post-session supervision with no observation of me by my supervisor or vice versa) during the actual placement. But having completed my second placement I was then (not unexpectedly) much more dissatisfied with my third experience and, in retrospect, I was very acutely aware of how little I had learnt during my first placement because the relaxed style of supervision was supportive but not challenging enough to actually help me learn new skills.

Bearing these issues in mind we would therefore remain cautious in interpreting Sharrock and Hunt's results – half a loaf is after all much better than no loaf at all. Our approach to this issue gains credibility from considering accounts by trainees who receive a different training experience when they have graduated as clinical psychologists. Interestingly, we have discovered two retrospective accounts of training written by psychologists who received additional psychotherapeutic training. These accounts are much more critical of clinical psychology training but they too concern trainings undertaken in the 1970s.

One of these accounts by Crockatt (1976) was referred to by Adams in one of the ten ex-trainees' accounts but it is striking how Crockatt's different life experience influences his/her account of basic training. The level of criticism is noticeably much deeper and more fundamental, as the following quotation illustrates:

I feel the profession has failed up until now to realise the aspirations embodied in the title 'Clinical Psychologist' ... there has been a failure to develop a truly clinical profession. ... Linked to this failure has been a continuing reluctance to place therapy at the centre of the role ... inspite of growing evidence both of the need for therapists in the health service ... (MIND, 1974) and of the desire of clinical psychology trainees to fill this gap. ... Those individuals who *have* managed to create truly clinical roles for themselves . . . have been little helped by their training experiences but have had to carve their own tracks, usually by establishing links with psychiatrists and social workers in the years following post-graduate training.

(Crockatt, 1976, p. 13)

Crockatt's solution to the problem is radical and ironically runs counter to the evolution of clinical psychology as a profession:

> The centre of gravity of our work as clinical psychologists must shift yet further away from the roles of 'scientist-researcher' and 'mental tester' toward the role of 'clinician' specialising in the practice and development of methods of psychological help for those complaining of psychological distress, in other words, toward the role of therapist.
>
>   This may seem as if I am casting off completely the research and assessment roles of the clinical psychologist, not to mention the more recently defined roles of teacher and consultant. To some extent, I must admit, I would welcome this – but only as a temporary corrective to a continuing and premature over-emphasis on the former roles. The problem here is that through developing the assessment and research roles *before* the clinical, therapeutic role (and very possibly at the latter's expense) clinical psychologists have put the cart before the horse.

(Crockatt, 1986, p. 14)

This position, of course, challenges the Eysenckian-Shapiro position fundamentally, but it is clear that Crockatt's position is very well thought out. For example, he mobilises a very interesting quotation from Koch (1974), which also puts the skids under the evolution of psychology itself, to underpin his position. Crockatt, in fact, argues that the adoption of the academic scientist-researcher role mirrors a fundamental mistake made by academic psychology in the nineteenth century. He uses this crucial quote from Koch:

> Psychology was unique in the extent to which its institutional-isation preceded its content and its methods preceded its problems. . . . For close to a century now, many psychologists have seemed to suppose that the methods of natural science are totally specifiable and specified: that the applicability of these to social and human events is not only an established fact, but that no knowledge based on enquiry that is not saturated with the

iconology of science is worth taking seriously. From the earliest days of the experimental pioneers man's [sic] stipulation that psychology be adequate to science outweighed his commitment that it be adequate to man. From the beginning some pooled, schematic image of the form of science was dominant, respectability held more glamour than insight, caution than curiosity, feasibility than fidelity.

(Koch, cited by Crockatt, 1976, p. 14)

This swingeing attack on academic psychology is utilised by Crockatt to open up, once again, the issue of the research role of the clinical psychologist:

Koch's argument stimulates a vital question for clinical psychologists. How can clinical psychological research and assessment be at all meaningful or relevant if it is carried out by people who inhabit roles that insulate them from deep immersion in the very phenomena they claim to study so systematically, namely the experiences of people presenting with problems of psychological distress? The answer to this question is, surely, that it cannot – if clinical psychological research and assessment are to avoid becoming hollow activities, empty of meaning and relevance. In Koch's words, content must precede institutional- isation, problems must precede methods. Much of the peripheral quality of published clinical psychological work, judged by the criterion of clinical relevance, testifies to this failure to engage deeply with the experience of people we claim to be in business to help.

I am suggesting, then, that there is a need to further develop the clinical and therapeutic roles of the clinical psychologist, not only to give meaning to the 'clinical' bit of our title but also to aid the development of more meaningful and relevant assessment of research roles than exists at present. Nor I believe, can the roles of teacher, supervisor and consultant to other professions be authentically sustained without a secure clinical and therapeutic base.

(Crockatt, 1976, p. 15)

Crockatt's paper is now fifteen years old and yet the issues he raises remain largely unresolved. Sections of his paper are, of course, reminiscent of Eysenck's original paper that we explored in some detail in Chapter 3. (Crockatt, of course, argues the opposite case to Eysenck.) Ironically, Mollon (1989), another clinical psychologist who is also psychotherapeutically trained, has written a paper (published in *Clinical Psychology Forum*) which argues a case similar to Crockatt's. The title of the paper 'Narcissius, Oedipus and the psychologist's fraudulent identity' is calculated to set many psychologists' teeth on edge but since it is an unusual paper which confronts basic issues we will follow its arguments in some detail. Mollon writes from the standpoint of a clinical psychologist who has also undertaken a training as a (psychoanalytically orientated) psychotherapist. The main thrust of his argument flows from a comparison he makes between his identity as a psychotherapist and his identity as a clinical psychologist.

> My identity as a psychotherapist is much clearer to me. . . . I know what my clinical skills are, their application, their limits of applicability, the body of knowledge they arise from; I have a peer group with shared knowledge, skills and assumptions; I have a clear sense of professional lineage – I can situate my practice and theoretical assumptions in a historical line. . . . But . . . as I think of myself as a psychologist I am not sure what I am, not sure of my peer group, not sure what I have in common with other psycho- logists, not sure that I could define or describe very coherently to others what psychologists do; and, regarding the sense of lineage (which I think is an important part of identity), the history of psychology seems too broad and diverse to relate to. Clearly then I must feel that my own identity as a clinical psychologist is uncertain if not fraudulent. However, I believe there are problems inherent in the structure and culture of clinical psychology which make it difficult to establish an authentic professional identity.
>
> (Mollon, 1989, p. 7)

In the absence of any published British research on this issue of identity it is difficult to determine whether Mollon's position is a relatively isolated one or whether he speaks for a wider constituency within British psychology. Certainly not all psychologists lack identity in the way he suggests – many behaviour therapists we meet have a strong sense of identity which meshes strongly with the scientist-practitioner model which is central to the Eysenck-Shapiro concept of clinical psychology. But nevertheless we also meet many clinical psychologists who do suffer from the lack of identity Mollon talks about. This lack of identity is often felt most by newly qualified psychologists who have just left their training courses. That they should lack identity is scarcely surprising given the nature of training courses they have experienced. Placements, as we have seen from other accounts, are typically too short – often lasting only three or four months. Trainees have to undertake at least three (sometimes four) compulsory placements in widely differing specialties and further elective placements. Since they are supervised by different supervisors on these placements they often have to experience widely differing styles of working. At the same time they, of course, receive a wide-ranging academic input via seminars and lectures and, for at least part of the course, they must undertake research.

Mollon surprisingly does not pay attention to these structural difficulties which are endemic to clinical psychology training. Instead, his focus is on a deeper source of identity confusion which flows from a lack of agreement about the central task of clinical psychology:

There is . . . a problem inherent in the lack of clarity of the task of clinical psychology. Medicine did not begin with biologists thinking 'Well, we must have something to contribute to the care of people who are ill, let us sell ourselves to the NHS and see what we can do'. Medicine grew out of the necessity of caring for the sick, attempting to heal the sick; even if the reality was that the doctor could not heal, at least the general task was clear. . . . It could be argued the original task of the psychologist was clear; it was to carry out psychometric testing. But . . . the relative ease with which psychologists have freed themselves from this role . . . must mean that it was never very important. With the liberation from the role of psychometrician, supplementary to the doctor, psychologists seemed then to seek an exaggerated autonomy, reluctant to allow anyone else to define their task. This was very much a profession-centred rather than a task-centred stance. Interestingly, a current managerial trend in some districts is towards individuals being encouraged to develop a primary orientation to the task, the clinical service, and the team, rather than towards the profession.

I have mentioned the aim of the doctor to heal or care for the patient. How does it sound if a would-be clinical psychologist expresses a desire to heal? In the current climate I believe it would sound embarrassing, although many psychologists probably are motivated by just such a desire, one which is unsupported by our culture and training.

(Mollon, 1989, p. 8)

Mollon's comparison between medical and clinical psychology is somewhat naive – the history of the two professions is not as simple as he implies but nevertheless his point about clinical psychology lacking a central task does seem valid to us. He is acutely aware of Eysenck's original denial that clinical psychology should be concerned with therapy but he goes on to develop an interesting point about another salient difference between medicine and psychology:

> Unlike the doctor in training, the clinical psychologist in our system undergoes no apprenticeship in caring, in having clinical responsibility for patients. Moreover there is no training in learning to observe people carefully and make use of experience. Clinical psychology ... is not based on clinical experience. One might draw a distinction between 'learning from experience' (in an apprenticeship mode) which characterizes medicine and also psychotherapy, and 'learning from research' which characterizes clinical psychology. The latter tends to encourage a detached intellectual stance rather than one which facilitates emotional contact with the patient; it does not recognise authority based on experience but rather assesses the value of an opinion in terms of the cleverness of the research strategy; it can foster a tendency to learn from the literature rather than personally from teachers. It is in my view a stance appropriate to an academic university-based study, but it is quite unsuited to a clinical therapeutic role.
>
> (Mollon, 1989, p. 8)

We are basically sympathetic to Mollon's position but unfortunately his arguments cannot be accepted without careful evaluation. Throughout his paper he presents medicine very uncritically – he clearly has no idea how problematic medical training is. For example, he fails to appreciate that initial medical training is bewilderingly scientific. Medical students usually spend two pre-clinical years being pumped with scientific information (anatomy, biochemistry, cell biology, etc.) *before* entering the very long apprenticeship phase of their training. Admittedly, they are exposed to a strong caring ethos during this latter phase but they too have initially been invited to become scientists. Medical students often, therefore, suffer many of the same problems as clinical psychology trainees – they are trapped between a world of scientific investigations (and scientific theorising) and a world in which they have to provide care for patients whose individuality makes the application of scientific principles complex and even hazardous.

Mollon is also in error in the way that he presents clinical psychology training – despite what he says there is definitely an apprenticeship element in clinical psychology training. It may not be as close an apprenticeship relationship as Mollon encountered in his psychotherapy training but clinical psychology supervisors do in some sense apprentice trainees to themselves, and many trainees report (as we have already seen) that it is within this relationship that they learn most about their future role. The problem that they usually face is that the academic side of the course is nearly always frustratingly tangential or even irrelevant to their learning in clinical settings. Ironically, it is a common experience for trainees to be exposed to this problem even when they are lectured by clinicians. In academic settings, skilful clinicians often find it impossible to communicate successfully with their audience – their presentations become too abstract in the spurious attempt to be scientific.

What is at stake here is a central problem of learning which clinical psychologists (despite their supposed knowledge about learning processes) studiously ignore. Doing is the form of learning which is decisive to a would-be clinician – and yet most clinical psychology learning is, as Milne (1983) has commented, traditionally passive and out of touch with the wisdom contained in the ancient Chinese proverb:

> I hear and I forget
> I see and I remember
> I do and I understand.

The essence of apprenticeship is, of course, doing and this is why we support Mollon's position. The problem with the apprenticeship component in clinical psychology is that it is too fragmented (because of the inadequate length of placements and because of the fact that trainees have to experience so many supervisors). There is also an unresolved tension about what psychological knowledge is and how it can be related to practice. The pluralism of psychology itself and the eclecticism of clinical practice creates inevitable confusion, particularly for psychologists in training.

But why did clinical psychology training adopt a policy of too short placements? We would suggest that the answer is, of course, not a 'scientific' one but an historical one. When clinical psychology training was first initiated it was designed, as we have seen, to produce psychometricians. Short (three- or four-month) placements were just about feasible because the trainee could be inducted into using a number of relevant tests and an adequate number of assessments could be carried out. Admittedly there was a problem about the skilled interpretation of the results but this could be neatly glossed over – more experience of doing tests later on in the psychologist's career would overcome this pitfall. When therapy was added to the role of being a clinical psychologist the structure of placements was not radically modified. Or, as Mollon argues:

> The problem is that having freed itself from the role of psychometrician the profession attempted to move towards a therapeutic function without the necessary changes in culture and in training. In American trainings by contrast, where psycho-therapy was much more clearly seen as part of the role, the norm became four year postgraduate internship programmes.
>
> (Mollon, 1989, p. 9)

Admittedly, some British three-year training programmes have attempted to modify their placement programmes to include longer placements with the same supervisor but these are exceptions to the normal rule. The two-year courses are, naturally, even more open to criticism on this point.

Short placements, unfortunately, have a crucial impact on the nature of the work that trainees can undertake. Through Mollon's eyes they could be seen as an unconscious mechanism to limit trainees' involvement with clients. But Mollon's argument goes deeper than this – he is prepared to argue that academic psychology itself is, in practice, utilised by clinical psychologists as a defence against coming into emotional contact with any clients who are themselves in emotional pain. This is a very crucial point so it is important for us to explore how Mollon attempts to justify his position. His point of departure initially concerns the mismatch between psychological theory and clinical practice:

> The ill-fitting nature of academic psychology as a background for clinical work is illustrated by some of the remarks of the editor of *Readings in Clinical Psychology* (R.D. Savage, 1966). Having emphasised the importance in his view of an academic training in clinical psychology, and the necessity of the psychologist

approaching problems with 'well standardised, reliable and valid tests for diagnosis, sound experimentally based techniques' he goes on to add (perhaps in a tone of regret) 'at the same time it must be realised that the task of the clinical psychologist is a difficult one, because he has to confront patients. . . . The clinical psychologist has to be in contact with patients and this unavoidable complication complicates his work.' . . . As Savage [remarks] . . . the contact with the patient is indeed a complication of what might otherwise be a clean and tidy science. To be in emotional contact with a person in emotional pain is painful. It is likely that all professions involved in caring for people in pain develop their own organization of unconscious defence against the pain of emotional contact: clinical psychology is surely no exception. The prototype study of this kind of defence is that of Menzies *et al.* (1961) who showed how nursing practice on a ward was systematically organized unconsciously to protect against the pain of contact.

(Mollon, 1989, p. 8–9)

Again, this is a very interesting and challenging argument but before we evaluate it in our own terms it is important to point out that Mollon inadvertently distorts Savage's position. The distortion can be illustrated by reinstating the parts of Savage's argument that Mollon leaves out. The full quote is as follows:

At the same time it must be realised that the task of the clinical psychologist is a difficult one because he has to confront patients. He is unlike, for example, biochemists, or pathologists who are concerned with 'specimens'. The clinical psychologist on the other hand has to be in contact with patients and this unavoidable relationship complicates his work and its interpretation and introduces the 'magic elements' – suggesting transference and the like. He must, therefore, also receive training and experience in this field.

The traditional gap between the academician and the applied psychologist is narrowing, and indeed for the benefit of both, it must.

(Savage, 1966, p. 4)

It's very curious to us that Mollon should edit out Savage's insistence that clinical psychologists should at least receive some psychodynamically orientated training. By omitting this part of the quotation he is able to imply that Savage devalues the clinical role of clinical psychology. But Savage is far more of an eclectic than Mollon would allow. Indeed elsewhere in his introduction to his book he insists on arguing that there was an important 'dynamic tradition' in British clinical psychology.

But defending Savage on this point does not, paradoxically, really detract from Mollon's argument because Savage's eclectic position leaves an important issue unanswered. How is experimental psychology (and the associated use of behaviour therapy techniques) to be married to the 'magic elements' that Savage also thinks are important? Unfortunately, Savage does not resolve this issue in any way but neither was his position heeded by the profession in any significant way. Training courses have mostly ignored such issues and through doing so have helped create a problematic method for training therapists, as Mollon argues:

> Clinical psychology trainings do not on the whole prepare the trainee for the fact that they may have to face people's emotional pain, overwhelming trauma and despair, and that the client may generate very powerful interactional pressures which can be very disturbing and incapacitating to the inexperienced clinician (Mollon, 1990). None of these interactional pressures are hinted at in the literature on behavioural and cognitive therapy. The student contemplating the research literature on the efficacy of different modes of therapy is far removed from the emotionally charged encounter with the despairing person in pain. The attempt to distance oneself from this person, to apply a technique to him, or her, to manipulate the person out of or into some behaviour, all these may contain elements of a manic defence against mental pain. Whenever this manic state of mind predominates the profession may be regarded as essentially fraudulent, based on illusion and mental trickery.
>
> (Mollon, 1989, p. 9)

Not unexpectedly, Mollon singles out behaviour therapy for special criticism – through his eyes behaviour therapy is a prime example of an overly manipulative and prescriptive therapy which is based on a delusion of omnipotence:

> Of course behaviour therapy has made an important contribution but in its enthusiastic embracement by clinical psychologists some years ago it lent itself to manic and obsessional controlling states

of mind.... It did not develop out of work with people in emotional pain; it is not based on human relationships....

When I did my training in the mid-1970s some psychologists seemed preoccupied with technical gadgetry. To respond to a person's request for help with emotional problems by wiring them up to a biofeedback machine is an attack on emotional meaning and quite perverse. To imagine that it might be possible to change something as fundamental as a person's sexual orientation by means of a shock box is a truly manic and very crazy idea, yet one which was around at that time.

(Mollon, 1989, p. 9–10)

So through Mollon's eyes clinical psychology is basically a fraudulent profession but, instead of exploring the profession's history in order to establish how and why it adopted behaviour therapy as its main credo, Mollon, not unexpectedly for an analytical therapist, seeks to explain the fraudulence by utilising ideas derived from Freudian developmental psychology. The essence of his argument is that there are basically two ways of achieving professional identity: 'The dichotomy is between an omnipotent assumption of identity based on projective identification and one derived from the slow and at times painful process of learning and development'.

Mollon's description of the projective identification method of achieving professional identity is best presented, once again, in his own words:

A little girl aged about three steps into her mother's shoes and walks proudly round the room holding her doll, which she announced is her baby. She is pretending to be her mother. This is a normal, healthy and transient form of projective identification (a term which covers all kinds of fantasies of getting inside another person). The little girl has a lot of growth and development to go through before she can in reality become a mother. But what happens if this projective identification, this false assumption of characteristics becomes chronic, within the individual or the group, or institutionalised, or part of the culture? The wish to avoid the pain of learning and gradual development, and omnipotently to assume the desired identity is probably ubiquitous; however the potential for resort to projective identification may be particularly enhanced when the person is faced with a difficult task or role, without sufficient guidance and supervision of a kind which recognises the reality of what the person can and cannot do; a situation which at times characterizes that of the initiate into clinical psychology, certainly it did when I was training.

(Mollon, 1989, p. 10)

Mollon's criticism of clinical psychology training is very damning on this point but his position is in step both with his own experience as a trainee and the experiences reported by many trainees attending the annual Tavistock one-week course for probationer psychologists. This course is much valued by trainees who attend it because it creates an unusual situation for trainees – a forum in which *feelings* about being a trainee can be safely shared. According to Mollon:

A recurring theme emerging from the discussion group . . . is the feeling many students have that they are discouraged from expressing doubt, anxiety and feelings of inadequacy as if they felt under pressure to assume a stance of omnipotence and denial of doubt. Under these conditions the initiate is faced with the choice of either going along with institutionalized defence, or else facing shame, isolation and contempt. The pressure towards projective identification in place of learning is towards a mimicry of appearance of externals. When I was a trainee we often seemed to become preoccupied with what to wear, and hot to 'look professional', as if the donning of appropriate garments would solve the problem of learning. In a two year course there is simply no time genuinely to learn, to acquire gradually an authentic professional identity based on skills and understanding, developed bit by bit through struggle and some emotional pain. Moreover there is no formal structure for continued clinical learning after basic qualification. Instead the pressure is on to 'learn' projectively a few concepts, phrases, attitudes, technical tricks and so on. The sheer length, or lack of it, of clinical training seems itself to reflect and undoubtedly foster, attitudes of omnipotence.

(Mollon, 1989, p. 10)

Once again we think Mollon's assessment is basically correct. The pressure for a trainee to knuckle down and not to express doubt or raise difficult issues varies from course to course and even from supervisor to supervisor. However, unless a supervisor has herself been trained within a model which legitimates the exploration of difficult personal issues, then there is a tendency for supervisors merely to recapitulate the errors that they experienced when they themselves were at the receiving end of training.

A classic example of this type of problem was reported to one of us recently by a trainee who was experiencing difficulty on her placement because of the style of supervision she was receiving. The situation had arisen whereby the trainee felt increasingly uncomfortable in sessions with a male client who had originally been referred for help with anger control. During recent sessions the client had been exploring the fact that he got angry when he was sexually frustrated. He was intent on exploring his sexual fantasies in the sessions and was quite open in reporting that his therapist (the trainee) was included in these fantasies. On reporting this difficulty to her supervisor (a behaviour therapist) she was curtly recommended to ignore the client's fantasising and to concentrate on devising anger control methods.

Clearly the supervisor in question was not able to help the trainee with the transference issues involved – and yet the supervisor's difficulty could be directly attributed to the behaviourist training he himself had received from a course which is notorious for its narrow adherence to traditional behaviour therapy. Such courses run the risk of creating psychologists who are incapable of working on anything other than superficial issues. This is bad enough from the client's point of view but when psychologists of this stamp are in a position of supervising trainees who have the courage to work on deeper issues (concerning both themselves and their clients) the mismatch between supervisor and trainee is potentially very damaging.

Faced by such situations some trainees flounder but others manage to develop despite bad supervision – usually by actively searching for another supervisor who would be prepared to handle such issues in supervision. Unfortunately bad supervisors are rarely challenged around such issues because to do so would set the cat amongst the pigeons. A basic assumption of clinical psychology training is, as Mollon argues, that psychologists 'should somehow be healthy enough, well adjusted enough not to need help themselves, as if psychologists and their clients have to be kept in clearly differentiated categories, another naive assumption' (Mollon, 1989, p. 10).

This defensive posture is, of course, indefensible but Mollon quite rightly pursues this point further by using it to explain the flight into management which is currently a marked feature of clinical psychology:

Those who are caught in this culture (of denying the need for personal work) and who make no further effort to obtain further clinical skills will be left with outwardly a valid professional identity but inwardly will feel fraudulent. There may then ensue the common phenomenon of flight from clinical work into management, a dynamic also prevalent in social work, another profession where training in clinical skills often seems inadequate. Whilst management is a perfectly valid and legitimate function if it is undertaken out of an underlying, perhaps partly unconscious, disillusionment with clinical work, it is essentially a manic activity, and obviously, if the clinical skills are not substantial and well grounded, the whole structure is flawed. Like any manic defence this flight to management would involve contempt, and denigration, of clinical skills.

(Mollon, 1989, p. 10)

Mollon's argument is quite complex at this point but we are not entirely in agreement with his position. In our opinion he does validly describe the development of some psychologists who become managers before they have accumulated a level of experience which equips them for the role. Given the enormous shortfall of clinical psychologists in the NHS (due to the provision of far too few training places) it is not surprising that this process is occurring but Mollon fails to acknowledge that the profession has been forced to respond to political pressures which were not of its making. (Chapter 6 will explore these issues in much greater depth.)

We have followed Mollon's argument step by step because it is one of the few serious attempts to come to terms with the current malaise of clinical psychology. However, it is important for us to make clear that we part company with the concluding part of his argument which is concerned with establishing the reasons why psychologists have tended to adopt the fraudulent identity described in his paper. Mollon unfortunately commits the classical error of the psychologist – he seeks to explain historically determined processes by utilising a psychological theory (in this case a developmental hypothesis derived from psychoanalysis). Once again we find it difficult to summarize Mollon's argument so we cite the relevant section in full:

A number of ... writers all describe a broadly similar phenomenon. They locate perversion and fraudulent identity in the small child's wish to avoid a genuine identification with the parent; to avoid the painful comparison between the capacities of the child and those of the parent. For example, in normal Oedipal development the little boy surrenders the desire to do away with the father and gives up the illusion that he can be mother's perfect partner, in favour of acknowledging the reality of the need to grow and develop and learn from the father in a gradual authentic identification. He is helped in this by the friendly and sympathetic availability of the father. In fraudulent and perverse development this task of facing reality, including the necessity of learning and development is avoided, or indefinitely postponed, a wish to avoid and deny inheritance in a retreat from Oedipus to Narcissus.

(Mollin, 1989, pp. 10–11)

Having established an hypothesis about fraudulent development in an individual (male) child Mollon then commits himself to the type of conceptual leap that psychoanalysts are particularly willing to make. He assumes that the development of an individual child is essentially similar to the development of a profession:

Some comparisons with trends in clinical psychology are obvious: its origins in hostility to fathers, the consultant psychiatrists and the psychoanalysts; the locating of the field outside any well-established tradition, coupled with the tendency towards a preference for eclecticism in therapies, scraps gathered from here and there, each individual putting together his or her own pseudo-original mix of this and that therapy i.e. the denial of inheritance and the avoidance of an apprenticeship model. Most crucial of all is the pervasive absence of clinical trainings of sufficient length to allow genuine growth and learning to take place.

(Mollon, 1989, p. 11)

The epistemological problems of Mollon's method of arguing are too familiar to detain us here but it is important to point out that Mollon presents the history of the development of clinical psychology in a most partisan way. His argument that clinical psychology should have identified itself with the fathers (psychiatry and psychoanalysis) is very problematic. For a child to develop normally he argues that the father must demonstrate 'friendly and sympathetic availability', but is he really saying that psychiatrists and psychoanalysts adopted such positions in relation to clinical psychologists? Curiously his developmental metaphor deals only with childhood, but what of adolescence? Is a child merely to be a parental look-alike or is there to be permission to rebel – to find new sources of identity and grow away from the model that is offered by the parent?

Curiously, Mollon is half aware of the difficulty in his own argument because in his very next paragraph he adds the following comment:

> Clinical psychology had rebellious origins in breaking away from . . . paternalistic psychiatry and psychoanalysis overthrowing the old order, the tyranny of the medical model. Undoubtedly there is something partially positive in this. Without some degree of Oedipal struggle there can be no development but here is the dilemma: that the same impulse that can lead to innovation and creativity can also take another course and lead to sterility, perverse posturing and a failure to develop. Without rebellion there can be no separate identity, but only sterile conformity yet it is delusional to suppose that we can situate ourselves outside of any tradition, competently hoisting ourselves with our own bootstraps.
>
> (Mollon, 1989, p. 11)

Clearly the concession to the positive nature of Oedipal rebelling that Mollon makes in this paragraph is dangerous for his argument. His discussion of a child's development insists that successful resolution of the Oedipus complex requires the child to identify with the parent but in this quotation we are told that conformity can be a problem. Mollon wants to have his cake and eat it too, but if we go back to the early origins of clinical psychology it's difficult to see how the profession could have emerged as a profession if it had taken the path that Mollon suggests.

We have already cited Smail's (1973) assessment of the professional climate that actually confronted clinical psychology as it attempted to establish its independence, but Mollon's assumption that psychoanalysis could provide a route for authentic development fails to confront a number of crucial issues about psychoanalytic training. The central core of such a training is, of course, the undertaking of an enormously costly training analysis – the cost of which is prohibitive and usually requires the analysand to live in London because the cabalistic nature of the profession is so marked that it is almost impossible to achieve a training outside the capital. The sacrifices that analysands make in order to complete their training can be remarkable and it is fully expected that analysands should make a total commitment to their training. For example some years ago a colleague of one of us explored the possibility of undertaking a training. She was told by her potential trainer in London that she should sell her house in Bristol, give up her job there, and move to London so that she could undertake the necessary training sessions four or five times a week.

The fallacy of Mollon's argument seems to us to be predicated on his uncritical attachment to psychoanalysis. Underlying his argument is the assumption that psychoanalysis is the *only* tradition that psychologists should respect and follow. This is a curious position – Mollon's acceptance of psychoanalysis clearly leads him to ignore other psychotherapeutic traditions. In the most recent (4th edition) of his book *Current Psychotherapy*, Corsini, the major American reviewer of psychotherapeutic methods, lists no less than fifteen major approaches to psychotherapy (Corsini and Wedding, 1989). Is it possible just to accept that psychoanalysis is *the* approach and dismiss the other fourteen. Does Mollon have no knowledge of the history of psychotherapy. For example, how does he come to terms with the fact that two major schools (Adlerian psychotherapy and analytical (Jungian) psychotherapy) have histories almost as old as psychoanalysis itself because they reflect very early attempts to develop ideas which the psychoanalytic model failed to encompass?

Mollon's own solution for resolving the identity confusion that is so prevalent in the profession is remarkably imprecise, as the ending of his article demonstrates:

> We should not sell ourselves or our students short by providing too little time and opportunity to learn clinical skills and thereby acquire a substantial and authentic foundation for our professional identity, a clinical base for clinical psychology, for if we continue to do so, we may one day wake up to find that a department called 'Psychotherapy' has been established in an adjacent building, leaving us with greatly diminished role and credibility.

> (Mollon, 1989, p. 11)

Surprisingly, Mollon doesn't indicate which model of psychotherapy should provide the backbone for learning – is it to be psychoanalysis? If it is, then Mollon would have to explain how courses could possibly be organised given the overconcentration of psychoanalysts in London. Equally surprising is Mollon's emphasis only on skills training. Surely he would want to stress not just skills training but training which also focused on the personal aspects of therapy?

Otherwise training becomes (yet again) narrowly defined as a didactic task involving the communication of techniques.

We believe that the personal aspects of training are crucial. As we have demonstrated in this chapter the chief opinion makers who shaped the early development of clinical psychology – people like Eysenck and Shapiro – succeeded in imposing a scientistic framework upon clinical psychology. Experimental psychologists, despite interesting research findings implicating the person of the experimenter in determining experimental results, traditionally do not consider themselves as a variable in determining the results of the experiments they undertake. It is therefore not surprising that clinical psychologists (because of being profoundly influenced by experimental psychology) have elected to ignore the personal in training new initiates to the profession. Eysenck's bitter attacks on the efficacy of psychoanalysis helped create an intellectual climate that prevented psychoanalytic theories concerning the client– therapist relationship from receiving adequate attention as far as the majority of training courses were concerned. Shapiro's more client-orientated approach paradoxically did not help to correct the over-concentration on the clinician as experimenter – instead, it deepened a tradition of scientism within clinical psychology which reinforced the notion of therapy as the application of techniques by an omniscient scientist who was not himself (male pronoun used advisedly, DP/AT) a possible object (or subject) for scientific investigation.

Historically, as we have seen, clinical psychologists were only peripherally involved with clients. But gradually their role as therapists (and consultants to people undertaking therapy) has deepened. During the last forty years training courses have not remained static; many have attempted to reflect the changing role of the clinical psychologist, but the question remains – have these changes been sufficient to equip psychologists for their new tasks? The twelve accounts given by ex-trainees give us a confused answer to this question – Crockatt and Mollon clearly say no and so do several of the other ex-trainees but clearly some of them felt well enough equipped to undertake their professional role. We can only guess at why their positions are so different. We would suggest that the differences can be explained partly in terms of the different roles that they may be performing as clinical psychologists. If a psychologist on graduation is primarily involved in research then obviously she is not likely to experience the angst of Crockatt or Mollon, committed to working with clients who may have profound therapeutic needs which can only be met by an extremely well-trained therapist.

A psychologist working with learning disabled clients on graduation may find that she is expected to do as much work with staff as with clients. So the role is a complex one requiring credibility as a practitioner but also as a source of ideas, support and consultancy as far as other staff are concerned. A psychologist working with older clients will need all the skills required by workers in adult mental health settings, but will also need to be reliant enough to deal with clients who are experiencing loss in all its many facets – loss of loved ones, loss of functioning, loss of social role. A psychologist working with children needs to have all the skills for working with children and yet at the same time be able to work with parents and also be a skilled couple therapist who can deal with unresolved couple issues which can prevent effective parenting from being undertaken.

The profession of clinical psychology in Britain has opted for generic training with all courses insisting that trainees must undertake clinical training (i.e. placements) in child health, adult mental health and learning disability specialities. Some courses (e.g. Exeter) have now introduced a compulsory placement to equip trainees to work with older clients. Preoccupation with the content of training – reflecting the expanding role of clinical psychologists – has taken precedence over the issue of process. Predictably new tensions will arise: for example, why shouldn't a compulsory placement in physical disability and general health care be introduced given that psychologists have already demonstrated their ability to be very effective in such settings? The implication here is that clinical psychology training should follow in the footsteps of medicine which has produced a form of training that resembles a multi-layered cake. New layers are added without any thought that the cake could become totally indigestible.

These ineluctable pressures within the profession have, given its scientific credo, militated against placing personal issues at the centre of training. As one former Exeter trainee has eloquently complained, the philosophy of training most predominant in Britain is the 'empty bottle' model (Yates, 1987). Trainees are assumed to require filling up with information before they are launched on their careers – what is studiously ignored is the fact that a trainee may already have vintage wine in her bottle before joining the course and that the wines that are then poured in are not of the same vintage and inadvertently form a near lethal mixture.

Not unexpectedly the person of the trainee is profoundly lost in this process. Historically the scientist-practitioner emphasis, as we have seen, militated against psychologists focusing their attention on the personal in therapy. And yet there is a growing consensus that it is the person of therapist that is a primary factor in making therapy effective. The recently published book *On Becoming a Psychotherapist*, edited by Dryden and Spurling (1989), is an example of the renewed thinking about this issue. In the opening chapter of the book Gilbert, Hughes and Dryden explore the crucial relationship between caring and the ability to deal with one's own feelings – a topic singularly ignored by most behaviouristically orientated frameworks:

> The ability to deal more effectively and honestly with one's own affect is probably central to the development of caring. Coming to know oneself is not always a joyful experience. Mair poses three questions that therapists should ask themselves: 1) Who or what do I trust? 2) How can I enter into another's way of experiencing? and 3) How much of myself or others am I willing to know? As he points out, our knowing is about focusing: 'Every way of knowing is at the same time a way of ignoring, of turning a particular blind eye or seeking not to know' (Mair, 1987, p. 118). If a therapist turns a blind eye to things in himself so may the client; dark areas are projected or denied. Therapists may care for their clients, as they themselves would like to be cared for, unaware that this is not what the clients need. So long as technique becomes the new touchstone of psychotherapeutic practice these issues remain secondary concerns. As trainers, we are increasingly under pressure to 'pass on skills' ... comparatively little attention is given to the 'people' these skills are imparted to.
>
> (Gilbert, Hughes and Dryden,
> in Dryden and Spurling, 1987, pp. 7–8)

The overall conclusion that Gilbert, Hughes and Dryden reach is worth quoting in full because it poses a crucial challenge to the current training of clinical psychologists (and, needless to say, several other professions as well).

We believe that in common with much anecdotal evidence the person of the therapists matters (Kottler, 1986, McConnaughty,

1987). Why people end up practising psychotherapy, their choice of approach, and the way they put this approach into practice are important research questions. Therapists require a certain kind of interpersonal intelligence and to be able to apply science. But like musicians or artists techniques will only carry a person so far. Those therapists who are probably the more successful are able to marry pragmatically different sets of styles and approaches which are not a mish-mash of eclecticism but a carefully considered application of approaches to suit different clients at different points on their journey. Therapists who are themselves heavily defended will tend to focus on what they are doing and on their techniques. There will, of course, always be some clients who will be helped even by the most defended of therapists. Nevertheless, many clients and professionals have expressed the view that the success of a therapy depends on finding the right person (i.e. therapist) as much as in finding the right school of therapy.... [T]herefore it is as important to focus on the style of the therapist as it is on the technique of therapy; we need both the singer and the song.

> (Gilbert, Hughes and Dryden, in
> Dryden and Spurling, 1989)

Clinical psychology training has concentrated on the song not the singer. Courses have generally moved away from the narrowness of the behavioural paradigm to embrace other frameworks but a recourse to eclecticism does not in itself solve the underlying problem that the heritage of the scientist-practitioner role has created for clinical psychologists.

Skadegaard and Grabelsky (1975) have written an interesting 'consumers' account' of what it is like to be at the receiving end of an eclectic teaching programme, albeit in America rather than Britain. At the time of writing their paper they were both interns completing their clinical psychology training. Their experiences are, of course, not identical to their British counterparts' but we believe they touch upon issues which are of common concern.

> Traditionally graduate training in clinical psychology has taught us how not to be psychologists.... Psychology departments working within the framework of the academic scientific tradition have served to block out human creativity and to put technological precision in its place. Involvement with one fellow man has been replaced by scientific detachment so that the people of Rollo

May's 'schizoid world' will be coming to psychologists afflicted
with the same condition. . . . The academic rationale reasons that
no particular theoretical system should be taught in detail for to
do so is at expense of academic freedom. Hence, theories are
presented to us in castrated form. . . . While students were once
encouraged to be critical of the theories in which they were
trained, today's students are taught to be critical of theories of
which they have merely superficial knowledge. Criticism without
knowledge of what is being criticized leads to apathy, not creative
thought. Apathy, the step-child of sterility, has become the current
value system taught to graduate programs.

(Skadegaard and Grabelsky, 1975, p. 201)

Skadegaard and Grabelsky then go on to explore the impact of this
apathy on clinical practice.

Theoretical systems, even when discussed, are often looked upon
as novelties by so many academicians so that students are often
reluctant to think about theories or other important clinical
issues. Thinking unscientifically (i.e. outside of the framework of
the traditional experimental design) does not sit well with the elite
in academia. Thus we are taught not to trust our thoughts, and,
along with this, our feelings.

Paradoxically the clinician, in working with people and with
theories must rely primarily on his [sic] inner resources, thoughts,
and intuitive feelings in order to help the people to understand,
modify, or create the theories. When the student is cut off from his
inner resources and becomes a stranger to himself, he must
struggle the rest of his career to come to know himself, his feelings
and thoughts again. We have difficulty committing ourselves to
treatment procedures and philosophies because we are taught to
disregard the very aspects of ourselves so necessary in our field.

(Skadegaard and Grabelsky, 1975, p. 202)

Unfortunately we have no empirical evidence that enables us really
to understand how new British trainee clinical psychologists
experience the increasingly eclectic courses they are exposed to, but
we know from first-hand discussion with trainees that there is a
general feeling of being beleaguered by an information overload. An
eclectic approach which does not help the trainee to create an
overarching integrated model of therapy can be hopelessly confusing

and leave the trainee suffering from an embarrassment of riches.

Clearly eclecticism has its problem but it is also important to stress that skills training is problematic too. Many courses try to overcome their theoretical weaknesses by attempting to impart interviewing skills to their trainees. However, such attempts are usually problematic because of inadequate curriculum time and because the length of placements is usually too short to allow the trainee really to practise skill development in a real life setting.

Equally, supervision rarely includes meticulous exploration of audiotapes or videotapes of trainees' active therapeutic work with clients. Defenders of current training courses will perhaps acknowledge these criticisms but argue that it is post-qualification training and supervision (at basic grade level) that can correct the inevitable inadequacies of training courses. Again, we have little space to go into this argument in any detail, but a recent paper by Houston, Revell and Woolett (1989) has once again drawn attention to the very great variability of training experiences, with some trainees feeling that their post-qualification needs were being met while a significant minority reported that they were not. Clearly post-qualification training needs to be strengthened but it cannot be used as a panacea for basic inadequacies in initial training.

Clinical psychology training in Britain, as we have demonstrated in this chapter, is many-faceted. Some courses retain a strong behaviourist orientation whilst others have evolved an eclectic approach. However, despite this apparent diversity, no course has elected to tackle the central historical issue that we have attempted to trace through the forty-year history of training. Training courses, despite important evidence to the contrary, still avoid exploring the role of the person in therapy. Initiates to the profession are put through all sorts of selection rituals at the point of being recruited to training courses. Their 'personalities' and 'interpersonal behaviour' are assessed in interviews but, tellingly, once they have been recruited to a course there is a built-in assumption that they will achieve competence solely through acquiring technique and knowledge. They therefore become largely invisible as people – people who may quite naturally have very genuine problems of coping with the very difficult task of being able to survive in a role which demands an ability to deal with other people's distress. As Mollon has eloquently pointed out, their difficulties in taking on this difficult role are not a central preoccupation of training. The scientist-practitioner model, as we have documented, has traditionally helped to distance a practitioner from distress emanating from clients, but it has also had a tendency to distance the practitioner from his or her own personal distress. And yet, contemporary discussions of therapy, as we have seen, are beginning to focus once again on the role of the therapist (rather than techniques of therapy) in helping clients.

Clinical psychology is clearly in a period of crisis. Its scientistic traditions have created training courses which are largely insensitive to the underlying needs and difficulties of trainees who are inducted into a profession which has a macho tradition which prevents any real discussion of vulnerability. This tradition, which we will briefly explore in the next section of this chapter, is inadvertently propagated by certain factions within the profession who seek to sell the profession to management on the basis that psychologists have skills and knowledge superior to those of other professions within the NHS. Clearly, if the profession were to draw attention to the arduous and hazardous nature of training (and the fact that considerable more resources need to be mobilised to enable effective training to take place), then the profession's attempt to justify its superiority would be subject to considerable scrutiny by managers. The rhetoric of the scientist-practitioner model is effectively used to paper over such difficulties but the actual effects of this process are conveniently ignored so psychologists are often catapulted into situations which expose their inadequate training. Their articulateness and their ability to quote research often enable them to survive but they have to cope with feeling very exposed, and even fraudulent, as Mollon has argued.

At a deeper level the neglect of the personal in training must be seen, we believe, as a reflection of a professional secret which is rarely discussed within clinical psychology. Professional burnout is now a well recognised issue within the caring professions (Rippere and Williams, 1985) but, as Sue Walsh (1990) has recently pointed out, we know surprisingly little about how clinical psychologists cope with this problem:

> [L]ittle is known about the ways that psychologists take care or 'refuel' themselves. Penzer (1984) and Nichols (1988) have both commented on the fact that though psychologists teach self-care skills to other professionals we fail to practise them ourselves. . . . One primary difficulty of the process for the psychologist is that it requires a role-reversal, with the professional experiencing a sense

of their own powerlessness. Nichols (1988) argues that for the psychologist to receive support it requires that we respect our own feelings, talk about them openly, are trusting, and that we take the time and the attention from another professional.

(Walsh, 1990, pp. 3–4)

On theoretical grounds it is possible to predict that a clinician who has been professionally socialised within the straightjacket of the scientist-practitioner model will find it difficult to achieve this role reversal. But it is possible to argue that the constraints may be even more powerful, or, as Walsh argues:

Helping and caring for others can be a very effective way of concealing personal needs. Storr (1979) and Malan (1979) have both noted that most therapists acknowledge that their interest in therapy stemmed from their own problems. Reinforcement of self-image as a caring person, fantasies of omnipotence, denial of our neuroses ('us and them' attitude) and voyeurism are just some of the motives described by the professional helper (Edwards, 1985).

Thus the tendency to experience one's sense of self-esteem and self-definition in terms of professional accomplishments is heightened for psychologists. One potential cost of [receiving support] . . . may arise out of the fact that professional work may be an extension of one's own intrapsychic pain. A fear of exposing our own emotional needs (potentially met in the process of caring for our clients) may be an important block to receiving support. Furthermore, to be disillusioned and dissatisfied with the job may be experienced as a deeper split, or alienation from our own selves.

(Walsh, 1990, p. 5)

As Walsh points out, two factors clearly militate against clinical psychologists being able to face their feelings of vulnerability:

The irony of our profession is that though the 'currency' of our work is with emotions, our background is an academic one which places the onus on objectivity (the applied scientist) as opposed to listening, giving space and listening (the practitioner).

Thus a potential block to the acceptance of a helping exchange lies in the confused nature of our professional ethos. The mis-match between objectivity and emotion may set up a contradiction within the clinical psychologist which may invalidate the process of self-care. . . .

The interface between the ... profession and the culture and climate of the NHS may also inhibit the process of self-care. ... Psychologists (along with other health service staff) are trying to maintain services in the face of decreased resources. ... Jick (1987) states that little attention has been paid to the human side of budget-cut stressors. As NHS employees are being put under intolerable pressure to organize the provision of client care around targets of efficiency and economy, self-care strategies may have little place in the current requirements for larger caseloads.

(Walsh, 1990, p. 7)

Walsh, a trainee at the time she wrote this piece, is acutely aware of the pressures that the profession is subject to but she is also acutely aware of the yawning gap that exists between theory and practice. 'Yes in theory self-care is necessary but haven't we a job to get on with?' is a catch-phrase which summarises many psychologists' attitude to the problem.

For us, the issue of self-care links to the question of professional ethos and professional persona. Succeeding cohorts of trainees have been inducted into the profession of clinical psychology in a specific, historically determined way. The rhetoric of the scientist-practitioner model has successfully precluded any real discussion of alternative models. From our point of view it is highly significant that alternative models are not seriously debated within clinical psychology. Unfortunately, we haven't sufficient space to explore this issue in any depth, but it is intriguing that the reflective practitioner model advocated by Rein and White (1981) and Schon (1983) has not been widely discussed in British clinical psychology. To argue that theory often develops in helping occupations from a reflective process which emanates from practice activities (Pilalis, 1984) is anathema to a profession which seeks to justify its superiority *vis-à-vis* other professions by insisting that it has special access to research and a special ability to undertake research. If practitioners, through reflective practice, can develop practical and effective knowledge then a profession that claims that research is the source of knowledge becomes very vulnerable to accusations that its knowledge base is both suspect and irrelevant to effective practice. Intriguingly, the spectre of psychoanalysis resurfaces at this point. It has a reflective knowledge base which is very appealing to many practitioners. Eysenck's attempts to banish it from clinical psychology appear increasingly to have been a disaster for the profession so perhaps the wheel has now come full circle (albeit on a time basis of forty years) and clinical psychology will be forced to re-examine its relationship with a body of knowledge that has continued to flourish and develop in ways which continually challenge the disconnected and disorganised empiricism of clinical psychology.

Conclusion

The last three chapters of our book have attempted to explore the way that trainee clinical psychologists are socialised within a professional culture which emphasises the primacy of research knowledge. Practical knowledge derived from day to day experience with clients is, for rhetorical and political reasons, downgraded because clinical psychology has traditionally justified its superiority, vis-à-vis other professions, in terms of the allegedly unique ability of clinical psychologists to undertake and consume scientific research.

We would argue that the success of training courses in producing scientist-practitioners is extremely debatable. Clinical psychologists may be fairly sophisticated in their understanding of research methodology but it is time the profession acknowledged that the production of valid, clinically relevant research cannot be achieved by psychologists who receive only part-time research training on a clinical training course. At a deeper level we would agree with Eysenck's original position – the role of the scientist and the role of the practitioner are virtually impossible to combine because the occupational characteristics of the two roles are much more incompatible than is usually admitted.

The contemporary role of the clinical psychologist is complicated enough without having to include the role of researcher. But advocates of the scientist-practitioner model facilely overlook the uncomfortable fact that the majority of psychological research is either trivial, methodologically unsound or so specific to a particular research setting that its generalisability to other settings is extremely problematic.

Training courses have unfortunately concentrated on uncritically preserving the scientist-practitioner tradition and have at the same time largely ignored the personal difficulties that trainees experience as they attempt to grapple with a role which is both diffuse and personally threatening. The macho tradition of the scientist-practitioner precludes any real discussion of vulnerability and the notion of personal work is dismissed because of clinical psychology's traditional antipathy to psychoanalysis or any framework that places the person of the therapist at centre stage. Eclecticism has been utilised by the profession to fudge the issue but ironically the impact of eclecticism has been to make the trainee's task even harder because it has created an information overload. It can even be argued that the situation has been made worse because rigorous training in one model at least creates a certain security for a trainee. Being fragmentarily trained in a number of competing models is predictably more confusing and creates greater insecurity.

It is no surprise to us that these crucial training issues are not often discussed openly by the profession. Predictably, a profession that prides itself on being so scientifically organised will have difficulty in putting its own activities under the microscope. Self-reflexivity is not strongly valued by clinical psychologists so it is therefore not surprising that clinical psychologists are reluctant to examine their own vulnerabilities or to come to terms with the fact that the way that they train new initiates requires fundamentally rethinking.

It is a continuing puzzle why house officers are forced to work such long hours that their own health and the health of their patients are put at risk. But it is more puzzling as to why a profession that is predicated on caring for clients psychologically should be so uncaring of its own trainees.

Clearly the historical roots of the profession are partly responsible for this state of affairs. A male-dominated profession that sought to establish a role for itself (*vis-à-vis* the state) by claiming that it had diagnostic and scientific skills and credentials could not at the same time afford to pay attention to its own vulnerabilities. To be human and to accept human vulnerability does not mesh well with claiming to be scientific and understanding of the psychological basis of patients' distress. But a profession in making claims to scientific objectivity of course cuts itself off from its ability to build any links with patient (client) groups. This provides a partial explanation of why clinical psychologists have tended to be little involved in patient-based movements, unlike, for example, many of their social work colleagues.

As we shall see in our next chapter, in the 1980s training issues were inevitably forced to one side as the profession's main preoccupations have been with survival. Thatcher's attacks on public services, including, of course, the NHS itself, posed a serious threat to the survival of the profession. Obviously, in the context of a struggle to survive the problems that have accumulated within the area of training have tended to be neglected. But, we would argue, it is perilous to neglect these issues. Mollon's warning about fraudulence cannot be easily dismissed but at the same time it is genuinely difficult to understand how a defensible alternative method of training could be devised.

Unfortunately, we have no space in which to explore alternatives in any detail. The most radical solution, and one we would favour, would be to reverse the historical trend of making training more and more élitist. Trainees must have completed a first degree in psychology and in the vast majority of cases must have achieved a 2.1 or better. Are these really the correct criteria for recruiting people to a caring profession? Equally, does it really make sense to recruit people who are under 30, given that the role requires a rich experience of life? Would, for example, recruiting mature candidates by means of a one-year induction course (followed by a three-year training) be preferable to the current system which is increasingly recruiting young, white, middle-class women (hence reflecting the basic recruitment to psychology degrees).

The recruitment of more women than men may well be justified since it would reflect the fact that more women than men seek help from psychological services, but clearly the ethnic and class background of recruits to clinical psychology is much too narrow and requires significantly broadening, as Davenhill *et al.* (1989) have recently pointed out.

The mere raising of such issues is perhaps to tilt, like Don Quixote, against windmills. The leaders of the profession, as we shall see in our next chapter, are intent on deepening the processes of professionalisation that have influenced clinical psychologists during the last forty years. Mowbray, the management expert called in by the Manpower Planning Advisory Group to monitor clinical psychology, has clearly pointed the profession in the direction of further professionalisation. For him, medicine is the ideal model and yet how ironic it would be for clinical psychology to follow this path given its attempts to break free from the power of a 'parental' profession which has always sought to dominate other professions.

Chapter 6

The profession after 1979

The last five chapters have tried to build up a picture of the profession for the reader by tracing its history and critically reviewing the socialisation of its practitioners. Hopefully, the emerging style of British clinical psychology, after its inception soon after the Second World War, should be evident. This was inherited from deeper cultural traditions: empiricism; an aversion to grand theory; pragmatism. However, these mutually supporting and intertwining historical threads, which spawned initially a form of aggressive scientism, did not go on to determine the whole fabric of clinical psychology. The attempt to banish permanently the threat of Continental depth psychology failed. The counter-cultural period of the 1960s, with its cacophony of existentialism, Californian humanism, systems theory, Marxism and eastern religion had left its mark. By the end of the 1970s eclecticism (itself facilitated by pragmatism and the avoidance of grand theory) characterised the profession.

In Chapter 2, we summarised Barrie Richards' research, which pointed up three phases (psychometrics, behaviour therapy and eclecticism) which characterised the profession up to 1979. The profession was on course at this point for a lengthy period of entrenchment and the bland epistemological compromise of 'scientific humanism'. Its practitioners could vary legitimately in their orientation and its clients might be offered a mixed bag of tricks (to their relief or confusion). Indeed, the profession has, over the past dozen or so years, evolved in a stable eclectic direction but there are also strong signs that clinical psychology is in a state of confusion. It is still confused about the tension between science and humanism but this is the least of its problems. As this chapter will demonstrate, by the end of the 1980s the profession showed signs of both arrogance, associated with expansionist aspirations, and profound anxiety about its future role in the health industry. How did this contradictory picture emerge?

1979: THE WATERSHED YEAR

Whilst there existed a political backdrop of consensus and compromise in British society, neophyte professions, such as clinical psychology, were free to develop their own emerging identities. History had set in motion the tensions between science and humanism but an accommodation could be, and was, worked out. The National Health Service, the jewel in the crown of post-war social democracy, offered a safe nursery for development. Metaphorically, it contained the fractious relationships of squabbling generations and siblings (disputes with psychiatry and within the profession itself). However, after 1979, consensus politics, which had nurtured the British welfare state, broke down. Cultural commentators began to construct a personalised discourse about neo-liberal economics and authoritarian government. The British welfare state, which had overseen, both the birth and the development of clinical psychology, came under an attack spearheaded by a ruthless and implacable leader. The country had entered a period of elected dictatorship.

'Thatcherism' was a phenomenon which could be seen all around us. It suffered the weakness of psychological reductionism by accounting for a wide range of political changes in terms of the actions of a solitary, over-bearing, middle-class woman. (Could one person really be responsible for such widespread social and economic re-structuring?) None the less, leftist academics (Jessop *et al.* 1988) and popular liberal journalists (Young, 1989) alike set to work analysing the phenomenon. Maybe 'Thatcherism' was a reified concept, which subsumed a variety of political processes, such as the resolution of problems of recession and the fiscal crisis of the welfare state in the capitalist system, but it served as an ideological focus (of adoration or resentment). If the unbroken period of conservative government, with its strong ideological leadership, was exerting such a totalitarian grip on British society, no group was immune from its influence. Looking back, it would have been remarkable then for clinical psychology not to show signs of Thatcherite influence. So, the question to be addressed now is in what way did the social context of the 1980s influence the development of the profession?

THE THREE PHASES OF MANAGERIALISM

Following the scheme laid out by Barrie Richards, the profession went through three broad periods of development after the Second World War (psychometrics, behaviour therapy and eclecticism). Essentially what was ushered in by the 1980s was a fourth period of *managerialism*. This period itself will be discussed, for convenience, in terms of three phases during the 1980s: early turbulence; the intensification of professionalisation; the crisis of survival. These are not self-evidently discrete temporal units but they do square with the accounts given of the period by professional leaders and with documentary evidence available for the reader's scrutiny in the published professional discourse of the *Bulletin of the British Psychological Society* and the *Division of Clinical Psychology Newsletter*. (These were re-labelled during the 1980s as respectively *The Psychologist* and *Clinical Psychology Forum*.) The three phases of managerialism were built on conflicting messages, inherited from the 1970s, about the organisation of the profession and about the regulation of psychological therapies.

1979–1983: early turbulence

By the time Thatcher was elected, the 1978 Trethowan Report (*The Role of Psychologists in the Health Service*) was beginning to have an impact on the actions of professional leaders and NHS administrators. The first phase of turbulence arose because of this baggage from the pre-1979 years. The first problem for the profession was that the official review of its work in the NHS was both liberating (from traditional medical dominance) but also ill fitted for an organisational framework which itself was being reformed. Trethowan had a contradictory impact, as this quote from Bernard Kat highlights:

> Trethowan had two impacts. It validated the management structure emerging from the 1974 NHS re-organisation for the profession by organising us into Area services. It also gave Area Psychologists a formal strategic and planning function. Of course all this was undone by the 1982 re-organisation into Districts and the arrival of the first Griffiths recommendations about general management. . . . At first the 1982 events seemed to be cata-strophic for the profession. The new Area services were immediately

fragmented and the profession lost its direction but then there was a paradoxical effect because we actually got more professional managers. We leapt from developing 92 Area Psychologists on paper to being given 192 District Psychology posts – a doubling of our expectations. Operationally we lost our way but managerially we gained massively.

(Kat, 1990, cited in Pilgrim, 1990)

For those unfamiliar with NHS organisation, Kat is talking here about Trethowan making recommendations fitted for a layer of administration (the Area health authority) which disappeared in 1982 leaving two layers – the coordinating superordinate role of the Regional Health Authority and the direct management of local services by District Health Authorities. So the official report on the profession's work stimulated contradictory developments but other factors contributed to this. On the one hand, there was an extensive re-grading exercise in the profession. On the other, the first Thatcher administration demanded a review of the management of the NHS. The first of these is commented on by Eric Bromley, one of the chief trade union negotiators (ASTMS now MSF) for the profession in the Whitley Council system:

Before 1982, decisions about Top Grades in the profession were made by a sort of quango (the Top Grade committee). Basically, the Tories did not like these so they set about dismantling them. What that led to was civil servants in the Whitley system agreeing to negotiate a set of principles or criteria for how people were graded in the profession. This, along with the 1982 re-organisation, suddenly gave us all these new Top Grade posts.

(Bromley, 1990, cited in Pilgrim, 1990)

So, the Trethowan report, which encouraged greater autonomy for the profession from medical control, also triggered a new managerial structure. In turn this was amplified by other developments which led to an expansion in its upper echelons. This marked the beginning of a pattern in the profession during the 1980s: the focus of interest in the profession was becoming less and less about the type of psychology which was to be practised, and more and more about an ethos of managerialism. This tendency was then amplified by the publication of the first Griffiths Report.

The Griffiths Report was commissioned by the then Secretary of

State for Health and Social Services, Norman Fowler, on 3 February 1983. Roy Griffiths (subsequently knighted by Thatcher for his 'service to the NHS') was managing director of Sainsbury's. Fowler invited him to chair an inquiry into NHS management. He was joined by other doyens of British industry (Michael Bett from British Telecom, Jim Blyth from United Biscuits and Sir Brian Bailey from Television South West). The report from this tight-knit group of profit-motivated men was originally to be provided, in confidence, to Fowler. However, pressure from media speculation prompted the government to publish the report (on 25 October 1983). Petchey (1986), discussing the report, notes that a series of other cost-cutting exercises had already been initiated by the first Thatcher government: the privatisation of support services (catering, laundry and cleaning); the expansion of private medicine (via the encouragement of private insurance schemes); and increases in NHS fees and the introduction of charges for spectacles and other services (between 1979 and 1985 revenue from NHS charges increased by 50 per cent). Also, by the time of the Griffiths Report Lord Rayner from Marks & Spencer had been asked to review the efficiency of non-ambulance transport and NHS recruiting.

The Rayner and Griffiths reviews were to set in motion a set of cost-cutting and 'value-for-money' initiatives during the 1980s which were to form a backdrop to developments in clinical psychology. One of the most important general ideological motifs of the decade, associated with the Griffiths Report, was an attack on the power of the clinical professions. From the beginning of the NHS there had been an oscillating power tussle between the medical profession and service administrators. The former was winning the battle for dominance during the 1970s. However, traditional professional élites in society (like doctors and lawyers) posed a potential threat to the 'Thatcher revolution'. One of the great myths associated with the latter was of 'rolling back the state'. In fact the Conservative administration of the 1980s increasingly sought to concentrate its own central powers. Nowhere was this more apparent than in the replacement of traditional professional power with centrally directed managerial power. The NHS was a crucial site for this political strategy. It was no longer to be merely 'administered', it was now to be 'managed', along the lines of a private business, but directed from the centre. In order to effect this strategy, the government systematically undermined the existing power of those professions which had enjoyed relative autonomy from the state. This tactic was not targeted narrowly on medicine, it was used as a blunderbuss against *all* clinical professions: psychology had to face the fire like the others.

Before we explore this development any further, it is important to comment on a second piece of 'baggage' from the 1970s. Whilst, in the longer term, the Thatcherite reforms of the NHS were to dictate much of what was to happen in the profession, it is crucial to understand that these external constraints also created potential *opportunities*. Leaders of any profession usually do the best they can with what is available in their social context. The leaders of clinical psychology were no different in this regard. One of the first opportunities which came the way of these leaders in 1979 was an unresolved debate about the regulation of psychological therapies.

This debate was traceable in immediate history to two reports. The first was the Foster Report into Scientology in 1972. At that time the Scientologists had attempted to take over the National Association for Mental Health (MIND). This stimulated the Foster enquiry. At the centre of this investigation was a scrutiny of 'dianetics', the form of psychotherapy espoused by Scientologists. Consequently, one of the recommendations emanating from Foster related to some form of state regulation of psychotherapy and other 'mindbending' techniques, to use a favoured term of the time. This recommendation lay fallow for a while until a group of therapists (mainly the organis-ations involved with private analytical psychotherapy) began to press the Department of Health and Social Security to activate the Foster recommendation on registration. This stimulated the government into another inquiry about such a possibility led by Paul Seighart.

The Seighart Report on the Registration of Psychotherapists was published in 1978 and the main NHS mental health professions were unimpressed. (The recommendations of Seighart did not lead to the enactment of any legislation.) Early in 1979 the Division of Clinical Psychology set up a working party to provide a response to the Seighart Report. The DCP almost pre-emptively considered the matter. At the same meeting of the DCP executive which recommended the setting up of the working party, the minutes also record that 'The Committee consider it a matter of urgency that a decision is made about the Statutory Registration of Psychologists in the UK.' (DCP executive minutes, 21.4.79). In less than a month the Seighart proposals on registration of psychotherapists were dismissed as 'restrictive and divisive' (DCP executive minutes, 14.5.79). The executive were of the view that only those trained in one of the core mental health professions should practise psychotherapy and that this was the only necessary safeguard. The attitude of the professional leaders was that if there was going to be any legislation to register practitioners it should be of *psychologists* not psychotherapists.

Reflecting on this period, Frazer Watts, now BPS President and an ex-Chair of the DCP, considers that the initiative for registration was traceable to his predecessor in the mid-1970s, Frank MacPherson (Watts, 1991, personal communication). Watts is of the opinion that the two types of registration being discussed together in the same meeting in 1979 was a mere coincidence. However, as with our discussion of the timing of the emergence of behaviour therapy earlier, it seems that innovations have to find their moment. MacPherson may have personally pushed for registration, but the events of the end of the 1970s and early 1980s provided a context in which the idea might germinate and grow into action.

It needs to be remembered that, until this point, clinical psychology had pursued its status as a profession by simply playing on the post-war cultural currency of applied science in the service of clients of the welfare state. This occupational strategy had been sufficient until the Thatcher years. By 1979, the Foster and Seighart Reports had roused psychologists from their complacency about who was allowed to possess psychological knowledge. After the psychometric period had receded and behaviour therapy had given way to therapeutic pluralism, there remained the problem of competing bids for ownership. If, as was the case, and still is, anybody could put a plaque on their door saying 'Psychotherapist', there was the spectre of a motley collection of self-styled therapists with no training in psychology or medicine competing for mental health clients. Had clinical psychology *only* identified itself with a set of behavioural techniques, the profession's identity could have simply been conflated with behaviour therapy. But, by the end of the 1970s, this was clearly not going to be the case.

The most obvious gambit to advance the interests of the profession was simply to seek state recognition for practitioners who held qualifications in academic and applied psychology, which were already regulated by the BPS. This would base registration upon existing higher education in general psychology. It would have the advantage of warding off the threat from the motley band of psychotherapists *and* it would not require the profession to actually define what psychology was (except in the circular sense of it being what is taught at a particular time to undergraduates studying psychology). The latter convenience was a very important consideration given that psychological knowledge is condemned to theoretical and methodological disputes. So the scene was set for a campaign from the DCP to persuade the BPS that the days of defining the profession by scholarship, but without formal state recognition of its practitioners, should be numbered. Before the year was out the DCP minutes recorded that they opposed the Seighart proposals and that 'the Professional Affairs Board [PAB] should be encouraged as a matter of urgency to work towards a register of applied psychologists' (DCP minutes, 23.11.79).

The external threat to the status of clinical psychologists was balanced by a threat from *within* the BPS. In 1979, a PAB working party had been reviewing the status of counselling and suggested the possibility of setting up a new Division of Counselling Psychology. There was already an academic interest group in the topic (i.e. a 'Section' in BPS terms). The possibility of this being converted to divisional status would have legitimised a new applied wing of psychology in competition with clinicians. The DCP minutes (14.4.80) record the executive's reaction to such a suggestion in the following terms: 'As counselling is a ubiquitous activity, the committee believes that a separate Division within the BPS would be superfluous.' In the same meeting a special resolution to be put to the Council of the BPS which 'unequivocally supports the proposal of a register of psychologists' was discussed. So the internal epistemological debate within the BPS about psychological therapies no longer emphasised 'their nature'. Now the issue was 'who will own and control them'.

1984–1988: the intensification of professionalisation

As the leaders of the profession began to grapple with a number of threats from without and from within the BPS, certain processes became discernible in the mid-1980s which pointed to an intensification of professionalisation. Reading through the minutes of the executive of the DCP, in the first half of the decade, there is an impression of increasing frenetic activity. By 1985 the following exemplified this trend. The business of the DCP was becoming too much for clinicians elected and delegated for the task. In response the BPS appointed a full-time officer to service the DCP (Bruce Napier in April 1985). Napier, reflecting on the period, comments:

> In the early eighties a couple of the DCP Chairs had turned the job into something that an ordinary human being couldn't do. So it was getting difficult to recruit anyone prepared to be the Chair for the term of three years. . . . So I was hired to service the committee in 1985. . . . At that time as well there was all the business created by registration.

(Napier, 1989, cited in Pilgrim, 1990)

It was the DCP which was both the prime mover and main advocate during the 1980s of the registration of psychologists, an issue to which we will return below. In addition, the profession became preoccupied with 'image building'. Discussion increasingly centred upon how to sell psychology better than had been the case in the past. This was first recorded in the executive minutes as early as March 1980 in the context of discussing the projected impact of public expenditure cuts from the newly appointed Conservative government. Cash limits in the NHS combined with the anti-clinician message emerging from the Griffiths Report were together 'turning the screw' on the professions. This unpropitious political context inevitably stung all the health professions into some form of activity.

For instance, the dominant profession, medicine, was spurred into reaction. The British Medical Association represented a profession which had been formally recognised by the state since the 1858 General Medical Act. Medical practitioners have been used to wielding their collective power in order to dictate or block health policy. The NHS was born in the image set by medicine. (Some would say it was born in spite of rather than because of doctors, with Aneurin Bevan having to 'stuff' the mouths of consultants 'with gold'.) As was mentioned earlier, as the dominant clinical profession it only had to ward off the power of administrators to ensure its complete domination of health policy in practice. In other words, medicine was a mature profession with sufficient confidence actually to challenge politicians about health service organisation. By contrast, clinical psychology in the mid-1980s was over a hundred years its junior. By then, its practitioners did not even enjoy the protected status of state registration, which other professions, like nursing, had secured. It was a small profession (compared with medicine and nursing), with only around two thousand practitioners in the UK, and it had no legal powers (even under the terms of the recently passed 1983 Mental Health Act). Because of these differences, the clinical professions reacted differently to the Griffiths assault.

For a while, clinical psychologists, like the BMA and the Royal College of Nurses, cooperated with the Griffiths implementation of general managers (as they hoped to fill the posts as much as possible from within their own ranks). However, by 1985 it was becoming obvious that clinical professionals were securing 'Griffiths manager' posts in only a minority of cases. Over 60 per cent were appointed from the ranks of hospital administrators. At this point the confidence of the different clinical professions, according to their maturity and track record of power, was revealed. The BMA embarked on an extremely pugnacious campaign against the government's treatment of the NHS. Prior to this the less powerful, but numerically dominant, nursing profession ran its own aggressive poster campaign against the government. In contrast to these older professions, the DCP opted for a different strategy of survival, which if successful would actually have led to an expansion and consolidation of the profession. The leaders of clinical psychology evaded an oppositional stance towards government, instead, controversially choosing to bare the throat of their profession to its state employers by requesting a manpower review.

Manpower levels in the profession had been a source of concern for many years. In some specialties, such as those working with elderly people and people with learning difficulties, recruitment was proving virtually impossible at times. And yet, training courses were massively over-subscribed. So, a paradoxical situation had arisen. Training was a bottle-neck, with many disappointed psychology graduates on one side and many empty posts on the other. This pattern in the profession had become a recurring concern for its leaders in the DCP since the mid-1970s. What the social context of the mid-1980s provided was an opportunity to rectify the problem by stabilising the structure, as well as expanding the ranks, of the profession.

Following some informal inquiries from the Committee on Training in Clinical Psychology to civil servants in the DHSS, a strategy emerged for the BPS to resolve the clinical manpower problem. It was a risky strategy determined very directly by government ideology about staffing and practices in the NHS clinical professions. If it paid off, the leaders would be recorded historically as shrewd strategists. If it were to fail they risked being condemned for their naivety. At that time health service managers, in the wake of Griffiths, were given *carte blanche* to challenge the traditional self-interest of clinicians. Officials in the DHSS, under the direction of their ministers, were emphasising that the worthiness of the clinical professions had to be proved rather than be taken for granted. So, when clinical psychology sought a review of its manpower it did so in a context in which these ideological principles would be applied.

In December 1987, a joint working group from the DCP and the Committee on Training in Clinical Psychology reported on its liaison with the National Health Service Training Authority and the Manpower Planning Advisory Group. The latter was a committee deployed by the DHSS to scrutinise manpower levels in the NHS. The joint working group recommended that the MPAG should give 'firm (rather than friendly) advice' to Regional managers about minimum levels of training posts. It also recommended that the MPAG 'with the cooperation of the profession initiate a major review of psychology in the NHS'.

The MPAG agreed to this suggestion and set about its task guided by the notion of a 'greenfield review'. Essentially this emphasised the idea of a clear greenfield, on which structures would have to be justified and built. This going-back-to-basics-with-nothing-taken-for-granted-approach, flowed from the post-Griffiths, anti-clinician, value-for-money ideology noted above. The BPS representatives, who negotiated with the MPAG, knew that this was a risky ideology to submit to, but they thought that the risk was worth taking, given the unrelenting manpower crisis. They were the 'realists' of the day. Little common support was evident in the profession for what Thatcher and her government were doing in the NHS and more widely in the welfare state. There was also little evidence at the time that the professional leaders advocating the MPAG exercise actively embraced Thatcherism. Instead, the 'realists' can be seen as a group who were trying to create an opportunity from a situation of adversity. However, their efforts were to meet with hostile opposition from many in the profession because the review exercise was potentially very threatening.

The MPAG hired a management consultant to review, 'greenfield style', what clinical psychologists did and what if anything they were worth to the NHS. This hiring of management consultants was becoming a vivid motif in the public sector. In the midst of cut-backs in services, the privatisation of ancillary staff and an assault on the power of clinical professional élites, the ministers in the DHSS positively sanctioned a massive explosion in hired consultancy. This followed from the central conclusion of the Griffiths report that, to date, inefficiency in the NHS had been a failure of management. The logic then was to hire hyper-critical management consultants to highlight the details of this claimed failure and recommend corrective action (Between 1979 and 1985, DHSS spending on NHS management consultants rose from £411,000 to £13.8 million (Petchey, 1986).) The organisation which found favour with the MPAG was the grandly titled 'MAS – Management Advisory Service to the NHS'. This comprised a psychology graduate, Derek Mowbray, and his assistant.

By September 1988, Mowbray was busily contacting a sample of psychologists throughout the country, announcing his role and laying out the purpose of the task set for him by the MPAG. He reported three main aims of his investigation in a covering letter to his invited sample thus:

- To identify common or core skills of the Clinical Psychologist by examination of representative and innovative patterns of service taking into account both the unique and transmissible skills of Clinical Psychologists for patient care and the current and future requirements of the service particularly in the main client group areas (punctuation in the original).
- To determine levels of staff and skill mix required, examining the possibility of introducing support staff and the feasibility of delegating or sharing tasks with some other groups and the managerial and professional implications of so doing to provide guidance on appropriate numbers of staff at the described level (punctuation in the original).
- To examine the educational role of Psychologists in training other people in the services.

These three aims were issued by Mowbray to his entreated respondents in late September. He added thirteen sub-headings about the inquiry, which required responses from those sampled by the end of October. In this light, the point is made above about the lack of punctuation, because it was symptomatic of the breathless urgency which characterised the review exercise. And yet, the review had potentially momentous implications for the profession. For instance, two of the BPS representatives who were proactive in engaging with the MPAG, John Hall and Glenys Parry, described the exercise as being 'of major significance for clinical psychology in Britain; the proposals which emerge from it are likely to establish the basic structure of clinical psychology until the next century'. The hopes of these leaders were genuine, and their tactics opportunistic, but the Mowbray review became controversial immediately.

Mowbray toured the country to review the profession, with his three composite aims and thirteen sub-headings in mind. Those cooperating with him in his data collection found him abrasive and a number of anxieties about his intentions emanated from these personal encounters. Word began to circulate rapidly that the worst should be expected from his report back to the MPAG and that the best was not to be hoped for. Indeed, anxiety eventually turned to anger about what was happening. Mowbray's research design offended the methodological sensibilities of the more scientifically minded and his style offended the sensitivities of those with a humanistic bent. On both counts, confidence was not inspired. This culminated in a rearguard campaign within the profession against the review, which was targeted on the 'realists' in the leadership who were deemed to be responsible. In November 1988, this rearguard campaign coalesced around NHS psychologists in Nottingham. They circulated a ten-page critique of the MPAG/MAS exercise and the proactive role played by the profession's leaders. The critique commented:

> We question the political wisdom of cooperating in an undertaking which seems unequivocally to be aimed at weakening the profession and perhaps undermining its viability totally. . . . In accepting at face value some of the aims of the review and the management strategy which underlies it, we do feel that the ability to defend our professional position has been seriously compromised. . . . We are not dealing with a properly considered approach (such as that undertaken by the Trethowan Working Party) but an exercise in 'scientific management' designed eventually to de-professionalise clinical psychology in accordance with simplistic and pre-conceived notions involving programmable skills and competencies. . . . Its glib resort to simple-minded managerial machismo displays the fundamental lack of balance and seriousness, which are the first priorities in a review of this importance.
>
> (Nottingham NHS psychologists, 1988)

This lengthy quote, and the subsequent one below, highlight some features of the rhetoric of this critical grouping. In particular, there is the rejection of a skills-based approach. This was favoured by Thatcher's NHS managers because it operationalises what workers do (or should do). It also, potentially, makes them more accountable to their managers, and even dispensable, if their skills can be bought at a cheaper price from other occupational groups. The Nottingham group wanted to vigorously reject this formulation of their work in favour of one more grandiose but also more vague:

> Clinical psychology is not a finite collection of technical skills. . . it embodies a scientific approach to clinically related psychological phenomena and entails a close and disciplined acquaintance with those phenomena – an approach informed by immersion in a long and not always specifiable tradition of scientific enquiry. Clinical psychologists don't have 'unique characteristics' or 'core competencies' (half-baked concepts uncritically taken over from Taylorist 'scientific management'), but training and experience in a form of knowledge the contributions of which need no justification in terms of some kind of simplistic evaluation. The significance of the contribution of clinical psychology to the conceptualisation, measurement and treatment of whole ranges of clinical phenomena within the field of mental illness alone could scarcely be calculated; such contributions have been generated by the creative and open-ended involvement of a self determining profession in the field of its application. The 'theory' underlying the approach adopted by MAS is not only a travesty, but an insult to our history as well as our intelligence.
>
> (Nottingham NHS psychologists, 1988)

The skills-based approach favoured by the DHSS employers of Mowbray thus provoked this angry diatribe from his critics. However, when the indignation is stripped away, the critique reveals some vital clues to the profession's view of itself and the organisational context surrounding it. A sub-text is the rejection or evasion of any notion of accountability (certainly to the government of the day and probably anyone else). There is the clear message that knowledge borne of practical professional experience is necessarily sovereign and beyond scrutiny. This has led to contributions which 'need no justification'. The more mature profession of medicine had long since learned the political value of rendering its knowledge base inscrutable, by the construction of the notions of 'clinical experience' and, the even more convenient, 'clinical judgement'. Theory and practice in medicine have been separated, but retained, as 'science' and 'art'. A similar process is discernible here within clinical psychology. The value of 'indeterminate' knowledge to professionals will be discussed in more detail in the next chapter.

The value of experience favoured by humanists in the critical group was balanced in the rhetoric by the solemn allusions to the importance of 'scientific enquiry'. Note how 'science' takes on the vague secular authority of God in religious ideology. Thus the 'radicals' had more in common with their opponents than the diatribe would at first suggest. They, like the objects of their critique, were committed to a vision of scientific humanism. This group of 'radicals' in damning the 'realists' for their lack of wisdom revealed an attitude which was in its own way élitist. Their notion of a profession was rather quaint and old-fashioned and had been prefigured by Mannheim. He depicted professionals as being a free-floating collection of scholars within society's liberal intelligentsia (Boronski, 1987). Given the radical re-structuring of society by three successive Conservative governments bent on removing pockets of political and ideological resistance to its own burgeoning centralised power, such a view was a utopian anachronism. By contrast, the 'realists' may have been in turn optimistic and unwise but they were more in tune with the discipline of Thatcherism, in terms of its constraints and opportunities. We would argue that it was only this difference, about whether to adapt to or defy Thatcherism, which really marked off the 'radicals' from the 'realists' in the dispute. In their own ways, both advocated a special blend of science and humanism to justify their privileged position as health workers. The 'radicals' succeeded in calling a General Meeting of the DCP in London on 21 December 1988. The BPS leaders were censured by their opponents but they survived, their egos bruised but intact.

The controversies surrounding the MAS report and the BPS instigated-MPAG review certainly were the most visible signs of efforts to expand the profession in the late-1980s. However, these events were intertwined with others involving professional politicking. The Trethowan Report had created a climate which gave psychologists confidence to break away from psychiatry. More and more articles began to appear in the *DCP Newsletter* about working with other client groups. Primary care work in particular was popular at first and this was followed on with other signs of liaison with physicians and surgeons. Ed Miller, Top Grade Psychologist in Cambridge and professional adviser to the DoH, summarised the change during the 1980s as follows:

> There has been a steady moving away from the traditional links with psychiatry and more towards new client groups – behavioural medicine, primary care, physical medicine. Also the profession has got itself involved more at national level in what people might mistakenly believe to be the centre of power, the Department of Health.
>
> (Miller, 1990, cited in Pilgrim, 1990)

The allusion about the centre of power, though slightly self-mocking, did confirm evidence in the DCP minutes from the beginning of the decade. The leaders of the profession were indeed increasingly interested in formalising their links with civil servants and with liaising with sympathetic MPs to lobby parliament about matters which might advance the profession's interests. Also, the liaison with medical specialities including, but also outside, psychiatry by practitioners was evident throughout the profession. From the beginning of the decade, the minutes of the DCP executive revealed moves to secure relationships with Royal Colleges, based upon equality rather than dominance. This may have been shaped by two considerations. First, in being granted independence by Trethowan, psychologists were testing the limits of associating with the more mature profession of medicine (which was still the dominant clinical one in the NHS). All sorts of non-specific pay-offs might arise from these alliances, including improved status ('glory by association') and support for manpower expansion. Second, in the context of the post-Griffiths attack, clinical professionals, whatever their disciplinary background, huddled together to ward off the threat from the DHSS and its NHS managers. As far as the Joint Standing Committee with the Royal College of Psychiatrists is concerned, its changing nature during the 1980s is summarised well here, in 1991, by David Bird from the BPS:

> I have become aware that there has been a subtle shift from the kind of 'unspoken confrontation' to one where not only quite serious issues are being discussed, but that they are being discussed with an understanding that mutual co-operation

between the two bodies is of increasing importance, given the fluid
state of the National Health Service at the moment.

(Bird, 1991, personal communication)

The escape from professional dominance by psychiatry also left open
some possibilities to be dominant over others. There were weak signs
of this during the 1980s. In the field of people with learning
difficulties, for instance, psychologists, despite their manpower
shortages, were often taking up a leadership role. The DCP also
sought to influence the psychology input to other professions such as
occupational therapy. In between the strategies of liaising with
medicine above and less qualified para-medical groups below, the
DCP also sought the non-specific pay-offs of contact with other
groups such as the Police Federation.

The wheeling and dealing with other occupational groups was only
one side of professional expansion. As was mentioned earlier, image
building was becoming important throughout psychology. As early as
November 1982, the BPS had set up a 'Forum on the Public Image of
Psychology'. By 1988, the BPS produced a programmatic document
The Future of the Psychological Sciences: Horizons and Opportunities.
This placed impression management centre stage and left no
opportunity for self-doubt in the profession. Differences of opinion,
which are necessarily endemic to human science, were discouraged in
the interest of a common front to those on the outside. This might
then reinforce the impression that psychology was a thoroughly
worked out body of knowledge and its practitioners could be called
upon on an *ad hoc* basis (by paymasters) to offer expertise on
demand. In other words the document set out to market the
profession in a social context where market principles had come to
displace other values based upon social justice and intellectual
criticism.

What became important then was not only what psychologists
were really capable of knowing and doing, but what they could
convince the world they were capable of. The language and the ethos
of the market-place permeated the document. Moreover, in those
areas of applied psychology like clinical work, this bolstered the
notion that a 'technical fix' really did exist: that clinicians really were
experts in human misery. In the light of the publication of this
'mission statement' (another bit of Thatcher argot of the 1980s) it is
worth noting how Glenys Parry, an MPAG steering committee
member, summarised the profession in the 1980s:

The 80s has been about establishing who we are, what we can do and what is our core identity. If you like it has been about establishing a proper rhetoric of justification. The hostile climate for professionals has put pressure on us to clarify and justify what we are about.

(Parry, 1990, cited in Pilgrim, 1990)

Bringing together the wider issue of image building in psychology as a whole and the specific set of justificatory rhetorics feeding into the MAS report, this is how Parry then goes on to sell the special features of clinical psychology:

Community psychiatric nurses cannot do what we can do. The fact that we have an undergraduate degree and post-graduate qualification does make us different... (DP-Why?)... Well I think that for too long, clinical psychologists pinned their credibility on their cookbook credentials. And yes on these grounds CPNs could say offer a similar therapy package to psychologists. But what we should be doing is saying that we can tackle problems that do not have standardised solutions. We can think through from first principles *in ways which other professionals cannot.* Our strength, which we have got to get across, is that we are special because we combine knowledge of a wider client group, with knowledge about clinical skills with knowledge about psychological theories. Other professions may be skilled in one of these three areas, *but only clinical psychologists* can combine all three (draws a Venn diagram with overlapping sets, with clinical psychology at the centre of the overlap).

(Parry, 1990, cited in Pilgrim, 1990, emphasis added)

This position from Parry was elaborated in *The Psychologist* (Parry, 1989) in a special edition which focused on the implications of the MAS report, which we will return to below. Clinical psychologists elsewhere in the correspondence columns of *The Psychologist* were vying in competing claims about expertise in the psychological therapies with others making similar bids. Opportunities, such as the emotional aftermath of the Zeebrugge ferry sinking, the Lockerbie explosion and the Hillsborough football stadium tragedy, were becoming fortuitous sites of employment for all in the 'psy professions'. Newly emerging groups making a bid for legitimacy, such as counselling psychologists, announced to the world that they were natural experts in the field:

Clinical psychologists do excellent work in their own field, but it is only counselling psychologists whose training in inter-personal and enabling skills specifically equips them to deal with the trauma suffered by victims of disasters. Although some clinical psychologists may possess these skills, it cannot be presumed that it is a major part of their training.

(Noyes *et al.*, May 1989, p. 214)

Many clinical psychologists were clearly worried about this competition and that coming from other groups like CPNs. This insecurity prompted them to make grandiose claims about their peculiar expertise. For instance, here is a snippet of a letter to *The Psychologist* expressing concern about non-psychologists using psychological techniques:

As trained clinical psychologists, who have received intensive training, supervision and accreditation, we are skilled in all the various therapeutic methods such as anxiety management, psycho-dynamic psychotherapy, psychosexual and marital counselling, rational-emotive therapy, transactional analysis, guided grieving, to name but a few.

(Hallam *et al.*, September 1989, p. 375)

Our earlier discussion of training revealed the dubiousness of this type of posturing. But, by the end of a decade of Thatcherism, self-aggrandisement, not scientific caution, characterised the public rhetoric of psychologists. The Conservative attack on professional power, along with its legitimation of aggressive individualism, provoked responses which were typically devoid of humility but which were traceable in part to the arrogant scientism endemic in the profession since its inception.

All these claims and counter-claims about the special and indispensable abilities of varieties of applied psychology, within the discourse of the discipline, were also operating at a time when the efforts of the DCP leadership in connection with chartering had at long last succeeded, at least in part. The fate of the campaign, which ran for the full decade, got off to a bad start. Civil servants, in line with the anti-professionalism of their political masters, had given the BPS leadership strong cues early on that the government would not support the introduction of legislation to grant full registration of psychologists. It will be recalled that this aspiration, in the wake of

Foster and Seighart, was the preferred option advocated by the DCP. The BPS adapted to the signal from the civil servants by seeking a weaker but more feasible version of registration: chartering. Registration proper would have involved new legislation to set up an independent register of practitioners. By contrast, chartering involved the BPS itself keeping its own register and did not require parliament to consider new legislation.

Colin Newman, executive secretary of the BPS, formally described the success of the campaign with hyperbole typical of the Thatcher years and influenced by the traditional pomp of British Royal assent (the Privy Council acts on behalf of the monarch):

> as in the theory of evolution, cataclysmic events occur which result in more dramatic, sudden revolutionary changes. . . . One such cataclysmic event has just occurred in the national environment in which the Society exists. In 1987, the Privy Council granted the order in Council amending the Royal Charter and Statutes of the Society, thereby authorising the Society to maintain a Register of Chartered Psychologists.
>
> (Newman, 1988)

Just in case anyone was under any doubt about the motives involved in the chartering campaign, a member of the Charter Promotion Group and BPS President, Ian Howarth, professor of psychology at Nottingham University, sent a letter to all academic psychologists saying why they should take advantage of an 'introductory offer'. Early applicants (before 18 June 1989) were to be guaranteed their name in the first published register and they were to sign up at a reduced cost. The form of the letter adhered to a marketing ethos; its content was in the same vein.

Howarth gave five reasons why he was making an offer his colleagues should not refuse. First, chartered status would help academic psychologists advance their careers. Second, it would reinforce the 'good image' of the profession to employers, government, schools and the general public. Third, it would signal to current and prospective students of psychology that there was a 'concern for the preservation and development of the profession'. Fourth, 'psychology is a science-based profession and depends upon the kind of research and teaching we do.' Consequently, academics were urged by Howarth to influence its professional development. He goes on, 'It is also important for the credibility (and funding) of research that a close link is maintained between academic and professional members of the Society.' Fifth, echoing the thrust of *The Future of the Psychological Science* document, he appeals for professional coherence – 'It is one of the strengths of psychology in this country that we present a coherent image of our subject.' His rallying call then concludes:

> The Society is the main source of publicity about the promotion of psychology in this country. Join me and other academics who have taken chartered status and help to make sure that academic psychologists benefit from the publicity.

(Howarth, 1989)

These messages are quoted to underline the ethos of marketing dominating the discourse of the professional leadership by the end of the 1980s. Once more science is claimed to be at the heart of the profession's legitimacy. Once more only its name, like that of God for theists, needs to be used to assure a taken-for-granted authority. This plea for conformity to the chartering initiative also reveals an anxiety on the part of the profession's leadership. The run up to chartering was not straightforward for them. Many academic psychologists were ambivalent or hostile to chartering on both political and financial grounds (inevitably it would involve paying recurrent fees). Remember that the pressure for chartering came from applied psychologists (especially from the DCP). Howarth's entreaty was an attempt to sell the package to a target group (academics) predicted to be resistant. Ironically, it was clinicians who were slowest on the uptake when the charter was finally effected, to the disappointment of the DCP executive and paid officials in the BPS. This would suggest that the ideology of the professional leadership and that of grassroots practitioners cannot be assumed to coincide – a point to be returned to in the next chapter.

It is also instructive to contrast the balance of the content of the letter which Howarth sent to his academic colleagues with the more formal description he had given earlier in *The Psychologist* reporting in his capacity as Chair of the Membership and Qualifications Board, the new committee set up in the BPS to vet applications to the charter (Howarth, 1988). In this, more public statement, the bulk of the space is given over to the more solemn concerns of 'protecting the public' in the light of the code of conduct by which chartered psychologists would be bound. He draws particular attention to the four duties of care about: client welfare; confidentiality; consent; and competence.

Even though space-wise these dominated the article, they were also sandwiched between briefer statements which revealed the same self-interest as his later letter. At the start he says:

> We must be careful not to claim too much or we shall lose credibility. We must also bear in mind that the ability of professional bodies to protect the public by disciplining their members, is being questioned in many quarters, especially the media. Too many professional organisations have protected their members rather than the public. If we are seen to behave in the same way we shall be easy targets, less able to defend ourselves than some longer established and more prestigious organisations.
>
> (Howarth, 1988, p. 96)

Thus Howarth's main concern seems to be about the rhetorical advantages of the new charter in competition with other professions. Note the phrase 'If we are seen to behave. . .'. This suggests an ambivalence about which is more important – the behaviour or the impression it creates. One incontestable point he makes is that, in the past, profes- sions have put their own interests before those of the public – the question is whether psychologists are really capable of being any different.

Nearing the end of the article, under the candid marketing title 'Is a Chartered Psychologist a "best buy"?' he goes on:

> Our new Charter will improve the status of psychology and increase the employability of psychologists, only if we can persuade the public, that, for certain purposes, psychology can provide a 'best buy'. So we cannot avoid the need to compare ourselves with other people who provide similar or competing services. In doing so it is doubly important not to 'make claims beyond our competence', because the credibility and validity of our claims is our only effective and unstoppable weapon.
>
> (Howarth, 1988, p. 98)

Indeed, it is persuasive, on both logical and democratic grounds, that professional competence should be evident to recipients of services. This stance compares favourably with the more open-ended position taken up by the 'radicals', above, whose professional actions needed 'no justification'. However, Howarth's (and presumably the BPS') stance on democracy and accountability still provides a subtle revision and maintenance of professional dominance over its clients. This is revealed under another rhetorical heading in the article ('An egalitarian approach'), where it is argued that the new approach to professionalism ushered in by the charter is 'less authoritarian' as it 'sees the client as the expert in his or her problems and the professional *as having expert knowledge about, and perhaps personal expertise in, the solution to certain categories which have been solved successfully in the past*' (emphasis added). It can be seen from this statement that the power differential between professional and client is not to be imposed by 'irrational authority', to use Erich Fromm's notion, typical of, say, the doctor-centred discourse of medicine. Instead the new client-centred discourse is to be characterised by one party having more formal knowledge than the other. As psycho-therapists have known for years, an approach to professional work which actually minimises authoritative directiveness is, itself, an extremely effective way of having power over clients (Haley, 1963). Non-directiveness and contrived neutrality are themselves evidence of professional power and choice. Client-centred practices do not necessarily make professionals actually more amenable to public accountability, although they may be more benign and user-friendly compared to more professional-centred interactions.

After 1988: the crisis of survival

Derek Mowbray, the man from MAS, presented a draft report to the project steering group of the MPAG on 17 April 1989 and a final version on 12 June. His report was released to the public on 21 September. Contrary to the worst fears of the radicals, the report was highly complimentary about the profession and even provided a formula for its expansion and increased status. He suggested that psychologists have a particular skill level, as a product of their scientific training, unmatched by others in the NHS.

The MAS Report commended the notion that clinical psycho-logists are experts at a third level of skill. Level 1 skills were constructed by Mowbray as being about rapport and simple techniques of counselling clients or stress management. Level 2 skills were about undertaking, cookbook fashion, circumscribed activities such as behaviour therapy. Clinical psychologists, but also lots of other professionals, attained levels 1 and 2.

Mowbray argued that only psychologists can theorise about new problems and how to solve them because of their higher education in academic and applied psychology. This level 3 marked off clinical psychologists from other workers, according to Mowbray. They could be, according to him, unique consultants on hand to theorise, analyse and make suggestions about a variety of psychological issues in a variety of health care settings. This unique role was a function of their 'broadly based psychological knowledge.'

The Report also reviewed models of service delivery for the future. It favoured one of 'shared care' in which psychologists would support, complement and provide alternatives to medical care. The model on offer emulated that of medicine. A psychological service would be 'consultant psychologist-led'. In this scheme, the consultant psychologist would 'be responsible not only for the services provided by other psychologists working in the area, but also for co-ordinating the psychological services provided by certain other disciplines to that client group'. This seemingly optimistic scenario of course assumed that other professionals would actually accept the special consultancy expertise of psychologists, a moot point which we will return to in the next chapter. Mowbray admitted his own strategic guidance to the profession entailed a conciliatory attitude to medicine in the light of its dominant history.

In an interview with Celia Kitzinger in *The Psychologist* with the individualistic and grandiose title, 'Turbulent Visionary', Mowbray said of clinical psychology and its medical context:

> It is a fledgling profession, growing, changing, grabbing what it can and it's done so on the back of the medical profession, and it's allowed to survive because doctors let it. So to bite the hand that's fed them [*sic*] is a risky thing to do.
>
> (Mowbray, 1989, p. 441)

Another encouraging recommendation (for expansionists) from Mowbray was that the profession should be enlarged well beyond the current number of just under 2500 in the UK. Mowbray did not review Wales, Scotland and Northern Ireland but suggested that by the year 2000 there should be 4000 clinical psychologists in England alone. When the MAS findings and recommendations began to filter out to the profession, it seemed that the fears of critics of the MPAG exercise had been unfounded. However, not only were the expectations of the 'radicals' not fulfilled, but the optimistic ones of the 'realists' also came to nought. The government (via the Department of Health) showed no signs of destroying the profession in the wake of the MPAG review. Their preferred option was to preserve the status quo temporarily and let the impact of new legislation, following on the White Paper *Working for Patients*, set in motion a new philosophy for the NHS which would define its organisation and its staffing patterns.

In this light, the response of the Department of Health was neither to endorse the MAS report about the future of the profession nor to seek any other direct policy change about manpower. The report was sent out to Regional Health Authority Directors of Personnel on 12 October. It was covered by a letter from the MPAG Secretary which emphasised that:

> Some of the more far reaching recommendations, particularly those concerned with advancing the models of service develop- ment and staff gradings, are such that neither the MPAG nor the Department of Health sees them as relevant or appropriate to current circumstances and plans for change within the NHS. Because of this both MPAG and the DoH would not wish the review's findings and recommendations to be regarded as their considered view on future arrangements for the profession of clinical psychology.

This was civil servicespeak for saying that the MAS report was, like any other not fitting the government of the day's intentions, going to be shelved to gather dust. The DCP leadership, ever-optimistic, hoped that it could be used on a local basis to provide guidance and advice in negotiating post levels in both training and higher grades. They knew that even if this were to take place this would be very much a second best compared to a warm endorsement of the MAS recommendations by the government.

In tandem with the MPAG/MAS review the DCP had hedged its bets over the manpower crisis by asking Bernard Kat, District Psychologist in Newcastle and an MPAG steering group member, to draw up his own recommendations about improving the training bottle-neck problem. He presented his 'short term strategy' to meetings of RHA officers and training course organisers in Harrogate and at the DoH in London in November 1989. Kat's proposals were guided, in part, by his knowledge of the MAS report. He offered proposals for the first half of the 1990s which would work towards boosting the number of newly qualified staff per annum nationally to 300. Kat recognised that this would first require that a round of promotions would be needed to boost the numbers of required supervisors to underpin an expansion in trainees.

The MAS proposals, positive but unendorsed by those who mattered, might be used to negotiate these changes. However, this was in a context where the decade of value-for-money ethos in the NHS had left funding arrangements for any innovations highly precarious. It seemed that two constraints were imposed on the profession in the wake of the controversial MAS report. First, the report was effectively shelved and the incipient *Working For Patients* was signalled as the real determinant of NHS staffing. Second, recommendations or no recommendations, cash limits, as elsewhere in the NHS, were over-determining policy outcomes. For all the hopes of the DCP leadership and the fears of its radical critics, at the end of the day money not ideology was to determine the fate of the profession – at least until the practical effects of *Working for Patients* were to be discovered.

In anticipating the new legislation (the 1990 NHS and Community Care Act), some practitioners were pessimistic about the survival of the profession. They pointed towards a 'doomsday scenario' in which clinical psychology might disappear from sight in some localities. Two trends gave the pessimists support for their anxieties. First, the new legislation would separate provider and purchaser functions in the NHS. One logical possibility when this occurred would be that consortia of mental health professionals from one discipline might compete with those from another in selling a 'treatment package' to the local health authority. If say a group of CPNs could convince a purchaser of psychological therapies that they could do the job well and at a cheaper price than their clinical psychology colleagues, the latter might be out of a job. This is why the arguments of Parry above, when talking about the superiority of psychologists' skills over those of nurses, were important. To the relief of the profession, Mowbray had indeed endorsed this higher skill level claim for clinical psychology in his report. This emphasised the deployment of psychologists as a scarce consultancy resource. The problem was that the value of his recommendations was now in serious doubt (following the MPAG/DoH disclaimer).

A second trend had been developing during the 1980s, as result of another policy shift, which might also undermine the viability of the profession. As a result of de-institutionalisation and a move towards community care, the psy professions were beginning to test out the problems of working together away from the ritualised certainties of hospital routines. One consequence of this, particularly in the new community mental health centres, was that role blurring or genericism was beginning to characterise practice. Whilst many from all the professions contributed to this trend, those which had no statutory powers or duties, such as clinical psychology, became vulnerable. Doctors were needed to prescribe drugs and nurses to administer them. Doctors and social workers had statutory duties under the 1983 Mental Health Act when patients were compulsorily detained and nurses had new holding powers.

These examples highlight that psychiatry, psychiatric nursing and social work were guaranteed mandates of practice in the community or in the new district general hospital acute units. This was not the case for psychologists. Also, because all of the mental health professions working in the community increasingly aspired to be applied psychologists (by practising variants of psychological therapy or counselling), a defined role for clinical psychologists was becoming unclear. In what way exactly were they needed? These doubts about the profession's necessity were elaborated in the article in *Clinical Psychology Forum* with the telling title 'Community mental health teams and clinical psychology – the death of a profession?' (Anciano and Kirkpatrick, 1989). Whilst in some localities psychologists were negotiating a credible role for themselves (sometimes even as leaders) this was by no means inevitable.

Thus, despite all the efforts of the leadership, throughout the 1980s, to improve the standing of the profession and guarantee its survival, wider forces were threatening its viability. Moreover, these efforts were not always received with gratitude, as the dispute between the 'radicals' and 'realists' demonstrated. Also the push for full legal registration failed and the chartering compromise seemed to find greater support from its advocates in the vanguard rather than with ordinary practitioners (be they academics or clinicians). Maybe now the contradictory claim made at the beginning of this chapter, that the profession was both expansionist and insecure by the end of the 1980s, can be understood. The profession tried to make its own history but was constrained by forces well beyond its control.

These constraints were external (an unrelenting de-stabilisation of the welfare state by the most authoritarian Conservative government in British history) and internal (the ambivalence of its practitioners). More will be said about both of these in the next chapter. However, before moving to a summary of this one, it is worth returning to Parry's opinion about the plight of the profession by the end of the decade:

> The move towards Chartering to gain professional closure is incomplete because unlike in say medicine, being Chartered is not an obligatory condition for employment in the NHS. Consequently, I still see closure in the profession as being ramshackle and reversible. Theoretically the whole chartering process could be reversed if enough psychologists took an anti-professional stance. . . . The thing to do is not to over-adapt to temporary circumstances. Present government ideology may be forgotten in ten years time. Historically though we are unusual in that we have grown up with the welfare system, we expect to operate inside the NHS because we imbibed it with our orange juice. Personally I would like to get back to that old involvement with the NHS but if we get sold off that would provide us with new opportunities.
>
> (Parry, 1990, cited in Pilgrim, 1990)

The first point made by Parry is crucial. Chartering is of little value *collectively* to the profession unless it is enforced (by making it a pre-condition of employment). There are signs, for this reason, in some localities that, by stealth, pro-charter professional leaders are indeed enforcing this condition. However, during the run up to chartering, one of its selling points (from its advocates to reluctant colleagues) was that this would be a *voluntary* arrangement. Now that chartering has been achieved, all the signs are that the profession's leadership will push to make it obligatory for practice. Parry's final comment highlights the difference between her position as an optimistic leader and those of her colleagues who predict a 'doomsday scenario'. Both recognise that the profession is under pressure but one party believes this could be fatal, the other suggests a new beginning.

This chapter has tried to explore the main features of clinical psychology as a profession during the 1980s – a period when Thatcherism, with its emphasis on marketing, value for money and self-promotion, clearly influenced clinical psychology in a variety of ways. It was a decade when social justice and intellectual integrity were disvalued in British society and it showed at all levels. The profession was certainly shaken into action but it was diminished by its attempts at adapting in order to survive. The 'radicals' may not have been totally self-critical about their own brand of professional élitism, but at least they made an attempt to oppose some of the consequences of living in an elected dictatorship. To put this in perspective though, all they were really trying to do was preserve the status quo – ironically a conservative strategy. However, Thatcher was in power for so long that, with hindsight, any whimper of opposition deserves some recognition.

A sign of the depressed fatalism which had gripped most public sector employees by the 1980s was that the 'realists' did not encounter a large enough opposition to risk defeat. Moreover, there was little or no sign of a substantial presence of a *genuine* client-orientated radicalism in the profession. The 'radicals' were simply concerned to promote a form of disobedience in order to hang on to current professional privileges. The mental health users movement was making great strides in the 1980s – clinical psychologists, with one or two exceptions, were notably absent from this emerging new social movement. This and other issues will be reconsidered at the end of the next and final chapter.

Chapter 7

Past, present and future?

The last chapter attempted to explore the development of clinical psychology in its fourth period of managerialism. This final chapter will extend the implications of this account and focus on two key areas of discussion. The first of these concentrates on how the profession's characteristics can be understood in terms of their social context. The second, following on from this, relates to the problems facing its practitioners in the future. Put differently, there is one set of considerations about how clinical psychology might be understood, as an object of enquiry, by social scientists. There is another set of considerations about what clinical psychologists themselves might want to reflect on in order to take their role in society seriously.

CLINICAL PSYCHOLOGY IN ITS SOCIAL CONTEXT

The previous chapters have highlighted a number of interweaving factors which shaped the emergence and development of the British profession. Any convincing rather than reductionist account of clinical psychology has to take account of the relationship between these factors which include the following:

- The empiricist cultural traditions of British philosophy.
- The industrial and social administrative requirements of the British state during war and peace.
- The organisational influence of British medicine.
- The centrality of the National Health Service in stimulating and constraining professional developments.
- The pro-active influence of meritocratic élites within the modern welfare state.

If the profession were to be described in its simplist terms the following would seem a fair summary:

- It is a small profession (about 2500 practitioners).
- It began life and developed overwhelmingly in the NHS.
- Its practitioners vary in their approach to their work.
- They have no peculiar statutory powers delegated by the state.
- Their only certain commonality is their standardised qualification in higher education, studying psychology to graduate and post-graduate levels.
- Their training courses are highly variegated and typically eclectic in espoused philosophy.
- They claim an allegiance to science to justify their existence – hence there is a strong emphasis on the 'scientist-practitioner' model of practice.
- They compete with other professionals who claim similar expertise. (There is no disciplinary monopoly on psychological knowledge.)

What will be attempted now is a review of the second list in the light of the first. The pre-history and history of the profession were summarised in Chapters 1 and 2 and the socialisation of its neophyte practitioners was described separately in Chapters 3, 4 and 5. Our discussion will start with a summary of the main conclusions of these chapters.

The foundations of the profession were unambiguously a reflection of the cultural legacy of British philosophy. Despite the clinical identity of the profession being a by-product of medical discourse and practices, the psychology identity was strongly rooted in the strengths and weaknesses of British philosophy. These roots meant that the profession started with a view of the world which was empiricist and positivist. The transition from philosophy to psycho- logy, exemplified by the developments at University College, London, led to a paradoxical situation. Psychologists, in the first half of the twentieth century, were driven by a scientific ethos and yet that very empiricist character disabled them from reflecting on their work (an idealist enterprise).

The certainty encouraged by the assured 'scientific' pursuit of 'facts' meant that practitioners, be they academic or applied psychologists, became experts at gazing outwards, not inwards. Reflexive scrutiny was excluded from the socialisation of trainees. At the individual level, this meant the rejection of the 'pre-scientific' and self-indulgent habit of personal knowledge associated with psychoanalysis. At the collective level, it meant that approaches from sociology or idealist philosophy (i.e. outside the profession) were, by and large, ignored or scorned. This was highlighted by the dispute between Eysenck and Portes in their competing accounts of the growth of behaviour therapy. Eysenck was insistent that the logic and achievement of empiricist science both justified and explained the existence, form and content of applied psychology. Portes suggested that the issue may have been a little more complicated.

Empiricism as a scientific ideology not only generates empirical knowledge claims (a quite legitimate and democratic enterprise) but it also disables its adherents from addressing pre-empirical and non-empirical questions. The latter are intimately bound up with moral and political values. This is why, more generally in academia, British empiricism encourages both a liberating attention to the details of external reality *and* a blinkered attitude towards value analysis (Bhaskar, 1989; cf. Thompson, 1978). Neophyte psychologists are typically led to believe in the importance of a 'disinterested' and 'value-free' attitude towards human scientific investigation. If this belief is held by graduates, by default they will be unable to think critically about their role in modern society.

By the time clinical psychology evolved after 1950, a mixture of misplaced scientific self-confidence and inevitable social naivety characterised its practitioners. First, psychometrics, with its commitment to reducing the complexities of human existence to points on a few pre-constructed dimensions, marked off its professional identity. Second, behaviour therapy, with its commitment to reducing the complexities of human distress to a few principles of faulty conditioning, enabled practitioners to don a different cloak of scientific respectability, which continued to blinker them from acknowledging their normative role in society. Even at this stage, the curious onlooker may have wanted to know *which* version of 'science' was the public and the state (let alone psychiatrists) supposed to take seriously? Was it to be the eugenic, Galtonian 'nomothetic science' of sorting people into categories for the purposes of industrial efficiency, social administration and the war effort? Or was it to be the 'science' of behaviour therapy built on a selective mixture of Pavlovianism and American learning theory? Were these alterations in the views of Eysenck (or was it Gwynne Jones?) to be joined by the tentative and scrupulous experimental approach to the individual favoured by Shapiro? If so, was *his* the 'real' psychological science?

Also, if psychoanalysis was condemned for being 'pre-scientific', was this name calling going to be enough to establish a 'proper' version of scientific psychology? If not, how might the retention of 'non-scientific' discourses be accounted for and responded to by clinical psychology? All these questions were unresolved even before clinical psychologists were softened by the adaptation to humanism in the 1970s. Essentially what starts as a simple proposition – that human conduct can be studied scientifically by clinical psychology – soon generates a whole set of complicated considerations.

The removal of reflexivity, in the separation from philosophy, meant that these legitimate epistemological questions were disputed privately but avoided in public. From the 1950s onwards, the surface rhetoric of the profession has been one of scientism. This certainly reached its most advanced form in the marketing days of the 1980s, but it has been the hallmark of the profession since its inception. Thus, by the 1980s, both conservative advocates of chartering, such as Howarth, or 'radical' critics of Taylorism, such as his Nottingham colleagues working in the NHS, solemnly invoked 'science' when justifying their position in public statements.

Of course, hidden from the public, competing tendencies within academia were indeed troubled by what a psychological science was, or should be. To this day, students of psychology are encouraged to respect relativism in the discipline, and textbooks often emphasise differences of theory and methodology (Lambie, 1991). And yet, when practical disputes have broken out, or when psychology has had to be 'sold' to the outside world, suddenly the scientific status and coherence of the profession have been deemed to be self-evident. This poses a genuine difficulty for clinicians. Their original training contained, typically, two conflicting messages. The first was that everything they were being taught was under the general rubric of a scientific approach. The second was that psychological knowledge, though scientifically generated, was perennially problematic. When faced with 'making out' or being personally effective in their daily activities, the confidence borne of the first message is highly seductive and useful for practitioners. But, when addressing their professional lives seriously, they invariably confess a commitment to one approach amongst many or an eclectic confusion. Consequently, even during the 1980s, the rhetoric of the professions' leaders, discussed in the last chapter, did not necessarily coincide with the private views of grassroots practitioners, who may have been humble or uncertain about their knowledge base (Pilgrim and Barnes, 1989).

These characteristics and confusions can only be understood if we attempt to develop a socio-historical account of their emergence. Work within the sociology of professions and the sociology of knowledge may help in this regard. Before considering some of the contributions from these, let us recap on some of the most recent features of the profession.

The previous chapters emphasised that the profession has not developed in a social vacuum. During the 1980s it was driven by or adapted to demands of the state. Four points in particular can be made to justify this claim. First, there was the stimulus for state registration (which became chartering) in the wake of the Foster and Seighart reports. Second, there was the spur to independence prompted by the Trethowan report. Third, there was the impact of de-institutionalisation, which created new opportunities and threats in terms of working in the community. Fourth, there was the de-stabilisation of expert authority in the wake of the Conservative government's attack on the clinical professions. These four key examples reflected state initiatives which engendered opportunistic (or desperate) activity on the part of the profession's leadership. Thus any sociological understanding of the profession's development needs to take account of the interaction of demands and constraints imposed 'from above' by the state and the initiatives attempted by the leadership of the profession in response.

How might these developments in the profession be understood in the light of knowledge derived from sociology? Probably the least satisfactory sociological account of professions is one which rests upon the uncritical assumption that they exist merely to provide a disinterested service to the public, based upon a set of specific personal skills and attributes. This view of professions as authoritative experts warranted by the possession of knowledge superior to that of their lay fellows is derived from the work of Talcott Parsons (1937). It accepts what professionals say about themselves on trust. In clinical psychology, the following type of uncritical account is offered by Kendall and Norton-Ford (1982):

> clinical psychologists share several common attributes. They are *psychologists* because they have been trained to use the guidelines of knowledge of psychology in their professional work. They are *clinicians* because they attempt to understand people in their

natural complexity and in their continuous adaptive transformation.... They are *scientists* because they utilise the scientific method to achieve objectivity and precision in their professional work. Finally they are *professionals* because they render important human services by helping individuals, social groups and communities solve psychological problems and improve the quality of life.

Note that this American definition endorsed in a recent British primer on clinical psychology (Marzillier and Hall, 1987) reduces the profession to a set of positive attributions preferred for its own advancement. However, we have already seen that clinicians have not always had a track record of respecting human complexity. We have seen that the notion of science is problematic. We have seen that professionals pursue their own interests, not those of their clients, much of the time. In other words, accounts of professions which depend upon practitioners themselves will be limited to professional rhetoric. This problem with the Parsonian view of professions led to the assertion of competing critical models within sociology (Saks, 1983).

Two of these critical models (neo-Weberian and neo-Marxian) will be utilised now to discuss the four government-derived agendas set out above. The neo-Weberian approach emphasises the strategies used by leaders of occupational groups to 'corner the market' in relation to certain client types. In order to do this they work towards claiming a mandate to have a special legitimate control over that group (either with formal state powers or through an informal acceptance of a unique knowledge base). If successful, this produces closure around the activities and the relations with clients, which excludes other workers making similar bids. Thereafter, the profession will resist encroachment from new bids. It will also seek to develop a dominant relationship with nearby professional groups. This subordination process, if successful, helps resist encroachment and it ensures and amplifies the social and financial status of the dominant profession. A fully fledged profession has control over its own training, in order to regulate its own professional boundaries, and it tends to lengthen that training increasingly in order to justify its special and peculiar expertise. It also regulates its boundaries by being in control of its activities in relation to its client group.

Applying this sketch of the neo-Weberian model to the features of clinical psychology discussed in previous chapters, we can identify some of these processes immediately. It was evident during the formative years of the profession that the issue of dominance was important in relation to psychiatry. The disputes it had with medicine began to emerge in the late 1950s when the therapeutic monopoly established after 1858 by doctors was challenged by clinical psychologists in relation to behaviour therapy. Psychiatry resisted that encroachment (the Lewis-Marks-Gelder initiative) but was only partially successful in warding off psychologists. It became evident to psychologists thereafter that their own professional autonomy was being defined *against* that already established by medicine. This culminated in the Trethowan Committee trying to negotiate an end to these hostilities by recommending the informal recognition of the profession's independent status. The opportunities afforded by the post-Foster and Seighart period then gave the DCP the chance to seek a formal recognition by the state of this independence in its bid for registration.

As far as controlling professional boundaries are concerned, two initiatives were evident, thereafter. First, the outcome of the manpower review if successful would have provided the profession with some control about trainee levels. Second, the review might also define the special expertise peculiar to clinical psychologists. These initiatives, of the registration campaign and the MPAG review, were totally consistent then with a strategy of professional closure. However, as the quote from Parry demonstrated, the fear was that such closure was vulnerable because of the weak achievement of voluntary chartering instead of compulsory registration as a condition of employment. As came to pass, the next vulnerability was whether the MPAG review was to have any genuine credibility about defining psychological expertise and regulating training levels.

Weber's model of professional closure was developed before one of his predictions (the increasing bureaucratisation of society) was proved depressingly correct. His original model assumed that professionals would have direct and exclusive control over their relationship with their clients. Once health care became bureaucratised, the state began to intervene or mediate in that relationship. The state, not the client, was the professional's employer. This posed a threat to the autonomous status of professionals (hence the resistance to the NHS by the medical profession in 1948). So, by the mid-1980s, tactics about closure had to be directed primarily towards the state, not patients (although credibility in the public's eyes would facilitate the negotiations – hence the image-promotion campaign). In this light, if the manpower regulation problem was to be resolved, some negotiation with state managers had to be risked at some time (whether it should have been risked at the time it was remains a moot point).

Another feature of closure by 1990 was the extension of the two-year training course to three years. Examples were also given of the weak attempts by psychologists to subordinate other professions in the 1980s, once Trethowan had cut them loose from the control of medicine. To date, these attempts do not appear to have been very successful, not least because of the shifting organisational sands of community care. Not only have psychologists failed to achieve a credible leadership role in community mental health teams, the role blurring in them may have even risked the obliteration of the special identity of the profession (Anciano and Kirkpatrick, 1989).

As we saw in the last chapter the Mowbray recommendations seemed to offer a formula for the special consultancy role of psychologists, which if effected would indeed given them a privileged and protected status in the NHS. However, three obstacles are in the way of this occurring. First, this report was effectively shelved by the DoH, in favour of superordinate NHS reforms, emerging from *Working for Patients*, determining the issue of staffing. Second, even if the MAS recommendations eventually trickle through at local level in the NHS, there remains a doubt as to whether most clinical psychologists actually want and are capable of such a 'level three' consultancy role. (Most seem to take a continued interest in patient contact.) Third, there is the reality of inter-disciplinary rivalry in the mental health professions. Whilst psychologists may have a good chance of being invested with credibility where they are not known, in the specialties of physical medicine (and even there they will be competing with the growth of liaison psychiatry), this is not the case where other mental health professionals are traditionally sited.

It is unlikely that professions already competing with psychologists in pursuit of their own occupational interests will willingly accept their authority. One of the reasons for this is that, although clinical psychologists may have sought to secure the unambiguous professional ownership of psychological knowledge in health care contexts, they have not succeeded. There are plenty of others, especially medical psychotherapists, who have already secured organisational control in this regard. Others such as social workers, psychiatric nurses and occupational therapists can equally point to their claimed expertise in cognitive-behaviour therapy, family therapy and dynamic psychotherapy, as well as organisational consultancy. In this light, why should these occupational groups passively accept the special authority of psychologists about psychological knowledge?

Thus any discussion of the profession guided by neo-Weberian considerations inevitably comes back to certain limitations on clinical psychology providing itself and its employers, the state, with a credible case for genuine closure and legitimacy. It is not surprising that, faced with such a legitimation crisis, many NHA psychologists have sought refuge in either private practice or Griffiths management roles.

Turning now to the insights that might be gained from testing a neo-Marxian model on the material discussed in earlier chapters, more emphasis would be placed on the economic function and characteristics of the profession and on its contradictory role in society. Some in this tradition have argued that the scientific middle classes are a progressive force whose interests are inherently opposed to those of the ruling class (e.g. Baran, 1973). However, many Marxian theorists have been highly critical of the role of service professionals including, and surrounding, medicine. For instance, Poulantzas (1975) dismissed them as inculcators of bourgeois ideology and agents of social control acting on behalf of the state. Navarro (1986) goes as far as arguing that medical élites are best formulated as segments of a dominant capitalist class. Presumably para-medical groups like psychologists aspiring to a similar status are attempting to enter such a class position. However, the Navarro argument seems to be at odds with the empirical reality of the Conservative government importing members of the capitalist class to curtail the superstructural power of the medical profession and its hangers on (the Griffiths report).

Increasingly, the Marxian analysis moved towards a view that incorporated both critical and commendable depictions, by emphasising the contradictory role of white-collar workers under monopoly capitalism. For instance, Carchedi (1977) argues that professionals constitute a 'new middle class' inside the capitalist system (which is expanding in proportion to the genuine proletariat). They are in an intermediate position between the capitalist class and the proletariat. As a result they share characteristics and interests with the classes both above and below them. They are agents of the state, yet they are also wage slaves. Their interests, being split, lead some of them to ally themselves with conservative forces in society and some of them to form alliances with reformist or revolutionary forces. This analysis of an ambiguous role is supported by Braverman (1974).

In the light of this ambivalence about health care professionals from Marxians, how does clinical psychology look? As far as Poulantzas' points about bourgeois values and social control are concerned, it is certainly true that psychologists make themselves particularly vulnerable to such claims. The pre-history of the profession points towards a series of collusions with the state in peacetime to regulate the population. The early interest of those following Galton, such as Burt, was clearly in children, the slow, the mad and other races. These were the groups which, unless put in their place conceptually and physically, constituted a threat to the socio-economic stability of the capitalist order. Most of these groups are, of course and tellingly, of continuing interest to clinical psychologists. More generally, psychology, by definition, responds to problems by individualising them. It is defined, *inter alia*, as the science of the individual; accordingly there is a continuing confusion within academia about whether it is a biological or social science. Psychological reductionism diverts attention from the social determinants of distress. The framing of social relations as individual characteristics is probably the most important occupational hazard of applied psychology hence it inevitably earns the sort of criticism expressed by Poulantzas and Navarro.

The claim by Carchedi that middle-class groups manifest a divided class loyalty (a 'cleavage' of class consciousness) seems apparent in clinical psychology. Their divided interest is reflected in the common situation of practitioners being members of both a professional association (the BPS) which pursues the path of élitism and expanded social status and a traditional trade union (MSF previously ASTMS) which defends their interests as workers. Equally it is true (following Baran) that many in the profession espouse left of centre political values, whilst others are preoccupied with increasing their personal status and wealth.

However, it could be argued, probably more convincingly, that what Carchedi would describe as a 'contradictory' position is actually a manifestation of a different but *unified* occupational strategy emphasised by neo-Weberians, such as Parkin (1979). When studying another group of applied scientists (engineers) McLoughlin (1982) noted that memberships both of a professional association and of a white-collar trade union were 'complementary alternatives' pointing towards the common goal of collective upward social mobility via social closure. What McLoughlin suggests for engineers could also apply to clinical psychologists: the BPS operates to fulfil the long-term goal of professional closure but this can be boosted at times by the tactical deployment of industrial solidarity of activity in MSF.

As an example of the complexity of this issue an important inter-professional argument will now be considered. The speech therapy dispute of 1986 spotlights the divided reaction in the profession about the rights of female health workers who are science graduates. In doing so, it demonstrates that clinical psychology not only has to be understood in class terms (using neo-Marxian or neo-Weberian accounts) but also raises the issue of *gender* and therefore questions of patriarchy.

In 1987, the trade union representing clinical psychologists (MSF) attempted to advance the interests of another group under its jurisdiction, speech therapists. These are graduates and like psycho-logists arguably applied scientists. They are also a predominantly female profession. Significantly, a female full-time official (less than 10% of MSF officials were female) argued that the similarity between the professions should be a basis for claiming parity of conditions and salaries from their employer, the NHS. Some in the profession reacted in a very hostile way to this exercise, arguing that it was inappropriate as psychologists were superior – they were not merely graduates but also had post-graduate training. Such was the anger in this reactionary lobby that they argued that MSF should cease to represent psychologists as a trade union and that the BPS should take over this function (the BPS considered this untenable). Others in the profession vociferously supported the speech therapists and the MSF initiative. The majority remained silent, maybe indicating their ambivalent support for continued dual representation. Carchedi's work could be mapped on to this dispute, as could the modified interpretation of McLoughlin. In addition, the issue of patriarchal, not class interests may be apparent, which will be reconsidered below.

Before considering this issue of gender further, another set of sociological enquiries within Marxian sociology has some relevance for our understanding of clinical psychology. These have addressed the changing role of the white-collar worker in advanced capitalism. Just as Marx and Engels emphasised that the old *petite bourgeoisie*, including handicraftsmen and artisans, became rapidly degraded in their labour power by capitalist developments during the nineteenth century, others have argued that a similar degradation has affected the 'new middle class' of the late twentieth century. The degradation brings them nearer to the economic status of manual workers, so has been called 'proletarianisation'. This notion addressed by Carchedi (1977) has been extended to all professional groups by Oppenheimer (1975).

According to Oppenheimer, professional work, especially that carried out in large bureaucracies such as the NHS, becomes increasingly fragmented. This makes the work vulnerable to 'routinisation'. Essentially this means that because of the sub-division of labour in health care, tasks may become reduced to a set of skills which could be learned by others. When and if this happens, the employer (the NHS say) could then argue that others capable of doing the job may do so in a more cost-effective way. At this point, the group being out-priced by their colleagues would be rendered redundant, unless they competed favourably. Labour costs can then be kept down by employers and, in the process, the special skills developed by some groups become eroded ('de-skilling').

Oppenheimer's work can be seen to have relevance to the market-driven NHS after the first Griffiths report, especially with regard to the fears of the 'doomsday scenario'. It will be remembered that this referred to the possibility of other mental health professionals out-bidding psychologists for work once the provider and purchaser functions were separated out, subsequent to the 1990 NHS Act in the wake of *Working for Patients*. Workers vulnerable to such moves of de-skilling then seek to defend their occupational position. (Another contributory factor in the resentment over the speech therapy dispute could have been the perception that MSF were failing to protect psychologists against de-skilling.) The strength of the Oppenheimer thesis is that it draws attention to the political status of middle-class workers: they are workers. Consequently, they are vulnerable to the vagaries of the goals of their employing bureaucracy (they are subject to 'bureaucratic subordination'). By this logic knowledge-based as well as manual health workers can have their activities subordinated to the objectives of their employer (the NHS).

The fears of psychologists about community mental health teams may also be rendered intelligible within this scheme. According to Oppenheimer, the drive towards de-skilling by management increasingly places white-collar workers in the same vulnerable and oppressed role as their blue-collar colleagues: hence the notion of the proletarianisation of the middle-class worker – they have become 'mental labourers'.

The weakness of the Oppenheimer thesis is that its workerist emphasis deflects attention away from the *élitist* role of middle-class health workers when resisting de-skilling. In particular, white-collar workers, like psychologists, have a tendency to *mystify* their activities in order to resist accountability and defend their existing privileges. What psychologists did in the dispute between the 'radicals' and the 'realists' was, in different ways, to mystify psychological knowledge in order to render it 'indeterminate'. The first group simply argued that they required 'no justification' to carry on with their work. It was borne of a special blend of scientific training and clinical experience. The second group argued that they could operationalise their knowledge as the peculiar overlap of the three types of knowledge outlined by Mowbray and Parry in the last chapter. This led to a unique role in which only psychologists could make *ad hoc* judgements about psychological knowledge. Both strategies, if successful, would ward off the direct jurisdiction of their managers. They would also be a bulwark against encroachment from other mental health professionals.

In other words, when is a resistance to 'de-skilling' a defensive attempt to preserve the privileges of the status quo? Knowing, as we do, the reactions of clinical psychologists at different levels during the 1980s, it would appear that this ambiguity must remain. On the one side, the professional leadership were seeking opportunities for status maintenance or even élitist expansion. On the other side, those practitioners concerned only with their patient contact and job security struggled simply to survive and keep up their flagging morale under conditions of constant organisational changes imposed by the 'new managerialism'. Once more we come back to the contradictory nature of professionalism. Within this contradictory picture is the use of indeterminate knowledge both to maintain or extend élitist status but also simply to cope and survive.

The role of indeterminate knowledge in health care organisation has been analysed by Jamous and Peloille (1970). According to them, the fragmentation and routinisation of knowledge in health care bureaucracies is resisted by knowledge-based occupational groups (like psychologists) rendering their work indeterminate. As we acknowledged earlier, notions of 'clinical judgement' and 'clinical experience' are the pertinent examples of the latter typically used by medical and para-medical practitioners. If professionals accepted a thoroughly operationalised version of their work, defined by their employers, they would risk losing control of their unique role, as operationalised skills could be disseminated outside the profession's boundaries to others. On the other hand, they cannot expect their employers simply to take on trust that what they do is special, worthwhile, cost-effective, etc. (as the 'radicals' pushed for).

Thus a tension exists between the 'technicality' of knowledge and its 'indeterminacy' in professional practice and rhetoric. The Mowbray formula was carefully calculated, and willingly endorsed by practitioners, to provide a ratio between these two. It operationalised psychological knowledge enough to convince employers about clinical psychology being a 'good buy' but insisted on the unique role of practitioners, by giving them the open-ended mandate to make *ad hoc* judgements in their work. The latter, by definition, could not be operationalised in advance as they were about new problems which would be context-specific. In the light of the Conservative attack upon clinical professional power, it can be seen now why the market formula of *Working for Patients* was a preferred ministerial option for NHS staffing compared to the particular, professionally influenced, enquiries orchestrated by the MPAG. (In 1990, shortly after the publication of their report on psychologists, the MPAG was disbanded.) Whilst the Mowbray formula satisfied professionals, it automatically contradicted the new managerialist emphasis upon imposing greater controls upon them. In such circumstances it is not surprising that the MAS/MPAG plan was shelved.

Work from within the sociology of the professions is not the only source of sociological enquiry which can be of help in making sense of clinical psychology. There are also studies which have addressed the issue of 'interest work', which links knowledge and profes-sionalism (Atkinson and Delamont, 1990). The relationship between the interests being served by the production of scientific knowledge and those involved in professional activity are clearly relevant to clinical psychology as its self-ascribed identity is that of a culture of 'scientist-practitioners' (e.g. Marzillier and Hall, 1987). The

Mowbray level 3 argument, if successful, ensures that a group of academic and applied psychologists justify and profit from the possession of a scarce brand of knowledge. By arguing for special expertise in this realm psychologists can justify and advance their personal and collective interests, in terms of salaries and status, in society (hence the direct appeal to these in the statements quoted in the last chapter of Howarth). This contributes to the reproduction of the division (or separation) of intellectual and manual labour, via the special sub-division of 'psychology' within the first of these.

In case the obvious needs pointing out, there are clear advantages to being on the intellectual rather than manual side of the divide: on average higher earnings; more control over one's life (e.g. not clocking on and off from work); an absence of physical stress and danger; greater respect and deference from strangers in everyday life; the absence of anti-social hours of work or shift work, etc. Thus the quality of a 'scientific-practitioner's' life is intimately bound up with the social status achieved by the knowledge they possess.

Clinical psychologists are not just a part of an amorphous middle class. They have certain peculiar characteristics, which have emerged from the particular material conditions surrounding their lives. They are part of the 'new' middle class of meritocrats which expanded in the first thirty years following the Second World War. This sets up certain ideological claims which are special to them, including a cultural commitment to the pursuit of rational knowledge (hence the high value attached to science) and an assumption that merit not inherited privilege should define social status. When the speech therapy dispute broke, the DCP minutes recorded indignantly that, if their pay claim was successful, 'it would imply that some kinds of academic achievement are of no value in determining appropriate rates of pay' (DCP, 2.11.87). Because the profession has been coterminous with the NHS, as Parry pointed out, its practitioners have 'imbibed' the welfare state with their orange juice. Unlike the pre-war mature professions, like law and medicine, with their predominance of nepotistic connections and their bias towards public school candidates, clinical psychology has been more in the state school/redbrick university tradition. Its élite base was not Oxbridge but the Institute of Psychiatry. This was reflected in the profession's expansion, when, until the 1980s, those running training course were overwhelmingly Institute graduates.

There are also necessary considerations, outside this issue of class interest, about gender and race. If meritocratic criteria define or determine advancement and status ('credentialism'), in theory these could lead to the advancement of *all* in society, including disadvantaged groups such as women and black people. However, as yet this has not been the case in clinical psychology: its upper echelons are predominantly male, even though the profession as a whole is biased numerically in favour of women. By the late 1980s seven in every ten entrants to the profession were female (Torpy, 1988). Similarly, it is a white-dominated profession, with black people being present well below the base rate for British society. In a survey of the ethnic background of applicants to twenty-two clinical training courses between 1957 and 1984, Bender and Richardson (1990) found that 96 per cent were white. Only two Afro-Caribbean people entered the profession from a sample of 454 after 1977. Bender and Richardson also found that Asian and Afro-Caribbean students were less likely to complete their training compared to white peers. Moreover, during the 1980s not a single black person was evident in the profession's leadership (judging by the recorded membership of the DCP committee). Basically, the notion that meritocracy is governed by the free interplay of ability and opportunity simply does not translate into practice, as far as race and gender are concerned.

Black psychologists have made their views felt about this exclusion. In response to a survey on the needs of ethnic minority clients (Goodwin and Power, 1986), Gurnami and Sayal (1987) gave their view of discrimination in the profession, claiming that, despite an excess of national vacancies, black psychologists were more likely than their white counterparts to be unemployed following training. The acknowledged structural inequalities affecting black people prompted the North East Thames DCP recently to draw up and promote a plan of action to work towards genuine equal opportunities (Davenhill *et al.*, 1989). This targeted current selection and training practices.

Focusing on gender, the trend of the profession seems to have been against, not for, women, despite the claimed equalising potential of meritocratic principles. When push came to shove about helping the advancement of a predominantly female group (speech therapists), most clinical psychologists were lukewarm and some were militantly hostile. How is this to be understood? The first point to make is that clinical psychology is similar to other 'knowledge-based' professions in reproducing male interests within its ranks. The second point to make is that, as with these other professions, certain male priorities can be identified, which succeed in keeping women in lower ranks once they are qualified as practitioners. A third point is that where women begin to outnumber men, as in clinical psychology (Morris *et al.*, 1990), the profession becomes particularly vulnerable to an inferior status and the arrest of collective upward social mobility. These points will now be developed, in the light of the observations of Crompton (1987) and Hearn (1982).

Clinical psychology operates within a 'caring' organisational context. Evidence from other professions (e.g. Rueschmeyer, 1986) suggests certain processes which culminate in the advancement of men at the expense of women. With regard to this claim about the *collective* status of clinical psychology, in competition with other occupational groups, observations of two conservative patriarchs in the early 1980s are relevant. Humphrey and Haward (1981) reported a survey which recorded a trend of more women entering the profession than men, a trend which amplified during subsequent years (Torpy, 1988). To the anger of female practitioners, the authors reported that this trend might lead to the profession 'losing status and momentum'. They claimed that other female-dominated professions were characteristically inferior and subordinated to male professions. In fact, they were absolutely correct in their observation.

What made their article offensive was the programmatic implication linked to their observation: that the presence of women was a bad thing to be rued or rectified. It is certainly true, as Hearn (1982) points out, that female-dominated caring professions (social work, nursing, occupational therapy, speech therapy) have been subordinated in status in relation to a male profession (medicine). Whether women in those professions should be struggling to change this, rather than feeling guilty about 'causing' the inferiority is what divided the conservatism of Humphrey and Haward from their feminist critics. Despite an angry female reaction to the Humphrey and Haward article, male psychologists persisted in bemoaning the 'problem' of having a female-dominated intake to the profession. For example, Crawford restates the sexist case in 1989, but tries to distance himself personally from his message by fatalistically invoking the 'world at large', in the following way:

Whilst the BPS adheres to a non-sexist policy, the world at large is not necessarily so enlightened. National pay rates for women are significantly below those of men ... as the profession becomes increasingly all female so it will become harder to persuade general managers, mostly male, to improve pay and status: a downward spiral of a declining profession.

(Crawford, 1989, p. 30)

Another way in which clinical psychology has reproduced the male characteristics of other caring groups is to do with *internal* gender divisions. As Hearn notes when reviewing these groups, they are characterised by their managerial layer being predominantly male (as with district psychologists and DCP committee members). In this way male domination is reproduced within the profession. But how does it arise within a meritocratic occupational group like clinical psychology? Gender exclusion operates, once in the profession, in a number of ways. Despite the nominal existence of equal opportunity policies, subtle decision-making processes favour male candidates based upon prejudicial assumptions about the vulnerability of women of child-bearing age to absent themselves from their work role. For instance, in their article, Humphrey and Haward talked of the problem of women in the profession resisting 'the distractions of maternity'.

This informal prejudice against young women has been demonstrated by Homans (1987) when studying female scientists in the NHS. Gender exclusion leading to male-dominated hierarchies has also been demonstrated in NHS clerical and administrative work (Davies and Rosser, 1986). Also, increasing professionalisation is associated with the deployment of codes of practice (this was the case with the chartering campaign in the 1980s). Duman (1979) points out that modern codes of practice are traceable to the 'gentlemanly reasonableness' of the professions of law and medicine maturing in the nineteenth century. In other words, formal rationality is associated more with male discourse and thereby favours its possessors.

This issue of formal rationality also applies to the emphasis within the profession on the scientific method and the technical knowledge flowing from it (Ussher, 1991). Within 'scientific medicine' men are repeatedly favoured for promotion, and posts within academia are biased in favour of males. (Until 1960 there was also a ceiling of a 20 per cent quota of females entering British medical schools.) This pattern extends to the para-medical world of psychology. In psychology women are the largest group as undergraduates (79 per cent) (Morris, Cheng and Smith, 1990) and yet they are well under-represented in the senior grades of academic staff (15.9 per cent) (Kagan and Lewis, 1989).

To summarise, the profession is dominated by white men from middle-class origins. This is the outcome of a number of social processes, operating over time, which defy the corrective logic of meritocracy. During schooling, a class bias operates which filters out people from lower class backgrounds. This class bias is reinforced later when richer graduates have an advantage by paying for themselves as self-financing post-graduates. Similar filters operate for black people. Women seem to be particularly disadvantaged later on, after becoming clinicians. A number of informal processes operate, which keep certain groups marginalised in the profession. Mary Rowe, studying health care professions, metaphorically dubbed these processes 'Saturn's Rings' (the swirling particles which allow those on the margins to glimpse but not enter the centre of power) (Rowe, 1977).

Atkinson and Delamont (1990), explaining gender exclusion in the 'knowledge-based' professions generally, consider that it is these subtle processes of white male domination which must be identified rather than crass discrimination (like the defunct medical school quota system). They point to informal rules of discourse (Jamous and Peloille's 'indeterminacy') being vital for knowledge and advancement in middle-class circles. Professions operate as a 'brotherhood', the wheels of which are oiled by the old school tie and being socialised in a professional family. At work the hidden decisions made in the pub are more likely to take place in male, rather than female, company. This is reinforced by women employees being more likely than men to return quickly at the end of the day to the domestic arena to tend their children. As with other professions, it matters within clinical psychology to know how to communicate, with whom and about what, in which context. These skills are nothing to do with passing examinations or working with patients but are about peer acceptance and validation. Accordingly they operate against the advancement of female and black psychologists.

A final point to make here is that the marginalisation of certain groups should not lead to an idealisation of their role. For instance, there is no evidence that, when and if women do make it to the top in the profession, they are any less preoccupied with personal power in their role than is the case with male colleagues. In a hierarchy, those at the top, whoever they are, are prone to oppressive action. Also, following the appearance of the Psychology of Women Section inside the BPS in 1988, there has not been much evidence to date that feminist psychologists are producing a sustained reflexive critique of professional power over their clients (Burman, 1990; cf. Blackman, 1990). Their focus remains that of *women* (their shared oppressed identity with their clients) not *professionals* (their potentially oppressing identity). In one case in point, feminist psychologists in the thrall of the psychoanalytical tradition failed to challenge it about its betrayal of sexually abused women clients, ironically leaving this task to men (e.g. Sayers, 1989; cf. Masson, 1989).

CLINICAL PSYCHOLOGY AND THE FUTURE

In the light of the above discussion, what does the future hold for clinical psychology? And what might clinical psychology be offering to the world in the future? Predictions are notoriously difficult but what we can do is try to map out certain trends and possibilities.

The first possibility is that the profession may collapse and disappear. The 'doomsday scenario', still worrying pessimists in the profession, remains a possibility. Remember that clinical psychologists hold no formal powers under mental health legislation. Consequently, the state could potentially dispense with their services without any loss to its formal coercive powers to enforce social stability. By contrast, doctors, nurses and social workers are required for the latter task. A buffer against this scenario is predicated on the fact that social order in complex societies has increasingly been achieved by relying on voluntary relationships. Indeed those analysing the psy professions within the Foucauldian tradition (Castel *et al.*, 1979; Rose, 1990; Donzelot, 1979) argue that during the twentieth century, with the decline of segregative control in institutions, coercive power has become less and less relevant. Within this analysis, psychological therapies, counselling and health education are examples, par excellence, of a new type of moral regulation favoured by both government and public.

Of course *Working for Patients*, by separating the provider and purchaser functions in the NHS, set up the possibility of local economics determining whether this generalised mandate in society would continue to be held by *clinical psychologists*. In other words, the Foucauldians may be correct, in general, that psychological techniques are now implicated deeply in modern society. They may well overstate their case about the degree of penetration of these techniques into everyday life but their general point is well taken. However, even if their case were to be accepted uncritically, this would not imply that any *particular* occupational group deploying such techniques would have a protected existence as a result. If clinical psychology does not disappear without trace, another possibility is that it will disappear in certain localities but not others (as a result of winning or losing bids for work).

Let us suppose then that the profession survives – what then? Another scenario, but an unlikely one, is that there will be a total triumph of the marketing campaign of the 1980s. The blocking of the MPAG/MAS report by the DoH when it was published does not augur well for the profession's ascent in the 1990s. This highlights the weakness of any account of professions which is over-reliant upon their 'action' potential, i.e. assumes that ascent follows from the acquisition of persuasive credentials (cf. Collins, 1979). It is certainly true that professional leaders will wheel and deal in all sorts of ingenious ways to advance their personal and collective interests, but this only marks aspirations not their inevitable achievement. In this light, maybe the 'radicals' were wise to caution the leadership about the timing of their manpower review strategy. The latter were making a move towards expansion built on scientific arrogance but at a time when the Conservative government showed an antipathy towards such traditional expert authority. The 'realists' were certainly in tune with the times, with their image building and their skills definitions, but they were also vulnerable to the goals of the times (the demolition of power in society not derived directly from ownership or central state control).

Of course, potentially, the reforms of the NHS along business lines may be reversed by an incoming Labour government. But even if Labour do manage to return to power before 2000 (still a big 'if') much of the restructured public sector may be deliberately left untouched, as a result of Labour's own problems with budget controls and the rise of new consumer expectations. In the past, in the tradition of Fabianism, the Labour Party has been fairly uncritical of the oppressive potential of expertise, emphasising only the optimistic view of science in service of the people. (The Wilsonian emphasis on technological and scientific advances in the 1960s typified this Labourist ideology). However, it has been the radical doubting of the

Conservative Party about professional power which has subverted this confidence in the eyes of many, including those not sharing their wider political position. The Conservative rhetoric about consumer choice helped legitimise the rise of the mental health users movement during the 1980s (Rogers and Pilgrim, 1989) in a way in which the old Labour deference to professional expertise had singularly failed.

What clinical psychology would have to do in the future is learn how to take the consumer view much more seriously than has been the case in the past. It is worth remembering that one of the main rhetoricians for the profession, Ian Howarth, argued that psychologists were more likely to be democratic and user-friendly, than members of other professions. This 'selling point' of course referred only to the appeal of voluntary negotiations for individual clients. However, if this emphasis on voluntarism and client rights becomes a collective issue about power then a wider notion of democratic accountability to clients will be required, which leads us to the next scenario.

Another possible future role for the profession, if it survives, is to ally itself with progressive forces 'from below' in mental health politics. At present psychologists have rarely come out and aligned themselves directly with users organisations (cf. Bell, 1989). Thus there is little current evidence that there is mass support from psychologists as full-blown activist-allies within the mental health service users movement. Having said this, psychologists may still be able to encourage a more user-sensitive service, whilst remaining within their professional boundaries. The increasing demand for involvement in the planning and running of services by users could be supported, and where possible facilitated, by psychologists in each locality. They could be involved in assessment of needs in a way which satisfies local users groups. They could help them evaluate levels of satisfaction with new community services. They could offer benign alternatives to physical psychiatric treatments, which find little favour with users (Rogers et al., 1992).

It would appear that, despite the attacks upon verbal psychotherapy by diverse critics (Eysenck, 1952; Howarth, 1989; Masson, 1989), clients do want this to be offered more by the state than has been the case in the past. For instance, in their founding charter, the largest mental health users group, Survivors Speak Out, demanded the universal free availability of counselling for people experiencing mental distress (Survivors Speak Out, 1987). However, users are not uncritical of psychotherapy and counselling: the power games experienced at the hands of therapists often provoke distaste (Rogers *et al.*, 1992). It should also be emphasised that the iatrogenic menace of drugs and ECT is so offensive to psychiatric patients that *any alternative* which primarily involves paying heed to experience, rather than interfering with the body, is probably a welcome relief. It may lead too readily though to complacency on the part of practitioners in clinical psychology and competing occupational groups.

None the less, it is in this scenario that both science and humanism, interwoven in the profession, may find a positive rather than mystifying or oppressive expression. The first of them could be used in terms of systematic quality assurance in service delivery. Whilst *empiricism* may generally be associated with conservative social forces, this need not be always the case for *empirical* knowledge. The second, humanism, could be directed towards services based upon empowerment rather than intervention. For this to happen, the issue of power in professional relationships would need to be examined more self-critically than has been the case in the past.

The dependency encouraged by long-term analytical therapy, the mystification of psychotherapeutic expertise, the manipulative relish of many family therapists and the smug language of personal responsibility in the growth movement are all legitimate targets here (Pilgrim, 1991). These professional characteristics have been associated with practitioners of varying orientations within clinical psychology enjoying power *over* clients. Only when they have been subjected to a thoroughgoing user-centred critique based upon race, class and gender will they have long-term credibility in the eyes of clients. In other words, the problem with Howarth's claim that psychologists are *already* offering a more democratic and therefore user-friendly service is that, at present, it is merely a professional assertion. When have women and black people (not dominant in clinical psychology but predominant as consumers of welfare services (Williams, 1990)) actually been provided with a form of therapy based upon their needs and view of the world, rather than those derived from the white patriarchs of Europe and the United States of America? Thus the potential for a progressive role for psychological therapists is there but these critiques are first required.

Another caution about being too enthusiastic about the progressive potential of psychological therapies is that they tend to individualise or psychologise problems (by definition) and thereby deflect attention from more important societal issues. Whereas we know that long-term recovery from mental health problems is a function of social opportunities, such as employment and housing (Warner, 1985), the case for the efficacy of both physical and psychological interventions from professionals is still problematic, as was noted above. As with curative medicine, there is not a strong case that mental health professions are offering convincing wares. At best, psychological 'treatment' can be described as being of 'marginal utility'. Indeed, the over-confident claims of rhetoricians in behaviour therapy, cognitive therapy and verbal psychotherapy need to be doubted or challenged.

This is not to argue that these professionals have *no* utility for clients. In a complex society the state should provide access to relationships which might ameliorate distress, if informal contacts are not there to do the job. Also, as indicated above, from what we know of user views of psychiatry, counselling is still in demand. The point here though is that the modest success of psychological therapies (when weighed against the hazards of induced dependency, deterioration effects, and sexual, emotional and financial abuse of clients) should be put into perspective. Moreover, a genuinely accountable mental health service would need to expose the findings of the research on these hazards to potential recipients. There is little point in accepting the traditional criticisms about medicine hiding its iatrogenic impact from patients (by failing to come clean on 'side-effects') if psychologists are going to do the same. It is also worth noting that the client demands for counselling come largely as a result of it being absent. They are asking for something *new* in the main. Thus, given that the overwhelming majority of people presenting to professionals with distress are denied access to such services at present, a large-scale client-centred evaluation is still awaited (cf. Rogers *et al.*, 1992).

A final doubt about the capacity of clinical psychology to demonstrate a strong support for the users' agenda in mental health services is the seductive power of status and money. At the time of writing, following on the most recent regrading exercise in the profession, many psychologists are enjoying enlarged salaries and statuses. The latter development is amplified when psychologists have become 'clinical directors' of services. Moreover, if, despite the lack of formal managerial endorsement, Mowbray's recommendations gain some purchase in particular localities, this élitist professionalising trend would be amplified further. The professional path will be one of an inward looking preoccupation with money and hierarchical power. This is essentially incompatible with an alliance with the users movement. Mowbray's model is very similar to that of a medical structure: a stratified power pyramid. Users of psychiatric services have learned from experience that this type of structure in psychiatry has simply added to their oppression at the hands of professionals.

If clinical psychology survives and is not to go the way of other professions, by pursuing self-interest, it has to be honest about its limitations, as well as its capabilities. In different ways, preoccupations with both science and humanism, when combined with the inherent tendency of professionals to emphasise only the positive about themselves, militate against an open, user-centred accountability. The scientist-practitioner model dominant in clinical psychology, predicated as it is on positivism, tends towards technocratic solutions to existential problems. It assumes the non-problematic status of 'facts' and the justified power of their possessors. The lack of value engagement and reflexivity of this approach, discussed at the start of this chapter, does not augur well for an accountable form of professional practice. For its part, humanism tends to drive its practitioners towards an uncritical form of relativism, where 'anything goes' and subjectivity is prized to the exclusion of external factors such as poverty and oppression. The oldest tradition of verbal psychotherapy, psychoanalysis, committed as it is to a view of expertise derived from clinical experience, has simply led to a set of pre-emptively expensive arcane practices. These are overwhelmingly limited to those who can afford to pay and they are shielded permanently from public scrutiny and accountability.

Thus both science and humanism can generate their own anti-democratic mystique. Each tradition in clinical psychology could of course act as a counterbalance towards the other. But the danger is that the mystique associated with each will simply cross-multiply and the public, as potential clients, will suffer a double mystification. They might be encouraged to believe that clinical psychologists really *are* experts in human misery, instead of practitioners who have a partial, confused or uncertain understanding of their fellows and a fairly modest set of current proposals for the amelioration of their distress.

Bibliography

Adams, M. and Kennard, D. (1988) 'What makes a good placement?', *Clinical Psychology Forum* 17: 19–28.

Adams, R. (1977) 'Clinical training: did it really happen to me?', *Newsletter of the Division of Clinical Psychology* 19: 13–17.

Allen, C. (1985) 'Training for what? Clinical psychologists' perceptions of their roles', unpublished MSc dissertation, Department of Psychiatry, University of Newcastle upon Tyne.

Anciano, D. and Kirkpatrick, A. (1989) 'CMHTs and clinical psychology: the death of a profession?', *Clinical Psychology Forum* April: 9–12.

Anderson, P. (1969) 'Components of the national culture', *New Left Review* 50 (July/August).

Anon (1977) *Newsletter of the Division of Clinical Psychology* 19: 10–11.

—— (1977) *Newsletter of the Division of Clinical Psychology* 20: 14–16.

Armstrong, D. (1980) 'Madness and coping', *Sociology of Health and Illness* 2 (3): 293–313.

Atkinson, P. and Delamont, S. (1990) 'Professions and powerlessness', *The Sociological Review* 38 (1): 90–110.

Bannister, D. and Mair, J.M. (1970) *The Evaluation of Personal Constructs*, London: Academic Press.

Baran, P.A. (1973) *The Political Economy of Growth*, Harmondsworth, Middx: Penguin.

Barlow, D. (1980) 'Behaviour therapy: the next decade', *Behaviour Therapy* 11: 315–28.

—— (1981) 'On the relation of clinical research to clinical practice: current issues, new directions', *Journal of Consulting and Clinical Psychology* 49: 147–55.

Barlow, D., Hayes, S. and Nelson, R. (1984) *The Scientist-Practitioner*, New York: Pergamon.

Barrom, C.P., Shadish, W.R. and Montgomery, L.M. (1988) 'Ph.D's, Psy D's and real-world constraints on scholarly activity: another look at the Boulder Model', *Professional Psychology: Research and Practice* 19: 93–101.

Bartlet, D. and Shapiro, M. (1956) 'Investigation and treatment of a reading disability in a dull child with severe psychiatric disturbance', *British Journal of Educational Psychology* 26: 180–90.

Baruch, G. and Treacher, A. (1978) *Psychiatry Observed*, London: Routledge & Kegan Paul.

Bean, P. (1980) *Compulsory Admissions to Mental Hospitals*, London: Wiley.

—— (1986) *Mental Disorder and Legal Control*, Cambridge: Cambridge University Press.

Beckman, L. (1974) 'Millions of homosexuals cured instantly!', *In a Nutshell: Mental Patients Union Newsletter* 3 (2): 4.

Bell, L. (1989) 'Psychotherapy and user empowerment', *Clinical Psychology Forum* 23: 12–14.

Beloff, J. (1973) *Psychological Sciences*, London: Staples.

Bender, M.P. and Richardson, A. (1990) 'The ethnic composition of clinical psychology in Britain', *The Psychologist* 3 (6): 250–2.

Bergin, A. and Strupp, H. (1972) *Changing Frontiers in the Science of Psychotherapy*, Chicago: Aldine-Atherton.

Bhaskar, R. (1989) *Reclaiming Reality: A Critical Introduction to Philosophy*, London: Verso.

Billig, M. (1979) *Psychology: Racism and Fascism*, London: Searchlight Publications.

Birley, J. (1990) 'The history of psychiatry as the history of an art', in R.M. Murray and T.H. Turner (eds) *Lectures on the History of Psychiatry*, London: Gaskell/Royal College of Psychiatrists.

Blackman, L. (1990) 'Review of Erica Burman's *Feminists and Psychological Practice*', *Psychology of Women Newsletter* spring: 34–7.

Bleuler, E. (1911) *Dementia Praecox*, trans. J. Zitkin (1950), New York: International Universities Press.

Boronski, Y. (1987) *Knowledge*, London: Longman.

Boyle, M. (1990) *Schizophrenia: A Scientific Delusion?*, London: Routledge.

Braginsky, B., Braginsky, D. and Ring, K. (1972) *Methods of Madness: The Mental Hospital as a Last Resort*, New York: Holt, Rinehart & Winston.

Braverman, H. (1974) *Labour and Monopoly Capital*, New York: Monthly Review Press.

British Psychological Society (1982) 'Training in clinical psychology: a statement of policy', *Bulletin of the BPS* 35: 153–5.

—— (1988) *The Future of the Psychological Sciences: Horizons and Opportunities for British Psychology*, Leicester: BPS.

Broad, W. and Wade, N. (1985) *Betrayers of the Truth: Fraud and Deceit in Science*, Oxford: Oxford University Press.

Burman, E. (1990) *Feminists and Psychological Practice*, London: Sage.

Burt, C. (1927) *The Young Delinquent*, London: London University Press.

—— (1949) 'Recent discussions of juvenile delinquency', *British Journal of Educational Psychology*, 19: 31–43.

Busfield, J. (1985) *Managing Madness*, London: Hutchinson.

Carchedi, G. (1977) *On the Economic Identification of the New Middle Class*, London: Routledge & Kegan Paul.

Castel, F. (1985) 'Moral treatment: mental therapy and social control in the nineteenth century', in S. Cohen and A. Scull (eds) *Social Control and the State*, Oxford: Blackwell.

Castel, F., Castel, R. and Lovell, A. (1979) *The Psychiatric Society*, New York: Columbia University Press.

Cattell, R.B. (1948) 'The meaning of clinical psychology', in I.A. Pennington and I.A. Berg *An Introduction to Clinical Psychology*, New York: Ronald Press Company.

Clare, A. (1977) *Psychiatry in Dissent*, London: Tavistock.

Claridge, G.S. and Brooks, D.N. (1973) 'A survey of applicants for the Glasgow M.Sc. course in clinical psychology: some applications for selection and training', *Bulletin of the BPS* 26: 123–7.

Cohen, L. (1979) 'The research readership and information source reliance of clinical psychologists', *Professional Psychology* 10: 80–5.

Cole, R.H. (1913) *Mental Diseases*, London: London University Press.

Collins, R. (1979) *The Credential Society*, Orlando, FL: Academic Press.

Committee on Training in Clinical Psychology (1947) 'Recommended graduate training program in clinical psychology', *American Psychologist* 2: 539–58.

—— (1982) *Criteria for the Assessment of Postgraduate Training Courses in Clinical Psychology*, Leicester: The Professional Affairs Board of the BPS.

—— (1987) *Guidelines on Clinical Supervision*, Leicester: BPS.

Cooper, D. (1967) *Psychiatry and Anti-Psychiatry*, London: Tavistock.

Corsini, R. and Wedding, D. (1989) *Current Psychotherapies*, 4th edition, Ifasca, IL: Peacock.

Coulter, J. (1973) *Approaches to Insanity*, Oxford: Martin Robertson.

Craig, J.R. and Reese, S.C. (1973) 'Retention of raw data: a problem revisited', *American Psychologist* 28: 723.

Crawford, D. (1989) 'The future of clinical psychology: whither or wither?', *Clinical Psychology Forum* 20: 29–31.

Crockatt, P. (1976) 'Reflections on training in clinical psychology', *Bulletin of the BPS* 18: 12–17.

Crompton, R. (1987) 'Gender, status and professionalism', *Sociology* 21 (3): 413–28.

Cullen, C. (1981) 'Supervisors' workshops: report of a survey conducted by the Standing Committee on Practitioner Training', *DCP Newsletter* 33: 21–2.

Dabbs, A. (1965) 'Personal reflections on training as a clinical psychologist', *Bulletin of the BPS* 18: 17–20.

—— (1972) 'The changing role of clinical psychologists in the National Health Service', *Bulletin of the BPS* 25: 107–9.

Darley, J.G. (1973) 'Opening address', in M. Korman (ed.) *Levels and Patterns of Professional Training in Psychology*, Washington, DC: American Psychological Association.

Davenhill, R. *et al.* (1989) 'Training and selection issues in clinical psychology for black and minority ethnic groups from an equal opportunities perspective', *Clinical Psychology Forum* 21: 34–7.

Davies, C. and Rosser, J. (1986) 'Gendered jobs in the Health Service: a problem for labour process analysis', in D. Knights and H. Wilmott (eds) *Gender and the Labour Process*, London: Gower.

Denburg, J. (1969) 'Registration of applied psychologists', *Bulletin of the BPS* 22: 19–20.

Department of Health and Social Security (1977) *The Role of Psychologists in the Health Service* (The Trethowan Report), London: HMSO.

Desai, M. (1967) 'The concept of clinical psychology', *Bulletin of the BPS* 20: 29–39.

Deutsch, A. (1959) *The Mentally Ill in America*, Columbia: Columbia University Press.

Dicks, H.V. (1970) *Fifty Years of the Tavistock*, London: Routledge & Kegan Paul.

Digby, A. (1985) 'Moral treatment at the retreat, 1796–1846', in W.F. Bynum, R. Porter and M. Shepherd (eds) *The Anatomy of Madness*, Volume 2, London: Tavistock.

Division of Clinical Psychology (1975) 'Training in psychotherapy', *Bulletin of the BPS* 28: 10–21.

Doerner, K. (1970) *Madmen and the Bourgeoisie*, Oxford: Blackwell.

Donnelly, M. (1979) *Managing the Mind*, London: Tavistock.

Donzelot, J. (1979) *The Policing of Families*, London: Hutchinson.

Dring, G. (1977) *Newsletter of the Division of Clinical Psychology* 19: 11–13.

Dryden, W. and Spurling, L. (1989) *On Becoming a Psychotherapist*, London: Tavistock/Routledge.

Duman, J. (1979) 'The creation and diffusion of a professional ideology in the 19th century', *The Sociological Review* 27: 113–38.

Edgell, B. (1961) 'The British Psychological Society 1901–41', special supplement of the *Bulletin of the BPS*.

Edwards, G. (1985) 'Helping and hindering', *Changes* 4: 20–3.

Eichenbaum, L. and Orbach, S. (1982) *Outside In Inside Out*, Harmondsworth, Middx: Penguin.

Ewins, D. (1974) 'The origins of compulsory commitment of the Mental Health Act, 1959', unpublished MA thesis, University of Sheffield.

Eysenck, H.J. (1949) 'Training in clinical psychology: an English point of view', *American Psychologist* 4: 173–6.

—— (1950) 'Function and training of the clinical psychologist', *Journal of Mental Science* 96: 710–25.

—— (1952) 'The effects of psychotherapy: an evaluation', *Journal of Consulting and Clinical Psychology* 16: 319–24.

—— (1953) *Uses and Abuses of Psychology*, Harmondsworth, Middx: Penguin.

—— (1958) 'The psychiatric treatment of neurosis', paper presented to the Royal Medico-Psychological Association, London.

—— (1960a) *Behaviour Therapy and the Neuroses*, London: Pergamon.

—— (1960b) *Handbook of Abnormal Psychology*, London: Pitman.

—— (1971) 'Behavior therapy as a scientific discipline', *Journal of Consulting and Clinical Psychology* 36: 314–19.

—— (1975) *The Future of Psychiatry*, London: Methuen.

—— (1990) 'Maverick psychologist', in E. Walker (ed.) *A History of Clinical Psychology - An Autobiography*, New York: Harper & Row.

Eysenck, H.J. and Rachman, S. (1965) *Causes and Cures of the Neuroses*, London: Routledge & Kegan Paul.

Foster, J. (1971) *Enquiry into the Practice and Effects of Scientology*, London: HMSO.

Foucault, M. (1965) *Madness and Civilisation*, New York: Pantheon.

Foulkes, S.H. and Anthony, E.J. (1957) *Group Psychotherapy: The Psychoanalytical Approach*, Harmondsworth, Middx: Penguin.

Frosh, S. and Levinson, F. (1990) 'Identifying clinical skill components of training in clinical psychology', *Clinical Psychology Forum* 25: 20–3.

Garfield, S. and Kurtz, R. (1976) 'Clinical psychologists in the 1970s', *American Psychologist* 31: 1–9.

Gaggs, A. (1977) *Newsletter of the Division of Clinical Psychology* 20: 16–17.

Gathercole, C.E., Kear Colwell, J.J. and Ben-Harari, M. (1962) 'Training of clinical psychologists in the University of Glasgow', *Bulletin of the BPS* 46: 53–7.

Gibson, H.B. (1981) *H. J. Eysenck*, London: Croom Helm.

Glover, E. (1945) 'An examination of the Klein system of child psychology', in *The Psychoanalytic Study of the Child*, Volume 1, New York: International Universities Press.

Goldie, N. (1974) 'Clinical psychology: statutory lackey or unwilling and informal handmaiden of psychiatry?', paper presented to the British Medical Sociological Conference, University of York.

—— (1975) 'Eclecticism as the dominant ideology, and its contribution towards the maintenance of the status quo in British psychiatry', paper presented at the British Sociological Society conference, University of Bath.

—— (1977) 'The division of labour among mental health professionals - a negotiated or an imposed order?', in M. Stacey and M. Reid (eds) *Health and the Division of Labour*, London: Croom Helm.

Goodwin, M. and Power, R. (1986) 'Clinical psychology services for minority ethnic groups', *Clinical Psychology Forum*, 5: 24–8.

Gray, S. (1977) *Newsletter of the Division of Clinical Psychology* 20: 13–14.

Gregg, A. (1948) 'The profession of psychology as seen by a Doctor of Medicine', *American Psychologist* 3: 397–401.

Griffiths, D. (1987) 'How successful is research training on clinical courses?', *Clinical Psychology Forum* 9: 16–20.

Gurnami, P.D. and Sayal, A. (1987) 'Ethnic minorities and clinical psychology: some further comments', *Clinical Psychology Forum* 7: 20–3.

Gwynne Jones, H. (1969) 'Clinical psychology', supplement to the *British Psychological Society Bulletin on the XLXth Congress of Psychology* 21–3.

Hadfield, J.A. (ed.) (1935) *Psychology and Modern Problems*, London: London University Press.

Haley, J. (1963) *Strategies of Psychotherapy*, New York: Grune & Stratton.

Hallam, R.S., Bender, M. and Wood, R. (1989) Letter to *The Psychologist* 2 (9): 375.

Harrower, M.R. (ed.) (1947) *Training in Clinical Psychology*, New York: Josiah Macy Jr. Foundation.

Hawks, D. (1981) 'The dilemma of clinical psychology practice - surviving as a clinical psychologist', in I. McPherson and A. Sutton (eds) *Reconstructing Psychological Practice*, London: Croom Helm.

Head, D. and Harmon, G. (1990) 'Psychologists and research: do we practise what we preach?, *Clinical Psychology Forum* 25: 15–16.

Hearn, J. (1982) 'Notes on patriarchy, professionalisation and the semi-professions', *Sociology* 16 (2): 184–202.

Hearnshaw, L.S. (1964) *A Short History of British Psychology*, London: Methuen.

—— (1979) *Cyril Burt*, London: Methuen.

—— (1986) *The Shaping of Modern Psychology*, London: Methuen.

Heim, A. (1979) 'The proper study of psychology', *New Universities Quarterly* 33: 135–54.

Hetherington, R. (1981) 'The changing role of the clinical psychologist', *Bulletin of the BPS* 34: 12–14.

Hogget, P. and Lousada, J. (1985) 'Therapeutic intervention in working class communities', *Free Associations* 1: 125–52.

Holden, P. (1977) *Newsletter of the Division of Clinical Psychology* 19: 18–19.

Holland, R. (1978) *Self and Social Context*, London: Macmillan.

Holland, S. (1979) 'The development of an action and counselling service in a deprived urban area', in M. Meacher (ed.) *New Methods of Mental Health Care*, London: Pergamon.

Holland, S. and Holland R. (1988) 'Depressed women: outposts of empire and castles of skin', in B. Richards (ed.) *Capitalism and Infancy*, London: Free Association Books.

Homans, H. (1987) 'Man made myths: the reality of being a woman scientist in the NHS', in A. Spencer and D. Podmore (eds) *In a Man's World*, London: Tavistock.

Horwitz, A. (1983) *The Social Control of Mental Illness*, New York: Academic Press.

Houston, J., Revell, J. and Woolett, S. (1989) 'The need for a basic grade training programme: results of a survey of basic grade psychologists in S.W. Thames Region', *Clinical Psychology Forum* 19: 29–32.

Howarth, I. (1988) 'Chartered psychologists: what can we claim for them?', *The Psychologist* 1 (3): 96–8.

—— (1989) Letter circulated to academic members of the BPS.

Humphrey, M. and Haward, L. (1981) 'Sex differences in recruitment to clinical psychology', *Bulletin of the BPS* 34: 413–14.

Ingham, J.G. (1961) 'Clinical psychology', *Bulletin of the BPS* 43: 6–11.

Ingleby, D. (ed.) (1980) *Critical Psychiatry*, Harmondsworth, Middx: Penguin.

—— (1983) 'Professionals as socialisers: the psy complex', paper presented at the British Sociological Association (Medical Section) Conference.

Jaques, E. (1951) *The Changing Culture of a Factory*, London: Tavistock.

Jamous, H. and Peloille, B. (1970) 'Professions or self-perpetuating systems? Changes in the French university-hospital system', in J.A. Jackson (ed.) *Professions and Professionalisation*, Cambridge: Cambridge University Press.

Jessop, B., Bonnett, K., Bromley, S. and Ling, T. (1988) *Thatcherism: A Tale of Two Nations*, Cambridge: Polity Press.

Jick, T. (1987) 'Managing and coping with budget-cut stress in hospitals', in M. Payne and J. Firth-Cozens (eds) *Stress in Health Professionals*, Chichester, Sussex: Wiley.

Jones, M. (1952) *Social Psychiatry*, London: Tavistock.

Kagan, C. and Lewis, S. (1989) 'Transforming psychological practice', paper presented at the BPS Annual Conference, University of St Andrews.

Kear-Colwell, J. (1972) 'A study of clinical psychologists' job movements during the period 1.10.67 to 30.9.70', *Bulletin of the BPS* 25: 25–7.

Kellner, R. (1965) 'Discussion in H.J. Eysenck. The effects of psycho-therapy', *International Journal of Psychiatry* 1: 322–8.

—— (1967) *The Evidence in Favour of Psychotherapy*, New York: Atherton Press.

Kelly, G. (1955) *The Psychology of Personal Constructs*, New York: Norton.

Kendall, P. and Norton-Ford, J. (1982) *Clinical Psychology: Scientific and Professional Dimensions*, New York: Wiley.

Kitzinger, C. (1989) 'Derek Mowbray: turbulent visionary', *The Psychologist* 2 (6): 440–1.

Kline, P. (1988) *Psychology Exposed or the Emperor's New Clothes*, New York: Routledge.

Koch, S. (1974) 'Psychology as a science', in S. Brown (ed.) *Philosophy of Psychology*, London: Macmillan.

Korman, M. (ed.) (1973) *Levels and Patterns in Professional Training in Psychology*, Washington, DC: American Psychological Association.

Kottler, J. (1986) *On Being a Therapist*, San Francisco: Jossey-Bass.

Kraepelin, E. (1895) *Psychiatrie*, Leipzig: Barth.

Laing, R.D. (1960) *The Divided Self*, London: Tavistock.

—— (1968) *The Politics of Experience and the Bird of Paradise*, Harmondsworth, Middx: Penguin.

Lambie, J. (1991) 'The misuse of Kuhn in psychology', *The Psychologist* 4 (1): 6–11.

Ledwidge, B. (1978) 'Cognitive behaviour modification: a step in the wrong direction?', *Psychological Bulletin* 83 (2): 353–75.

Liddell, A. (1977) 'Clinical psychologists as behaviour therapists', *Bulletin of the BPS* 30: 144.

McConnaughty, E. (1987) 'The person of the therapist in psychotherapeutic practice', *Psychotherapy: Theory, Research, Practice and Training* 24: 303–14.

McLoughlin, I. (1982) 'Misunderstanding the new middle class', *Sociology* 16 (4): 586–9.

Magaro, P., Gripp, R. and McDowell, D. (1978) *The Mental Health Industry: Cultural Phenomenon*, New York: Wiley.

Maher, B. (1978) 'Preface', *Journal of Consulting and Clinical Psychology* 46: 595.

Main, T. (1957) 'The ailment', *British Journal of Medical Psychology* 30: 29.

Mair, M. (1987) 'Pretending to care', in E. Karas (ed.) *Current Issues in Clinical Psychology*, Volume 3, New York: Plenum Press.

Malan, D. (1979) *Individual Psychotherapy and the Science of Psychodynamics*, Cambridge: Butterworths.

Marrow-Bradley, C. and Elliott, R. (1986) 'Utilisation of psychotherapy research by practising psychotherapists', *American Psychologist* 14: 188–97.

Martin, P.R. (1987) 'The scientist-practitioner model and clinical psychology: time for change?', paper presented to the BPS Annual Conference, Brighton.

Marzillier, J. and Hall, J. (1987) *What is Clinical Psychology?*, Oxford: Oxford Medical Publications.

Masson, J. (1989) *Against Therapy*, London: Collins.

Meehl, P. (1971) 'A scientific, non-research doctorate for clinical practitioners: arguments pro and con', in R.R. Holt (ed.) *New Horizon for Psychotherapy*, New York: International Universities Press.

Menzies, I. *et al.* (1961) 'The functioning of social systems as a defence against anxiety', *Tavistock Pamphlet* 3.

Miller, E. (1937) *The Growing Child and its Problems*, London: Kegan Paul.

Miller, Ed (1968) 'The case for automated clinical testing', *Bulletin of the BPS* 21: 75–8.

Miller, P. and Rose, N. (eds) (1986) *The Power of Psychiatry*, Cambridge: Polity Press.

—— (1988) 'The Tavistock programme: the government of subjectivity and social life', *Sociology* 22 (2): 171–92.

Milne, D. (1983) 'Some paradoxes and findings in the training of clinical psychologists', *Bulletin of the BPS* 36: 281–2.

Milne, D., Britton, P. and Wilkinson, I. (1990) 'The scientist-practitioner in practice', *Clinical Psychology Forum* 30: 22–30.

MIND (1974) 'Psychotherapy: do we need more talking treatment?', *Mind Report* 12, London: National Association for Mental Health.

Mollon, P. (1989) 'Narcissus, Oedipus and the psychologist's fraudulent identity', *Clinical Psychology Forum* 23: 7–11.

—— (1991) 'Anxiety, supervision and a space for thinking: some narcissistic perils for clinical psychologists in learning psychotherapy', *British Journal of Medical Psychology*.

Morris, B.S. (1949) 'Officer selection in the British army', *Occupational Psychology* 23: 219–34.

Morris, P.E., Cheng, D. and Smith, H. (1990) *How and Why Applicants Choose to Study Psychology at University*, report to the Association of Heads of Psychology Departments.

Morris, P.E., Holloway, J. and Noble, J. (1990) 'Gender representation within the British Psychological Society', *The Psychologist* 9: 408–11.

Navarro, V. (1986) *Class Struggle, the State and Medicine*, London: Martin Robertson.

Neimeyer, R.A. (1985) *The Development of Personal Construct Theory*, London: University of Nebraska.

Newman, C. (1988) *Evolution and Revolution*, Charter guide occasional paper, London: BPS.

Newsom, J., Newsom, E. and Gillham, B. (1983) 'Training in clinical psychology: a reply', *Bulletin of the BPS* 36: 77–9.

Nichols, K. (1988) 'Practising what we preach', *The Psychologist* February: 50–1.

Nitsun, M., Wood, H. and Bolton, W. (1989) 'The organisation of psychotherapy services: a clinical psychology perspective', *Clinical Psychology Forum* 23: 32–7.

Norcross, J. and Prochaska, J. (1982) 'A national survey of clinical psychologists: characteristics and activities', *The Clinical Psychologist* 35: 1–8.

Nottingham NHS Psychologists (1988) Unpublished circulated document.

Noyes, E., Franklin, B. and Val Baker, J. (1989) Letter to *The Psychologist* 2 (5): 214.

Oppenheimer, M. (1975) 'The proletarianisation of the professional', *Sociological Review Monograph* 20.

O'Sullivan, K. and Dryden, W. (1990) 'A survey of clinical psychologists in the S.E. Thames Health Region: Activities, role and theoretical orientation', *Clinical Psychology Forum* 29: 21–6.

Parkin, F. (1979) *Marxism and Class Theory: A Bourgeois Critique*, London: Tavistock.

Parry, G. (1989) 'Care for the future', *The Psychologist* 2 (6): 436–8.

Parsons, T. (1937) *The Structure of Social Action*, New York: Free Press.

Peck, D. and Gathercole, C. (1968) 'Automated techniques in clinical psychology', *Bulletin of the BPS* 21: 75–8.

Penzer, W. (1984) 'The psychopathology of the psychotherapist', *Psychotherapy in Private Practice* 2: 51–9.

Petchey, R. (1986) 'The Griffiths re-organisation of the health service: Fowlerism by stealth?', *Critical Social Policy* 17: 87–101.

Pilalis, J. (1984) 'The formalization of family therapy training issues and implications', *Journal of Family Therapy* 6: 35–46.

Pilgrim, D. (ed.) (1983) *Psychology and Psychotherapy*, London: Routledge.

—— (1990) 'Clinical psychology in the 1980s: a sociological analysis', unpublished MSc thesis, Polytechnic of the South Bank.

—— (1991) 'Psychotherapy and the social blinkers', *The Psychologist* 2: 52–5.

Pilgrim, D. and Barnes, B. (1989) 'Psychotherapy and contemporary British clinical psychology', *Clinical Psychology Forum* 23: 23–6.

Portes, A. (1971) 'On the emergence of behaviour therapy in modern society', *Journal of Consulting and Clinical Psychology* 36: 303–13.

Pottharst, K. (1973) 'A brief history of the professional model of training', in M. Korman (ed.) *Levels and Patterns of Professional Training in Psychology*, Washington, DC: American Psychological Association.

Poulantzas, N. (1975) *Classes in Contemporary Capitalism*, London: New Left Books.

Privy Council Office (1947) *The Work of Psychology and Psychologists in the Services: Report of an Expert Committee*, London: HMSO.

Prochaska, J.O. and Norcross, J.C. (1983) 'Contemporary psychotherapists: a national survey of characteristics, practices, orientations and attitudes', *Psychotherapy: Theory, Research and Practice* 20: 161–73.

Rachman, S.J. (1983) 'Clinical psychology in Britain - retrospect and prospect', in A. Liddell (ed.) *The Practice of Clinical Psychology in Great Britain*, Chichester, Sussex: Wiley.

Raimy, V.C. (ed.) (1950) *Training in Clinical Psychology*, New York: Prentice-Hall.

Ramon, S. (1985) *Psychiatry in Britain*, London: Gower.

Raven, J.C. (1966) *Psychological Principles Appropriate to Social and Clinical Problems*, London: Lewis.

Rees, J.R. (1945) *The Shaping of Psychiatry by War*, New York: Norton.

Rein, M. and White, S. (1981) 'Knowledge for practice', *Social Science Review* 55: 1–41.

Reisman, J.R. (1976) *A History of Clinical Psychology*, New York: Wiley.

Richards, B. (1977) *Newsletter of the Division of Clinical Psychology* 19: 9–10.

—— (1983) 'Clinical psychology, the individual and the state', unpublished PhD thesis, Polytechnic of North East London.

Rickman, J. (1938) 'The Medical Section of the British Psychological Society', *The Medical Press and Circular* 7 September.

Rippere, V. and Williams, R. (1985) *Wounded Healers - Mental Health Workers' Experiences of Depression*, Chichester, Sussex: Wiley.

Rogers, A. and Pilgrim, D. (1989) 'Mental health and citizenship', *Critical Social Policy* 26: 44–55.

Rogers, A., Pilgrim, D. and Lacey, R. (1992) *People First: Users' Views of Psychiatric Services*, London: Macmillan.

Rogers, C. (1957) 'The necessary and sufficient conditions for therapeutic personality change', *Journal of Consulting and Clinical Psychology* 21: 95–103.

Rose, N. (1990) *Governing the Soul: The Shaping of the Private Self*, London: Routledge.

Rowe, M. (1977) 'The Saturn's Rings phenomenon', *Proceedings of the Conference on Women's Leadership and Authority in the Health Professions*, Santa Cruz, CA.

Royal College of Psychiatrists (1975) 'Norms for medical staffing of a psychotherapy service for a population of 200,000', *Bulletin of the Royal College of Psychiatrists* September.

Rueschmeyer, D. (1986) *Power and the Division of Labour*, Cambridge: Polity Press.

Ryan, J.F. (1972) 'The IQ and the illusion of objectivity', in K. Richardson and J. Spears (eds) *Race, Culture and Intelligence*, Harmondsworth, Middx: Penguin.

Saks, M. (1983) 'Removing the blinkers? A critique of recent contributions to the sociology of the professions', *The Sociological Review* 1–21.

Salkovskis, P. (1984) 'Psychological research by NHS clinical psychologists: an analysis and some suggestions', *Bulletin of the BPS* 37: 375–7.

Salter, A. (1949) *Conditioned Reflex Therapy*, New York: Farrar, Straus.

Savage, R.D. (1966) *Readings in Clinical Psychology*, Oxford: Pergamon.

Sayers, J. (1989) in I. Parker and J. Shotter (eds) *Reconstructing Social Psychology*, London: Routledge.

Schon, D. (1983) *The Reflective Practitioner - How Professionals Think in Action*, New York: Basic Books.

Scull, A. (1977 (2nd edition 1984)) *Decarceration*, Englewood Cliffs, NJ: Prentice-Hall.

—— (1979) *Museums of Madness*, London: Allen Lane.

Sedgwick, P. (1982) *PsychoPolitics*, London: Pluto.

Shapiro, M. (1951) 'An experimental approach to diagnostic psychological testing', *Journal of Mental Science* 97: 748–64.

—— (1955) 'The training of clinical psychologists at the Institute of Psychiatry', *Bulletin of the BPS* 26: 15–20.

—— (1962) 'A two-year course for the training of clinical psychologists', *Bulletin of the BPS* 48: 30–3.

—— (1963) 'A clinical approach to fundamental research with special reference to study of the single patient', in P. Sainsbury and N. Krietman (eds) *Methods in Psychiatric Research*, London: Oxford University Press.

—— (1969) 'Recent trends in the training of clinical psychologists', *Bulletin of the BPS* 22: 13–17.

—— (1985) 'A reassessment of clinical psychology as an applied science', *British Journal of Clinical Psychology* 24: 1–11.

Sharrock, R. and Hunt, S. (1986) 'A national survey of trainees' satisfaction with supervision', *Clinical Psychology Forum* 6: 27–331.

Skadegaard, R. and Grabelsky, R. (1975) 'The dilemma of the emerging psychologist', *Professional Psychology* 6: 201–3.

Skinner, A. (1977) 'Out of the frying pan', *Newsletter of the Division of Clinical Psychology* 19: 17–18.

Skultans, V. (1979) *English Madness*, London: Routledge & Kegan Paul.

Smail, D. (1973) 'Clinical psychology and the medical model', *Bulletin of the BPS* 26: 211–14.

—— (1982) 'Clinical psychology - homogenized and sterilized', *Bulletin of the BPS* 35: 345–6.

Smith, L. (1977) *Newsletter of the Division of Clinical Psychology* 20: 17.

Smith, M. and Glass, G. (1977) 'Meta-analysis of psychotherapy outcome studies', *American Psychologist* 132: 152–70.

Sorokin, P.A. (1937) *Social and Cultural Dynamics*, Volume 2, New York: American Books.

Stoddard, W. (1919) *Mind and its Disorders*, London: Lewis.

Stone, M. (1985) 'Shellshock and the psychologists', in W.F. Bynum, R. Porter and M. Shepherd (eds) *The Anatomy of Madness*, Volume 2, London: Tavistock.

Storr, A. (1979) *The Art of Psychotherapy*, London: Secker & Warburg/Heinemann Medical.

Summerfield, D. (1958) 'Clinical psychology in Britain', *Bulletin of the BPS* 34: 9–18.

Sutherland, J. (1951) 'The Tavistock Clinic and the Tavistock Institute of Human Relations', *Quarterly Bulletin of the BPS* 2: 105–12.

Szasz, T. (1960) *The Myth of Mental Illness*, New York: Harper & Row.

Taylor, M. (1989) 'Do clinical psychologists agree about competence?', unpublished MSc thesis, University of Leeds.

Thompson, E.P. (1978) *The Poverty of Theory*, London: Merlin.

Tizard, B. (1990) 'Research and policy: is there a link?', *The Psychologist* 3: 435–40.

Torpy, D. (1988) 'New entrants to clinical psychology training 1987', *Clinical Psychology Forum* 13: 30–1.

Treacher, A. (1983) 'On the utility or otherwise of psychotherapy research', in D. Pilgrim (ed.) *Psychology and Psychotherapy*, London: Routledge & Kegan Paul.

Truax, C. and Carkhuff, R. (1967) 'Towards effective counselling and psychotherapy', Chicago: Aldine.

University of Leeds (1989) *Handbook of the Clearing House for Postgraduate Courses in Clinical Psychology*.

—— (1990) *Handbook of the Clearing House for Postgraduate Courses in Clinical Psychology*.

Ussher, J. (1991) 'Clinical psychology and sexual equality: a contradiction in terms?', *Feminism and Psychology* 1 (1): 63–8.

Vernon, P.E. and Parry, J.B. (1949) *Personnel Selection in the British Forces*, London: London University Press.

Walsh, S. (1990) 'Personal and professional threat: a model of self-care for clinical psychologists', MSc dissertation, University of Exeter.

Warner, R. (1985) *Recovery from Schizophrenia: Psychiatry and Political Economy*, London: Routledge.

Watts, F.N. (1984) 'Applicable psychological research in the NHS', *Bulletin of the BPS* 37: 41–2.

Weber, M. (1958) 'Bureaucracy', in H.H. Gerth and C.W. Mills (eds) *From Max Weber: Essays in Sociology*, New York: Oxford University Press.

—— (1965) *The Theory of Social and Economic Organisations*, New York: The Free Press.

Williams, F. (1990) *Social Policy: A Critical Introduction*, Cambridge: Polity Press.

Wolins, L. (1962) 'Responsibility for raw data', *American Psychologist* 17: 657–8.

Wollersheim, J. (1974) 'Bewail the vail or love is not enough', *American Psychologist* 29: 717–18.

Wolpe, J. (1958) *Psychotherapy by Reciprocal Inhibition*, Stanford, CA: Stanford University Press.

Wooton, B. (1959) *Social Science and Social Pathology*, London: Allen & Unwin.

Yates, A.J. (1970) *Behavior Therapy*, New York: Wiley.

—— (1987) 'The empty bottle model of training', presentation to a conference in celebration of the retirement of Jim Drewery, Exeter, September.

Young, H. (1989) *One of Us*, London: Macmillan.

Name index

Subject index